FREE Test Taking Tips DVD Offer

To help us better serve you, we have developed a Test Taking Tips DVD that we would like to give you for FREE. **This DVD covers world-class test taking tips that you can use to be even more successful when you are taking your test.**

All that we ask is that you email us your feedback about your study guide. Please let us know what you thought about it – whether that is good, bad or indifferent.

To get your **FREE Test Taking Tips DVD**, email freedvd@studyguideteam.com with "FREE DVD" in the subject line and the following information in the body of the email:

    a. The title of your study guide.

    b. Your product rating on a scale of 1-5, with 5 being the highest rating.

    c. Your feedback about the study guide. What did you think of it?

    d. Your full name and shipping address to send your free DVD.

If you have any questions or concerns, please don't hesitate to contact us at freedvd@studyguideteam.com.

Thanks again!

CSET English Test Prep 2018 & 2019
CSET English Exam Prep Book & Practice Test Questions

Test Prep Books English Prep Team

Table of Contents

Quick Overview

As you draw closer to taking your exam, effective preparation becomes more and more important. Thankfully, you have this study guide to help you get ready. Use this guide to help keep your studying on track and refer to it often.

This study guide contains several key sections that will help you be successful on your exam. The guide contains tips for what you should do the night before and the day of the test. Also included are test-taking tips. Knowing the right information is not always enough. Many well-prepared test takers struggle with exams. These tips will help equip you to accurately read, assess, and answer test questions.

A large part of the guide is devoted to showing you what content to expect on the exam and to helping you better understand that content. In this guide are practice test questions so that you can see how well you have grasped the content. Then, answer explanations are provided so that you can understand why you missed certain questions.

Don't try to cram the night before you take your exam. This is not a wise strategy for a few reasons. First, your retention of the information will be low. Your time would be better used by reviewing information you already know rather than trying to learn a lot of new information. Second, you will likely become stressed as you try to gain a large amount of knowledge in a short amount of time. Third, you will be depriving yourself of sleep. So be sure to go to bed at a reasonable time the night before. Being well-rested helps you focus and remain calm.

Be sure to eat a substantial breakfast the morning of the exam. If you are taking the exam in the afternoon, be sure to have a good lunch as well. Being hungry is distracting and can make it difficult to focus. You have hopefully spent lots of time preparing for the exam. Don't let an empty stomach get in the way of success!

When travelling to the testing center, leave earlier than needed. That way, you have a buffer in case you experience any delays. This will help you remain calm and will keep you from missing your appointment time at the testing center.

Be sure to pace yourself during the exam. Don't try to rush through the exam. There is no need to risk performing poorly on the exam just so you can leave the testing center early. Allow yourself to use all of the allotted time if needed.

Remain positive while taking the exam even if you feel like you are performing poorly. Thinking about the content you should have mastered will not help you perform better on the exam.

Once the exam is complete, take some time to relax. Even if you feel that you need to take the exam again, you will be well served by some down time before you begin studying again. It's often easier to convince yourself to study if you know that it will come with a reward!

Test-Taking Strategies

1. Predicting the Answer

When you feel confident in your preparation for a multiple-choice test, try predicting the answer before reading the answer choices. This is especially useful on questions that test objective factual knowledge. By predicting the answer before reading the available choices, you eliminate the possibility that you will be distracted or led astray by an incorrect answer choice. You will feel more confident in your selection if you read the question, predict the answer, and then find your prediction among the answer choices. After using this strategy, be sure to still read all of the answer choices carefully and completely. If you feel unprepared, you should not attempt to predict the answers. This would be a waste of time and an opportunity for your mind to wander in the wrong direction.

2. Reading the Whole Question

Too often, test takers scan a multiple-choice question, recognize a few familiar words, and immediately jump to the answer choices. Test authors are aware of this common impatience, and they will sometimes prey upon it. For instance, a test author might subtly turn the question into a negative, or he or she might redirect the focus of the question right at the end. The only way to avoid falling into these traps is to read the entirety of the question carefully before reading the answer choices.

3. Looking for Wrong Answers

Long and complicated multiple-choice questions can be intimidating. One way to simplify a difficult multiple-choice question is to eliminate all of the answer choices that are clearly wrong. In most sets of answers, there will be at least one selection that can be dismissed right away. If the test is administered on paper, the test taker could draw a line through it to indicate that it may be ignored; otherwise, the test taker will have to perform this operation mentally or on scratch paper. In either case, once the obviously incorrect answers have been eliminated, the remaining choices may be considered. Sometimes identifying the clearly wrong answers will give the test taker some information about the correct answer. For instance, if one of the remaining answer choices is a direct opposite of one of the eliminated answer choices, it may well be the correct answer. The opposite of obviously wrong is obviously right! Of course, this is not always the case. Some answers are obviously incorrect simply because they are irrelevant to the question being asked. Still, identifying and eliminating some incorrect answer choices is a good way to simplify a multiple-choice question.

4. Don't Overanalyze

Anxious test takers often overanalyze questions. When you are nervous, your brain will often run wild, causing you to make associations and discover clues that don't actually exist. If you feel that this may be a problem for you, do whatever you can to slow down during the test. Try taking a deep breath or counting to ten. As you read and consider the question, restrict yourself to the particular words used by the author. Avoid thought tangents about what the author *really* meant, or what he or she was *trying* to say. The only things that matter on a multiple-choice test are the words that are actually in the question. You must avoid reading too much into a multiple-choice question, or supposing that the writer meant something other than what he or she wrote.

5. No Need for Panic

It is wise to learn as many strategies as possible before taking a multiple-choice test, but it is likely that you will come across a few questions for which you simply don't know the answer. In this situation, avoid panicking. Because most multiple-choice tests include dozens of questions, the relative value of a single wrong answer is small. As much as possible, you should compartmentalize each question on a multiple-choice test. In other words, you should not allow your feelings about one question to affect your success on the others. When you find a question that you either don't understand or don't know how to answer, just take a deep breath and do your best. Read the entire question slowly and carefully. Try rephrasing the question a couple of different ways. Then, read all of the answer choices carefully. After eliminating obviously wrong answers, make a selection and move on to the next question.

6. Confusing Answer Choices

When working on a difficult multiple-choice question, there may be a tendency to focus on the answer choices that are the easiest to understand. Many people, whether consciously or not, gravitate to the answer choices that require the least concentration, knowledge, and memory. This is a mistake. When you come across an answer choice that is confusing, you should give it extra attention. A question might be confusing because you do not know the subject matter to which it refers. If this is the case, don't eliminate the answer before you have affirmatively settled on another. When you come across an answer choice of this type, set it aside as you look at the remaining choices. If you can confidently assert that one of the other choices is correct, you can leave the confusing answer aside. Otherwise, you will need to take a moment to try to better understand the confusing answer choice. Rephrasing is one way to tease out the sense of a confusing answer choice.

7. Your First Instinct

Many people struggle with multiple-choice tests because they overthink the questions. If you have studied sufficiently for the test, you should be prepared to trust your first instinct once you have carefully and completely read the question and all of the answer choices. There is a great deal of research suggesting that the mind can come to the correct conclusion very quickly once it has obtained all of the relevant information. At times, it may seem to you as if your intuition is working faster even than your reasoning mind. This may in fact be true. The knowledge you obtain while studying may be retrieved from your subconscious before you have a chance to work out the associations that support it. Verify your instinct by working out the reasons that it should be trusted.

8. Key Words

Many test takers struggle with multiple-choice questions because they have poor reading comprehension skills. Quickly reading and understanding a multiple-choice question requires a mixture of skill and experience. To help with this, try jotting down a few key words and phrases on a piece of scrap paper. Doing this concentrates the process of reading and forces the mind to weigh the relative importance of the question's parts. In selecting words and phrases to write down, the test taker thinks about the question more deeply and carefully. This is especially true for multiple-choice questions that are preceded by a long prompt.

9. Subtle Negatives

One of the oldest tricks in the multiple-choice test writer's book is to subtly reverse the meaning of a question with a word like *not* or *except*. If you are not paying attention to each word in the question, you can easily be led astray by this trick. For instance, a common question format is, "Which of the following is…?" Obviously, if the question instead is, "Which of the following is not…?," then the answer will be quite different. Even worse, the test makers are aware of the potential for this mistake and will include one answer choice that would be correct if the question were not negated or reversed. A test taker who misses the reversal will find what he or she believes to be a correct answer and will be so confident that he or she will fail to reread the question and discover the original error. The only way to avoid this is to practice a wide variety of multiple-choice questions and to pay close attention to each and every word.

10. Reading Every Answer Choice

It may seem obvious, but you should always read every one of the answer choices! Too many test takers fall into the habit of scanning the question and assuming that they understand the question because they recognize a few key words. From there, they pick the first answer choice that answers the question they believe they have read. Test takers who read all of the answer choices might discover that one of the latter answer choices is actually *more* correct. Moreover, reading all of the answer choices can remind you of facts related to the question that can help you arrive at the correct answer. Sometimes, a misstatement or incorrect detail in one of the latter answer choices will trigger your memory of the subject and will enable you to find the right answer. Failing to read all of the answer choices is like not reading all of the items on a restaurant menu: you might miss out on the perfect choice.

11. Spot the Hedges

One of the keys to success on multiple-choice tests is paying close attention to every word. This is never truer than with words like almost, most, some, and sometimes. These words are called "hedges" because they indicate that a statement is not totally true or not true in every place and time. An absolute statement will contain no hedges, but in many subjects, the answers are not always straightforward or absolute. There are always exceptions to the rules in these subjects. For this reason, you should favor those multiple-choice questions that contain hedging language. The presence of qualifying words indicates that the author is taking special care with his or her words, which is certainly important when composing the right answer. After all, there are many ways to be wrong, but there is only one way to be right! For this reason, it is wise to avoid answers that are absolute when taking a multiple-choice test. An absolute answer is one that says things are either all one way or all another. They often include words like *every*, *always*, *best*, and *never*. If you are taking a multiple-choice test in a subject that doesn't lend itself to absolute answers, be on your guard if you see any of these words.

12. Long Answers

In many subject areas, the answers are not simple. As already mentioned, the right answer often requires hedges. Another common feature of the answers to a complex or subjective question are qualifying clauses, which are groups of words that subtly modify the meaning of the sentence. If the question or answer choice describes a rule to which there are exceptions or the subject matter is complicated, ambiguous, or confusing, the correct answer will require many words in order to be expressed clearly and accurately. In essence, you should not be deterred by answer choices that seem excessively long. Oftentimes, the author of the text will not be able to write the correct answer without offering some qualifications and modifications. Your job is to read the answer choices thoroughly and completely and to select the one that most accurately and precisely answers the question.

13. Restating to Understand

Sometimes, a question on a multiple-choice test is difficult not because of what it asks but because of how it is written. If this is the case, restate the question or answer choice in different words. This process serves a couple of important purposes. First, it forces you to concentrate on the core of the question. In order to rephrase the question accurately, you have to understand it well. Rephrasing the question will concentrate your mind on the key words and ideas. Second, it will present the information to your mind in a fresh way. This process may trigger your memory and render some useful scrap of information picked up while studying.

14. True Statements

Sometimes an answer choice will be true in itself, but it does not answer the question. This is one of the main reasons why it is essential to read the question carefully and completely before proceeding to the answer choices. Too often, test takers skip ahead to the answer choices and look for true statements. Having found one of these, they are content to select it without reference to the question above. Obviously, this provides an easy way for test makers to play tricks. The savvy test taker will always read the entire question before turning to the answer choices. Then, having settled on a correct answer choice, he or she will refer to the original question and ensure that the selected answer is relevant. The mistake of choosing a correct-but-irrelevant answer choice is especially common on questions related to specific pieces of objective knowledge. A prepared test taker will have a wealth of factual knowledge at his or her disposal, and should not be careless in its application.

15. No Patterns

One of the more dangerous ideas that circulates about multiple-choice tests is that the correct answers tend to fall into patterns. These erroneous ideas range from a belief that B and C are the most common right answers, to the idea that an unprepared test-taker should answer "A-B-A-C-A-D-A-B-A." It cannot be emphasized enough that pattern-seeking of this type is exactly the WRONG way to approach a multiple-choice test. To begin with, it is highly unlikely that the test maker will plot the correct answers according to some predetermined pattern. The questions are scrambled and delivered in a random order. Furthermore, even if the test maker was following a pattern in the assignation of correct answers, there is no reason why the test taker would know which pattern he or she was using. Any attempt to discern a pattern in the answer choices is a waste of time and a distraction from the real work of taking the test. A test taker would be much better served by extra preparation before the test than by reliance on a pattern in the answers.

FREE DVD OFFER

Don't forget that doing well on your exam includes both understanding the test content and understanding how to use what you know to do well on the test. We offer a completely FREE Test Taking Tips DVD that covers world class test taking tips that you can use to be even more successful when you are taking your test.

All that we ask is that you email us your feedback about your study guide. To get your **FREE Test Taking Tips DVD**, email freedvd@studyguideteam.com with "FREE DVD" in the subject line and the following information in the body of the email:

- The title of your study guide.
- Your product rating on a scale of 1-5, with 5 being the highest rating.
- Your feedback about the study guide. What did you think of it?
- Your full name and shipping address to send your free DVD.

Introduction to the CSET English Test

Function of the Test

The California Subject Exam for Teachers (CSET) English test is designed to test the knowledge that entry-level educators have of the state of California's public-school standards in the area of English and Language Arts for certification purposes. The California Commission on Teacher Credentialing (also known as CTC) developed the exam, which can be taken by individuals who have earned a high school diploma, GED, or equivalent; or students who are actively taking college courses towards an education career. The exam is criterion-referenced. This means it is not designed to test an individual in comparison to another individual's performance. Instead, it is designed to test an individual's knowledge compared to an established standard. Pearson VUE administers and scores the CSET English at its testing centers throughout the state of California. The exam currently has a pass rate of around 80 percent.

Test Administration

The CSET English test can be taken year-round any day of the week, excluding Sundays, by appointment. Please note that some holiday dates may not be available. The exam is only offered as a computer-based test. An individual can register to take the exam by visiting Pearson VUE's website. An individual can choose to register for any of the four subtests or all four subtests in a single, six-hour session.

There is no waiting period to retake the CSET English test, and there is no limit on the number of times an individual can retest. If an individual has not passed a particular subtest, he or she can simply retake that subtest only, rather than the entire exam. While in the process of earning a certification, test scores are only valid for a period of five years. Therefore, all subtests must be successfully passed within a five-year period. Once that is accomplished, the certification is good for life.

All of the Pearson VUE test centers are wheelchair-accessible. Individuals taking the exam are also allowed to take breaks in order to address any type of medical need. However, no additional time is granted for breaks. The time is deducted from the available test-taking time. Any additional accommodations that may be needed by test takers can be requested by completing an Alternative Testing Arrangements Request form during the test registration process on Pearson VUE's website.

Test Format

The CSET English test is comprised of four subtests as outlined in the table below. Subtest I is made up of 50 multiple-choice questions split between two categories, and test takers are given 90 minutes. AN hour is allotted for Subtest II, which is made up of 50 multiple-choice questions in a single category. Subtest III is made up of two constructed-response questions. Each question focuses on one of the two categories of Subtest I. These questions require extended responses during a two-hour period (800-1,000 words on the assigned topic). These questions are scored based on four elements: purpose, subject matter knowledge, support, and depth/breadth of understanding. Finally, test takers are allotted 90 minutes to take Subtest IV, which is made up of four short, focused response questions in a single category (75-125 words on the assigned topic). These questions are scored based on three elements: purpose, subject matter knowledge, and support.

Here's a breakdown:

Sections of the CSET English Test – Subtest I		
Subject Areas	*Questions (multiple-choice)*	*Time Limit*
Reading Literature & Informational Texts	40	90 minutes
Composition & Rhetoric	10	
Total	50	

Sections of the CSET English Test – Subtest II		
Subject Areas	*Questions (multiple-choice)*	*Time Limit*
Language, Linguistics & Literacy	50	60 minutes
Total	50	

Sections of the CSET English Test – Subtest III		
Subject Areas	*Questions (constructed-response, extended responses)*	*Time Limit*
Reading Literature & Informational Texts	2	120 minutes
Composition & Rhetoric		
Total	2	

Sections of the CSET English Test – Subtest IV		
Subject Areas	*Questions (short, focused responses)*	*Time Limit*
Communications: Speech, Media & Creative Performance	4	90 minutes
Total	4	

Scoring

Individuals are not penalized for guessing when answering the multiple-choice questions on Subtest I and Subtest II. Each of the subtests is scored on a scale of 100-300, and a passing score for the CSET English test is a score of 220 or above on each of the subtests. Scores for Subtests I and II are made available within five weeks of testing, and

Subtest I: Reading Literature and Informational Texts; Composition and Rhetoric

Reading Literature

Major Literary Works and Authors

The CSET assumes test takers will have a familiarity with a wide range of American, British, World, and Young Adult literary works. In most cases, the test taker will be presented with a quoted literary passage and be required to answer one or more questions about it. This may involve having to identify the literary work presented from a list of options.

The ability of the test taker to demonstrate familiarity of major literary works is key in success when taking CSET exams. The following chart offers some examples of major works in addition to those listed elsewhere in this guide, but the list not exhaustive.

<u>American</u>
Fictional Prose
   Harriet Beecher Stowe | *Uncle Tom's Cabin*
   Ernest Hemingway | *For Whom the Bell Tolls*
   Jack London | *The Call of the Wild*
   Toni Morrison | *Beloved*
   N. Scott Momaday | *The Way to Rainy Mountain*
   J.D. Salinger | *Catcher in the Rye*
   John Steinbeck | *Grapes of Wrath*
   Alice Walker | *The Color Purple*
Drama
   Edward Albee | *Who's Afraid of Virginia Woolf?*
   Lorraine Hansberry | *A Raisin in the Sun*
   Amiri Baraka | *Dutchman*
   Eugene O'Neill |*Long Day's Journey into Night*
   Sam Shephard | *Buried Child*
   Thornton Wilder I *Our Town*
   Tennessee Williams | *A Streetcar Named Desire*
Poetry
   Anne Bradstreet | "In Reference to her Children, 23 June 1659"
   Emily Dickinson | "Because I could not stop for Death"
   Sylvia Plath | "Mirror"
   Langston Hughes | "Harlem"
   Edgar Allen Poe | "The Raven"
   Phillis Wheatley | "On Being Brought from Africa to America"
   Walt Whitman | "Song of Myself"
Literary Non-fiction
   Maya Angelou | *I Know Why the Caged Bird Sings*
   Truman | *Capote In Cold Blood*
   Frederick Douglass | *My Bondage and My Freedom*
   Archie Fire | *Lame Deer The Gift of Power: The Life and Teachings of a Lakota Medicine Man*

Helen Keller | *The Story of My Life*
Dave Pelzer | *A Child Called "It"*

British
Fictional Prose
John Bunyan | *The Pilgrim's Progress*
Joseph Conrad | *Heart of Darkness*
Charles Dickens | *Tale of Two Cities*
George Eliot | *Middlemarch*
George Orwell | *1984*
Mary Shelley | *Frankenstein*
Drama
Samuel Beckett | *Waiting for Godot*
Caryl Churchill | *Top Girls*
William Congreve | *The Way of the World*
Michael Frayn | *Noises Off*
William Shakespeare | *Macbeth*
Oscar Wilde | *The Importance of Being Earnest*
Poetry
Elizabeth Barrett Browning | "How Do I Love Thee? (Sonnet 43)"
Robert Burns | "A Red, Red Rose"
Samuel Taylor Coleridge | "Rime of the Ancient Mariner"
T.S. Eliot | "Love Song of J. Alfred Prufrock"
John Milton | "Paradise Lost"
Literary Non-fiction
Vera Brittain | *Testament of Youth*
T. E. Lawrence | *Seven Pillars of Wisdom*
Doris Lessing | *Going Home*
Brian Blessed | *Absolute Pandemonium: The Autobiography*
Virginia Woolf | *A Room of One's Own*

World
Fictional Prose
Anonymous | *The Epic of Gilgamesh*
Chinua Achebe | *Things Fall Apart*
Margaret Atwood | *The Handmaid's Tale*
Pearl S. Buck | *The Good Earth*
Miguel de Cervantes | *Don Quixote*
Fyodor Dostoyevsky | *Crime and Punishment*
Gabriel Garcia Marquez | *One Hundred Years of Solitude*
James Joyce | *Ulysses*
Nikos Kazantzakis | *Zorba the Greek*
Boris Pasternak | *Dr. Zhivago*
Amy Tan | *The Joy Luck Club*
Voltaire | *Candide*
Drama
Bertolt Brecht | *Mother Courage and her Children*
Anton Chekhov | *The Seagull*

Lady Gregory | *Workhouse Ward*
Henrik Ibsen | *A Doll's House*
Luigi Pirandello | *Six Characters in Search of an Author*
Molière | *Tartuffe*
Sophocles | *Antigone*
August Strindberg | *Miss Julie*
Vyasa | *The Bhagavad Gita*
Johann Wolfgang von Goethe |*Faust*

Poetry

Anonymous | *Beowulf*
Anonymous |*The Ramayana*
Dante Alighieri |*The Divine Comedy*
Federico García Lorca | *Gypsy Ballads*
Omar Khayyám |*The Rubaiyat*
Kahlil Gibran | *The Prophet*
Andrew Barton "Banjo" Paterson |*"Waltzing Matilda"*
Taslima Nasrin | *"Character"*
Kostis Palamas | *"Ancient Eternal And Immortal Spirit"*
Maria Elena Cruz Varela | *"Kaleidoscope"*
Unknown | The 23rd Psalm, the Judeo-Christian bible

Literary Non-fiction

Pavel Basinsky | *Flight from Paradise*
Jung Chang | *Wild Swans*
Confucius | *The Analects of Confucius*
Viktor Frankl | *Man's Search for Meaning*
Mahatma Gandhi | *India of my Dreams*
Nelson Mandela | *Long Walk to Freedom*
Fatema Mernissi | *Beyond the Veil*
Jonathan Swift | *"A Modest Proposal"*

Mythology

Homer | *The Iliad*
Homer | *The Odyssey*
Hesiod | *Theogony*
Ovid | *Metamorphoses*
Virgil | *Aeneid*
Valmiki | *Ramayana*
Vyasa | *Bhagavad Gita*
Epic of Gilgamesh
Ferdowsi | The Shahnameh
Beowulf
The Volsunga Saga

Young Adult

Fictional Prose

Jodi Lynn Anderson | *Tiger Lily*
Lois Lowry | *The Giver*
Scott O'Dell | *Island of the Blue Dolphins*
Katherine Paterson Jacob | *Have I Loved*
Antoine de Saint-Exupéry | *The Little Prince*

Ellen Raskin | *The Westing Game*
P. L. Travers | *Mary Poppins*
Marcus Zusak | *The Book Thief*
Drama
Peter Dee | *Voices from the High School*
William Gibson | *The Miracle Worker*
Poetry
Sandra Cisneros | "Eleven"
Eamon Grennan | "Cat Scat"
Tom Junod | "My Mother Couldn't Cook"
Tupac Shakur | "The Rose that Grew from Concrete"
Literary Non-fiction
Sherman Alexie | *The Absolutely True Diary of a Part-Time Indian*
Anne Frank | *The Diary of Anne Frank*
Philip Hoose | *The Boys who Challenged Hitler*
Cynthia Levinson | *We've Got a Job*
Malala Yousafzai and Christina Lamb | *I am Malala*

Literary Contexts

Understanding that works of literature emerged either because of a particular context—or perhaps despite a context—is key to analyzing them effectively.

Historical Context
The *historical context* of a piece of literature can refer to the time period, setting, or conditions of living at the time it was written as well as the context of the work. For example, Hawthorne's *The Scarlet Letter* was published in 1850, though the setting of the story is 1642-1649. Historically, then, when Hawthorne wrote his novel, the United States found itself at odds as the beginnings of a potential Civil War were in view. Thus, the historical context is potentially significant as it pertains to the ideas of traditions and values, which Hawthorne addresses in his story of Hester Prynne in the era of Puritanism.

Cultural Context
The *cultural context* of a piece of literature refers to cultural factors, such as the beliefs, religions, and customs that surround and are in a work of literature. The Puritan's beliefs, religion, and customs in Hawthorne's novel would be significant as they are at the core of the plot—the reason Hester wears the A and why Arthur kills himself. The customs of people in the Antebellum Period, though not quite as restrictive, were still somewhat similar. This would impact how the audience of the time received the novel.

Literary Context
Literary context refers to the consideration of the genre, potentially at the time the work was written. In 1850, Realism and Romanticism were the driving forces in literature in the U.S., with depictions of life as it was at the time in which the work was written or the time it was written *about* as well as some works celebrating the beauty of nature. Thus, an audience in Hawthorne's time would have been well satisfied with the elements of both offered in the text. They would have been looking for details about everyday things and people (Realism), but they also would appreciate his approach to description of nature and the focus on the individual (American Romanticism). The contexts would be significant as they would pertain to evaluating the work against those criteria.

Here are some questions to use when considering context:

- When was the text written?

- What was society like at the time the text was written, or what was it like, given the work's identified time period?

- Who or what influenced the writer?

- What political or social influences might there have been?

- What influences may there have been in the genre that may have affected the writer?

Additionally, test takers should familiarize themselves with literary periods such as Old and Middle English, American Colonial, American Renaissance, American Naturalistic, and British and American Modernist and Post-Modernist movements. Most students of literature will have had extensive exposure to these literary periods in history, and while it is not necessary to recognize every major literary work on sight and associate that work to its corresponding movement or cultural context, the test taker should be familiar enough with the historical and cultural significance of each test passage in order to be able to address test questions correctly.

The following brief description of some literary contexts and their associated literary examples follows. It is not an all-inclusive list. The test taker should read each description, then follow up with independent study to clarify each movement, its context, its most familiar authors, and their works.

Metaphysical Poetry

Metaphysical poetry is the descriptor applied to 17th century poets whose poetry emphasized the lyrical quality of their work. These works contain highly creative poetic conceits or metaphoric comparisons between two highly dissimilar things or ideas. Metaphysical poetry is characterized by highly prosaic language and complicated, often layered, metaphor.

Poems such as John Donne's "The Flea," Andrew Marvell's "To His Coy Mistress," George Herbert's "The Collar," Henry Vaughan's "The World," and Richard Crashaw's "A Song" are associated with this type of poetry.

British Romanticism

British Romanticism was a cultural and literary movement within Europe that developed at the end of the 18th century and extended into the 19th century. It occurred partly in response to aristocratic, political, and social norms and partly in response to the Industrial Revolution of the day. Characterized by intense emotion, major literary works of British Romanticism embrace the idea of aestheticism and the beauty of nature. Literary works exalted folk customs and historical art and encouraged spontaneity of artistic endeavor. The movement embraced the heroic ideal and the concept that heroes would raise the quality of society.

Authors who are classified as British Romantics include Samuel Taylor Coleridge, John Keats, George Byron, Mary Shelley, Percy Bysshe Shelley, and William Blake. Well-known works include Samuel Taylor Coleridge's "Kubla Khan," John Keats' "Ode on a Grecian Urn," George Byron's "Childe Harold's Pilgrimage," Mary Shelley's *Frankenstein*, Percy Bysshe Shelley's "Ode to the West Wind," and William Blake's "The Tyger."

American Romanticism

American Romanticism occurred within the American literary scene beginning early in the 19ᵗʰ century. While many aspects were similar to British Romanticism, it is further characterized as having gothic aspects and the idea that individualism was to be encouraged. It also embraced the concept of the *noble savage*—the idea that indigenous culture uncorrupted by civilization is better than advanced society.

Well-known authors and works include Nathanial Hawthorne's *The House of the Seven Gables*, Edgar Allan Poe's "The Raven" and "The Cask of Amontillado," Emily Dickinson's "I Felt a Funeral in My Brain" and James Fenimore Cooper's *The Last of the Mohicans.*

Transcendentalism

Transcendentalism was a movement that applied to a way of thinking that developed within the United States, specifically New England, around 1836. While this way of thinking originally employed philosophical aspects, transcendentalism spread to all forms of art, literature, and even to the ways people chose to live. It was born out of a reaction to traditional rationalism and purported concepts such as a higher divinity, feminism, humanitarianism, and communal living. Transcendentalism valued intuition, self-reliance, and the idea that human nature was inherently good.

Well-known authors include Ralph Waldo Emerson, Henry David Thoreau, Louisa May Alcott, and Ellen Sturgis Hooper. Works include Ralph Waldo Emerson's "Self-Reliance" and "Uriel," Henry David Thoreau's *Walden* and *Civil Disobedience*, Louisa May Alcott's *Little Women*, and Ellen Sturgis Hooper's "I Slept, and Dreamed that Life was Beauty*.*"

The Harlem Renaissance

The Harlem Renaissance is the descriptor given to the cultural, artistic, and social boom that developed in Harlem, New York, at the beginning of the 20ᵗʰ century, spanning the 1920s and 1930s. Originally termed *The New Negro Movement*, it emphasized African-American urban cultural expression and migration across the United States. It had strong roots in African-American Christianity, discourse, and intellectualism. The Harlem Renaissance heavily influenced the development of music and fashion as well. Its singular characteristic was to embrace Pan-American culturalisms; however, strong themes of the slavery experience and African-American folk traditions also emerged. A hallmark of the Harlem Renaissance was that it laid the foundation for the future Civil Rights Movement in the United States.

Well-known authors and works include Zora Neale Hurston's *Their Eyes Were Watching God*, Richard Wright's *Native Son*, Langston Hughes' "I, Too," and James Weldon Johnson's "God's Trombones: Seven Negro Sermons in Verse" and *The Book of American Negro Poetry.*

Young Adult Literature

Young Adult (YA) Literature is aimed at readers who are 13 years of age or older. As such, it should be appropriate to the age and interest level of its intended readers. Young Adult novels tend to deal with more mature themes such as sex, drinking, and death, and may also use profanity. Young Adult literature is not limited to any one genre, with popular novels running the gamut from fantasy to historical fiction. The YA novel typically features a teen protagonist who faces real issues that a teen might face. Adults are included in YA novels, but usually as secondary characters to the teen protagonist; typically, in such novels, the teen protagonist may need to face or stand up to an adult.

Literary Interpretation

Literary interpretation is an interpretation and analysis of a literary work, based on the textual evidence in the work. It is often subjective as critical readers may discern different meanings in the details. A test taker needs to be prepared for questions that will test how well he or she can read a passage, make an analysis, and then provide evidence to support that analysis.

Literal and Figurative Meanings

When analyzing and interpreting fiction, readers must be active participants in the experience. Some authors make their messages clearer than others, but the onus is on the reader to add layers to what is read through interpretation. In literary interpretation, the goal is not to offer an opinion as to the inherent value of the work. Rather, the goal is to determine what the text means by analyzing the *literal and figurative meanings* of the text through critical reading.

Critical reading is close reading that elicits questions as the reader progresses. Many authors of fiction use literary elements and devices to further theme and to speak to their audience. These elements often utilize language that has an alternate or figurative meaning in addition to their actual or literal meaning. Readers should be asking questions about these and other important details as a passage is analyzed. What unfamiliar words are there? What is their contextual definition? How do they contribute to the overall feel of the work? How do they contribute to the mood and general message? Literal and figurative meanings are discussed further in the informational texts and rhetoric section.

Drawing Inferences

An *inference* refers to a point that is implied (as opposed to directly-stated) by the evidence presented. It's necessary to use inference in order to draw conclusions about the meaning of a passage. Authors make implications through character dialogue, thoughts, effects on others, actions, and looks.

When making an inference about a passage, it's important to rely only on the information that is provided in the text itself. This helps readers ensure that their conclusions are valid. Drawing inferences is also discussed in the informational texts and rhetoric section.

Directly Stated Information vs. Implications

Engaged readers should constantly self-question while reviewing texts to help them form conclusions. Self-questioning is when readers review a paragraph, page, passage, or chapter and ask themselves, "Did I understand what I read?," "What was the main event in this section?," "Where is this taking place?," and so on. Authors can provide clues or pieces of evidence throughout a text or passage to guide readers toward a conclusion. This is why active and engaged readers should read the text or passage in its entirety before forming a definitive conclusion. If readers do not gather all the pieces of evidence needed, then they may jump to an illogical conclusion.

At times, authors directly state conclusions while others simply imply them. Of course, it is easier if authors outwardly provide conclusions to readers, because it does not leave any information open to interpretation. On the other hand, implications are things that authors do not directly state but can be assumed based off of information they provided. If authors only imply what may have happened, readers can form a menagerie of ideas for conclusions. For example, look at the following statement: "Once we heard the sirens, we hunkered down in the storm shelter." In this statement, the author does not directly state that there was a tornado, but clues such as "sirens" and "storm shelter" provide insight to the readers to help form that conclusion.

Development of Themes

<u>Theme or Central Message</u>
The *theme* is the central message of a fictional work, whether that work is structured as prose, drama, or poetry. It is the heart of what an author is trying to say to readers through the writing, and theme is largely conveyed through literary elements and techniques.

In literature, a theme can be often be determined by considering the over-arching narrative conflict with the work. Though there are several types of conflicts and several potential themes within them, the following are the most common:

- *Individual against the self*—relevant to themes of self-awareness, internal struggles, pride, coming of age, facing reality, fate, free will, vanity, loss of innocence, loneliness, isolation, fulfillment, failure, and disillusionment

- *Individual against nature*— relevant to themes of knowledge vs. ignorance, nature as beauty, quest for discovery, self-preservation, chaos and order, circle of life, death, and destruction of beauty

- *Individual against society*— relevant to themes of power, beauty, good, evil, war, class struggle, totalitarianism, role of men/women, wealth, corruption, change vs. tradition, capitalism, destruction, heroism, injustice, and racism

- *Individual against another individual*— relevant to themes of hope, loss of love or hope, sacrifice, power, revenge, betrayal, and honor

For example, in Hawthorne's *The Scarlet Letter*, one possible narrative conflict could be the individual against the self, with a relevant theme of internal struggles. This theme is alluded to through characterization—Dimmesdale's moral struggle with his love for Hester and Hester's internal struggles with the truth and her daughter, Pearl. It's also alluded to through plot—Dimmesdale's suicide and Hester helping the very townspeople who initially condemned her.

Sometimes, a text can convey a *message* or *universal lesson*—a truth or insight that the reader infers from the text, based on analysis of the literary and/or poetic elements. This message is often presented as a statement. For example, a potential message in Shakespeare's *Hamlet* could be "Revenge is what ultimately drives the human soul." This message can be immediately determined through plot and characterization in numerous ways, but it can also be determined through the setting of Norway, which is bordering on war.

<u>How Authors Develop Theme</u>
Authors employ a variety of techniques to present a theme. They may compare or contrast characters, events, places, ideas, or historical or invented settings to speak thematically. They may use analogies, metaphors, similes, allusions, or other literary devices to convey the theme. An author's use of diction, syntax, and tone can also help convey the theme. Authors will often develop themes through the development of characters, use of the setting, repetition of ideas, use of symbols, and through contrasting value systems. Authors of both fiction and nonfiction genres will use a variety of these techniques to develop one or more themes.

Regardless of the literary genre, there are commonalities in how authors, playwrights, and poets develop themes or central ideas.

Authors often do research, the results of which contributes to theme. In prose fiction and drama, this research may include real historical information about the setting the author has chosen or include elements that make fictional characters, settings, and plots seem realistic to the reader. In nonfiction, research is critical since the information contained within this literature must be accurate and, moreover, accurately represented.

In fiction, authors present a narrative conflict that will contribute to the overall theme. In fiction, this conflict may involve the storyline itself and some trouble within characters that needs resolution. In nonfiction, this conflict may be an explanation or commentary on factual people and events.

Authors will sometimes use character motivation to convey theme, such as in the example from *Hamlet* regarding revenge. In fiction, the characters an author creates will think, speak, and act in ways that effectively convey the theme to readers. In nonfiction, the characters are factual, as in a biography, but authors pay particular attention to presenting those motivations to make them clear to readers.

Authors also use literary devices as a means of conveying theme. For example, the use of moon symbolism in Shelley's *Frankenstein* is significant as its phases can be compared to the phases that the Creature undergoes as he struggles with his identity.

The selected point of view can also contribute to a work's theme. The use of first person point of view in a fiction or non-fiction work engages the reader's response differently than third person point of view. The central idea or theme from a first person narrative may differ from a third-person limited text.

In literary nonfiction, authors usually identify the purpose of their writing, which differs from fiction, where the general purpose is to entertain. The purpose of nonfiction is usually to inform, persuade, or entertain the audience. The stated purpose of a non-fiction text will drive how the central message or theme, if applicable, is presented.

Authors identify an audience for their writing, which is critical in shaping the theme of the work. For example, the audience for J.K. Rowling's *Harry Potter* series would be different than the audience for a biography of George Washington. The audience an author chooses to address is closely tied to the purpose of the work. The choice of an audience also drives the choice of language and level of diction an author uses. Ultimately, the intended audience determines the level to which that subject matter is presented and the complexity of the theme.

Analyzing Major Literary Works

An important part of the teacher's job is to interpret texts for students appropriately. Literary texts are one way for students to learn about history, culture, and politics. It is the teacher's responsibility to interpret the content of these texts so that students can read the material with a critical eye, and develop their own ideas about the information presented. Some strategies for interpreting texts include questioning what has been read, considering what the author wants the reader to believe, and making the decision to believe or disbelieve the author's claims. Readers should consider the author's authority, whether he or she is credible on the subject—and ideology—and what the author believes. They should also consider the author's use of logic – how the author presents the information. The cultural, social, and political influences on the author will affect many of these factors, particularly ideology. The author's beliefs inform the text, so knowing his or her belief system will help readers to interpret the intended meaning.

Craft and Structure of Literature

Characteristics of Literary Genres

Classifying literature involves an understanding of the concept of genre. A *genre* is a category of literature that possesses similarities in style and in characteristics. Based on form and structure, there are four basic genres.

Fictional Prose
Fictional prose consists of fictional works written in standard form with a natural flow of speech and without poetic structure. Fictional prose primarily utilizes grammatically complete sentences and a paragraph structure to convey its message.

Drama
Drama is fiction that is written to be performed in a variety of media, intended to be performed for an audience, and structured for that purpose. It might be composed using poetry or prose, often straddling the elements of both in what actors are expected to present. Action and dialogue are the tools used in drama to tell the story.

Poetry
Poetry is fiction in verse that has a unique focus on the rhythm of language and focuses on intensity of feeling. It is not an entire story, though it may tell one; it is compact in form and in function. Poetry can be considered as a poet's brief word picture for a reader. Poetic structure is primarily composed of lines and stanzas. Together, poetic structure and devices are the methods that poets use to lead readers to feeling an effect and, ultimately, to the interpretive message.

Literary Nonfiction
Literary nonfiction is prose writing that is based on current or past real events or real people and includes straightforward accounts as well as those that offer opinions on facts or factual events. The exam distinguishes between *literary nonfiction*—a form of writing that incorporates literary styles and techniques to create factually-based narratives—and informational texts, which will be addressed in the next section.

Major Forms Within Each Genre

Fictional Prose
Fiction written in prose can be further broken down into **fiction genres**—types of fiction. Some of the more common genres of fiction are as follows:

- **Classical fiction**: a work of fiction considered timeless in its message or theme, remaining noteworthy and meaningful over decades or centuries—e.g., Charlotte Brontë's *Jane Eyre*, Mark Twain's *Adventures of Huckleberry Finn*

- **Fables**: short fiction that generally features animals, fantastic creatures, or other forces within nature that assume human-like characters and has a moral lesson for the reader—e.g., *Aesop's Fables*

- **Fairy tales**: children's stories with magical characters in imaginary, enchanted lands, usually depicting a struggle between good and evil, a sub-genre of folklore—e.g., Hans Christian Anderson's *The Little Mermaid*, *Cinderella* by the Brothers Grimm

- **Fantasy**: fiction with magic or supernatural elements that cannot occur in the real world, sometimes involving medieval elements in language, usually includes some form of sorcery or witchcraft and sometimes set on a different world—e.g., J.R.R. Tolkien's *The Hobbit*, J.K. Rowling's *Harry Potter and the Sorcerer's Stone*, George R.R. Martin's *A Game of Thrones*

- **Folklore**: types of fiction passed down from oral tradition, stories indigenous to a particular region or culture, with a local flavor in tone, designed to help humans cope with their condition in life and validate cultural traditions, beliefs, and customs—e.g., William Laughead's *Paul Bunyan and The Blue Ox*, the Buddhist story of "The Banyan Deer"

- **Mythology**: closely related to folklore but more widespread, features mystical, otherworldly characters and addresses the basic question of why and how humans exist, relies heavily on allegory and features gods or heroes captured in some sort of struggle—e.g., Greek myths, Genesis I and II in the Bible, Arthurian legends

- **Science fiction**: fiction that uses the principle of extrapolation—loosely defined as a form of prediction—to imagine future realities and problems of the human experience—e.g., Robert Heinlein's *Stranger in a Strange Land*, Ayn Rand's *Anthem*, Isaac Asimov's *I, Robot*, Philip K. Dick's *Do Androids Dream of Electric Sheep?*

- **Short stories**: short works of prose fiction with fully-developed themes and characters, focused on mood, generally developed with a single plot, with a short period of time for settings—e.g., Edgar Allan Poe's "Fall of the House of Usher," Shirley Jackson's "The Lottery," Isaac Bashevis Singer's "Gimpel the Fool"

Drama
Drama refers to a form of literature written for the purpose of performance for an audience. Like prose fiction, drama has several genres. The following are the most common ones:

- **Comedy**: a humorous play designed to amuse and entertain, often with an emphasis on the common person's experience, generally resolved in a positive way—e.g., Richard Sheridan's *School for Scandal*, Shakespeare's *Taming of the Shrew*, Neil Simon's *The Odd Couple*

- **History**: a play based on recorded history where the fate of a nation or kingdom is at the core of the conflict—e.g., Christopher Marlowe's *Edward II*, Shakespeare's *King Richard III*, Arthur Miller's *The Crucible*

- **Tragedy**: a serious play that often involves the downfall of the protagonist. In modern tragedies, the protagonist is not necessarily in a position of power or authority—e.g., Jean Racine's *Phèdre*, Arthur Miller's *Death of a Salesman*, John Steinbeck's *Of Mice and Men*

- **Melodrama**: a play that emphasizes heightened emotion and sensationalism, generally with stereotypical characters in exaggerated or realistic situations and with moral polarization—e.g., Jean-Jacques Rousseau's *Pygmalion*

- **Tragi-comedy**: a play that has elements of both tragedy—a character experiencing a tragic loss—and comedy—the resolution is often positive with no clear distinctive mood for either—e.g., Shakespeare's *The Merchant of Venice*, Anton Chekhov's *The Cherry Orchard*

Poetry

The genre of **poetry** refers to literary works that focus on the expression of feelings and ideas through the use of structure and linguistic rhythm to create a desired effect.

Different poetic structures and devices are used to create the various major forms of poetry. Some of the most common forms are discussed in the following chart.

Type	Poetic Structure	Example
Ballad	A poem or song passed down orally which tells a story and in English tradition usually uses an ABAB or ABCB rhyme scheme	William Butler Yeats' "The Ballad of Father O'Hart"
Epic	A long poem from ancient oral tradition which narrates the story of a legendary or heroic protagonist	Homer's *The Odyssey* Virgil's *The Aeneid*
Haiku	A Japanese poem of three unrhymed lines with five, seven, and five syllables (in English) with nature as a common subject matter	Matsuo Bashō "An old silent pond . . . A frog jumps into the pond, splash! Silence again."
Limerick	A five-line poem written in an AABBA rhyme scheme, with a witty focus	From Edward Lear's *Book of Nonsense*: "There was a Young Person of Smyrna Whose grandmother threatened to burn her . . ."
Ode	A formal lyric poem that addresses and praises a person, place, thing, or idea	Edna St. Vincent Millay's "Ode to Silence"
Sonnet	A fourteen-line poem written in iambic pentameter	Shakespeare's Sonnets 18 and 130

Literary Nonfiction

Nonfiction works are best characterized by their subject matter, which must be factual and real, describing true life experiences. There are several common types of literary non-fiction.

Biography

A *biography* is a work written about a real person (historical or currently living). It involves factual accounts of the person's life, often in a re-telling of those events based on available, researched factual information. The re-telling and dialogue, especially if related within quotes, must be accurate and reflect reliable sources. A biography reflects the time and place in which the person lived, with the goal of creating an understanding of the person and his/her human experience. Examples of well-known biographies include *The Life of Samuel Johnson* by James Boswell and *Steve Jobs* by Walter Isaacson.

Autobiography

An *autobiography* is a factual account of a person's life written by that person. It may contain some or all of the same elements as a biography, but the author is the subject matter. An autobiography will be told in first person narrative. Examples of well-known autobiographies in literature include *Night* by Elie Wiesel and *Margaret Thatcher: The Autobiography* by Margaret Thatcher.

Memoir

A *memoir* is a historical account of a person's life and experiences written by one who has personal, intimate knowledge of the information. The line between memoir, autobiography, and biography is often muddled, but generally speaking, a memoir covers a specific timeline of events as opposed to the other forms of nonfiction. A memoir is less all-encompassing. It is also less formal in tone and tends to focus on the emotional aspect of the presented timeline of events. Some examples of memoirs in literature include *Angela's Ashes* by Frank McCourt and *All Creatures Great and Small* by James Herriot.

Journalism

Some forms of *journalism* can fall into the category of literary non-fiction—e.g., travel writing, nature writing, sports writing, the interview, and sometimes, the essay. Some examples include Elizabeth Kolbert's "The Lost World, in the Annals of Extinction series for *The New Yorker* and Gary Smith's "Ali and His Entourage" for *Sports Illustrated*.

Literary Elements

There is no one, final definition of what literary elements are. They can be considered features or characteristics of fiction, but they are really more of a way that readers can unpack a text for the purpose of analysis and understanding the meaning. The elements contribute to a reader's literary interpretation of a passage as to how they function to convey the central message of a work. The most common literary elements used for analysis are the presented below.

Point of View

The *point of view* is the position the narrator takes when telling the story in prose. If a narrator is incorporated in a drama, the point of view may vary; in poetry, point of view refers to the position the speaker in a poem takes.

First Person

The first person point of view is when the writer uses the word "I" in the text. Poetry often uses first person, e.g., William Wordsworth's "I Wandered Lonely as a Cloud." Two examples of prose written in first person are Suzanne Collins' *The Hunger Games* and Anthony Burgess's *A Clockwork Orange*.

Second Person

The second person point of view is when the writer uses the pronoun "you." It is not widely used in prose fiction, but as a technique, it has been used by writers such as William Faulkner in *Absalom, Absalom!* and Albert Camus in *The Fall*. It is more common in poetry—e.g., Pablo Neruda's "If You Forget Me."

Third Person

Third person point of view is when the writer utilizes pronouns such as him, her, or them. It may be the most utilized point of view in prose as it provides flexibility to an author and is the one with which readers are most familiar. There are two main types of third person used in fiction. *Third person omniscient* uses a narrator that is all-knowing, relating the story by conveying and interpreting thoughts/feelings of all characters. In *third person limited,* the narrator relates the story through the perspective of one character's thoughts/feelings, usually the main character.

Plot

The *plot* is what happens in the story. Plots may be singular, containing one problem, or they may be very complex, with many sub-plots. All plots have exposition, a conflict, a climax, and a resolution. The *conflict* drives the plot and is something that the reader expects to be resolved. The plot carries those events along until there is a resolution to the conflict.

Tone

The *tone* of a story reflects the author's attitude and opinion about the subject matter of the story or text. Tone can be expressed through word choice, imagery, figurative language, syntax, and other details. The emotion or mood the reader experiences relates back to the tone of the story. Some examples of possible tones are humorous, somber, sentimental, and ironic.

Setting

The *setting* is the time, place, or set of surroundings in which the story occurs. It includes time or time span, place(s), climates, geography—man-made or natural—or cultural environments. Emily Dickinson's poem "Because I could not stop for Death" has a simple setting—the narrator's symbolic ride with Death through town towards the local graveyard. Conversely, Leo Tolstoy's *War and Peace* encompasses numerous settings within settings in the areas affected by the Napoleonic Wars, spanning 1805 to 1812.

Characters

Characters are the story's figures that assume primary, secondary, or minor roles. *Central* or *major* characters are those integral to the story—the plot cannot be resolved without them. A central character can be a *protagonist* or hero. There may be more than one protagonist, and he/she doesn't always have to possess good characteristics. A character can also be an *antagonist*—the force against a protagonist.

Dynamic characters change over the course of the plot time. *Static* characters do not change. A *symbolic* character is one that represents an author's idea about society in general—e.g., Napoleon in Orwell's *Animal Farm*. *Stock* characters are those that appear across genres and embrace stereotypes—e.g., the cowboy of the Wild West or the blonde bombshell in a detective novel. A *flat* character is one that does not present a lot of complexity or depth, while a *rounded* character does. Sometimes, the *narrator* of a story or the *speaker* in a poem can be a character—e.g., Nick Carraway in F. Scott Fitzgerald's *The Great Gatsby* or the speaker in Robert Browning's "My Last Duchess." The narrator might also function as a character in prose, though not be part of the story—e.g., Charles Dickens' narrator of *A Christmas Carol*.

Dramatic Literature

Dramatic literature differs from other forms of literature in that instead of being read, it is meant to be performed. Dramatic literature includes some of the same elements of other literary forms, such as characters, plot, and setting. Unlike short stories or poems, dramatic literature includes set directions and dialogue. Often the set directions are used to show how characters feel through their actions, since readers are only able to see what they say through dialogue. The most prominent types of dramatic literature are comedies and tragedies. A tragedy is a play with an unhappy ending. It often includes a hero whose tragic flaw contributes to his or her downfall. A comedy typically uses a humorous or satirical tone and includes a happy ending. Its purpose is to amuse the audience.

Figurative Language

Whereas literal language is the author's use of precise words, proper meanings, definitions, and phrases that mean exactly what they say, *figurative language* deviates from precise meaning and word definition—often in conjunction with other familiar words and phrases—to paint a picture for the reader. Figurative language is less explicit and more open to reader interpretation.

Some examples of figurative language are included in the following graphic.

	Definition	Example
Simile	Compares two things using "like" or "as"	Her hair was like gold.
Metaphor	Compares two things as if they are the same	He was a giant teddy bear.
Idiom	Using words with predictable meanings to create a phrase with a different meaning	The world is your oyster.
Alliteration	Repeating the same beginning sound or letter in a phrase for emphasis	The busy baby babbled.
Personification	Attributing human characteristics to an object or an animal	The house glowered menacingly with a dark smile.
Foreshadowing	Giving an indication that something is going to happen later in the story	I wasn't aware at the time, but I would come to regret those words.
Symbolism	Using symbols to represent ideas and provide a different meaning	The ring represented the bond between us.
Onomatopoeia	Using words that imitate sound	The tire went off with a bang and a crunch.
Imagery	Appealing to the senses by using descriptive language	The sky was painted with red and pink and streaked with orange.
Hyperbole	Using exaggeration not meant to be taken literally	The girl weighed less than a feather.

Figurative language can be used to give additional insight into the theme or message of a text by moving beyond the usual and literal meaning of words and phrases. It can also be used to appeal to the senses of readers and create a more in-depth story.

Effect of Word Choice

An author's choice of words—also referred to as *diction*—helps to convey his or her meaning in a particular way. Through diction, an author can convey a particular tone—e.g., a humorous tone, a serious tone—in order to support the thesis in a meaningful way to the reader.

Connotation and Denotation
Connotation is when an author chooses words or phrases that invoke ideas or feelings other than their literal meaning. An example of the use of connotation is the word *cheap*, which suggests something is poor in value or negatively describes a person as reluctant to spend money. When something or someone is described this way, the reader is more inclined to have a particular image or feeling about it or him/her. Thus, connotation can be a very effective language tool in creating emotion and swaying opinion. However, connotations are sometimes hard to pin down because varying emotions can be associated with a word. Generally, though, connotative meanings tend to be fairly consistent within a specific cultural group.

Denotation refers to words or phrases that mean exactly what they say. It is helpful when a writer wants to present hard facts or vocabulary terms with which readers may be unfamiliar. Some examples of denotation are the words *inexpensive* and *frugal*. *Inexpensive* refers to the cost of something, not its value, and *frugal* indicates that a person is conscientiously watching his or her spending. These terms do not elicit the same emotions that *cheap* does.

Authors sometimes choose to use both, but what they choose and when they use it is what critical readers need to differentiate. One method isn't inherently better than the other; however, one may create a better effect, depending upon an author's intent. If, for example, an author's purpose is to inform, to instruct, and to familiarize readers with a difficult subject, his or her use of connotation may be helpful. However, it may also undermine credibility and confuse readers. An author who wants to create a credible, scholarly effect in his or her text would most likely use denotation, which emphasizes literal, factual meaning and examples.

Technical Language

Test takers and critical readers alike should be very aware of technical language used within informational text. *Technical language* refers to terminology that is specific to a particular industry and is best understood by those specializing in that industry. This language is fairly easy to differentiate, since it will most likely be unfamiliar to readers. It's critical to be able to define technical language either by the author's written definition, through the use of an included glossary—if offered—or through context clues that help readers clarify word meaning.

Authors' Intent with Text Structure

When it comes to an author's writing, readers should always identify a position or stance. No matter how objective a text may seem, readers should assume the author has preconceived beliefs. One can reduce the likelihood of accepting an invalid argument by looking for multiple articles on the topic, including those with varying opinions. If several opinions point in the same direction and are backed by reputable peer-reviewed sources, it's more likely the author has a valid argument. Positions that run contrary to widely held beliefs and existing data should invite scrutiny. There are exceptions to the rule, so be a careful consumer of information.

Though themes, symbols, and motifs are buried deep within the text and can sometimes be difficult to infer, an author's purpose is usually obvious from the beginning. There are four purposes of writing: to inform, to persuade, to describe, and to entertain. Informative writing presents facts in an accessible way. Persuasive writing appeals to emotions and logic to inspire the reader to adopt a specific stance. Be wary of this type of writing, as it can mask a lack of objectivity with powerful emotion. Descriptive writing is designed to paint a picture in the reader's mind, while texts that entertain are often narratives designed to engage and delight the reader.

The various writing styles are usually blended, with one purpose dominating the rest. A persuasive text, for example, might begin with a humorous tale to make readers more receptive to the persuasive message, or a recipe in a cookbook designed to inform might be preceded by an entertaining anecdote that makes the recipes more appealing.

Point of View

Point of view refers to perspective from which a story is told. A story can be told by a narrator or a character in the story. An author may choose to tell the story from the perspective of a single character, giving a limited view of the story's events. An author may also opt to use an omniscient point of view, where many characters tell the story, providing more than one view of the events in the story. This can be particularly effective when an author wants to show different perspectives on a single subject. An author can also use an objective point of view, where readers can only see what the characters do, say, and hear through dialogue, but do not have access to their inner thoughts. An example of this is Shirley Jackson's short story, *The Lottery*, where the objective point allows readers to consider their own perspective on the horrific events described. Factors such as race, class, beliefs, and cultural experiences can affect and shape an author's point of view. Where a particular text is written can influence the subject matter and point of view.

Reading Informational Texts

Textual Evidence

Once a reader has determined an author's thesis or main idea, he or she will need to understand how textual evidence supports interpretation of that thesis or main idea. Test takers will be asked direct questions regarding an author's main idea and may be asked to identify evidence that would support those ideas. This will require test takers to comprehend literal and figurative meanings within the text passage, be able to draw inferences from provided information, and be able to separate important evidence from minor supporting detail. It's often helpful to skim test questions and answer options prior to critically reading informational text; however, test takers should avoid the temptation to solely look for the correct answers. Just trying to find the "right answer" may cause test takers to miss important supporting textual evidence. Making mental note of test questions is only helpful as a guide when reading.

After identifying an author's thesis or main idea, a test taker should look at the supporting details that the author provides to back up his or her assertions, identifying those additional pieces of information that help expand the thesis. From there, test takers should examine the additional information and related details for credibility, the author's use of outside sources, and be able to point to direct evidence that supports the author's claims. It's also imperative that test takers be able to identify what is strong support and what is merely additional information that is nice to know but not necessary. Being able to make this differentiation will help test takers effectively answer questions regarding an author's use of supporting evidence within informational text.

Central Ideas in Informational Texts

Informational text is specifically designed to relate factual information, and although it is open to a reader's interpretation and application of the facts, the structure of the presentation is carefully designed to lead the reader to a particular conclusion or central idea. When reading informational text, it is important that readers are able to understand its organizational structure as the structure often directly relates to an author's intent to inform and/or persuade the reader.

The first step in identifying the text's structure is to determine the thesis or main idea. The thesis statement and organization of a work are closely intertwined. *A thesis statement* indicates the writer's purpose and may include the scope and direction of the text. It may be presented at the beginning of a text or at the end, and it may be explicit or implicit.

Once a reader has a grasp of the thesis or main idea of the text, he or she can better determine its organizational structure. Test takers are advised to read informational text passages more than once in order to comprehend the material fully. It is also helpful to examine any text features present in the text including the table of contents, index, glossary, headings, footnotes, and visuals. The analysis of these features and the information presented within them, can offer additional clues about the central idea and structure of a text. The following questions should be asked when considering structure:

- How does the author assemble the parts to make an effective whole argument?

- Is the passage linear in nature and if so, what is the timeline or thread of logic?

- What is the presented order of events, facts, or arguments? Are these effective in contributing to the author's thesis?

- How can the passage be divided into sections? How are they related to each other and to the main idea or thesis?

- What key terms are used to indicate the organization?

Next, test takers should skim the passage, noting the first line or two of each body paragraph—the *topic sentences*—and the conclusion. Key *transitional terms*, such as *on the other hand, also, because, however, therefore, most importantly*, and *first*, within the text can also signal organizational structure. Based on these clues, readers should then be able to identify what type of organizational structure is being used. The following organizational structures are most common:

- *Problem/solution*—organized by an analysis/overview of a problem, followed by potential solution(s)

- *Cause/effect*—organized by the effects resulting from a cause or the cause(s) of a particular effect

- *Spatial order*—organized by points that suggest location or direction—e.g., top to bottom, right to left, outside to inside

- *Chronological/sequence order*—organized by points presented to indicate a passage of time or through purposeful steps/stages

- *Comparison/Contrast*—organized by points that indicate similarities and/or differences between two things or concepts

- *Order of importance*—organized by priority of points, often most significant to least significant or vice versa

Summaries of Informational Texts

Informational text is written material that has the primary function of imparting information about a topic. It is often written by someone with expertise in the topic and directed at an audience that has less knowledge of the topic. Informational texts are written in a different fashion from storytelling or narrative texts. Typically, this type of text has several organizational and structural differences from narrative text. In informational texts, there are features such as charts, graphs, photographs, headings and subheadings, glossaries, indexes, bibliographies, or other guidance features. With the aid of technology, embedded hyperlinks and video content are also sometimes included. Informational material may be written to compare and contrast, be explanatory, link cause and effect, provide opinion, persuade the reader, or serve a number of other purposes. Finally, informational texts typically use a different style of language than narrative texts, which instead, focus more on storytelling. Historically, informational texts were not introduced until students were ready to read to learn versus still learning to read. However, research is now suggesting that informational text can be developmentally appropriate for students at a much younger age.

One very effective strategy for increasing comprehension of informational text is *reciprocal teaching*. Reciprocal teaching is a method of small group teaching that relies on students assuming different roles to practice four reading strategies particularly helpful for readers of informational texts. Predicting, summarizing, questioning, and clarifying will lead students to understand and apply what they read. Skilled readers have acquired a set of techniques that make informational reading effective for them. They begin by previewing text selections and making educated guesses as to what the content will include. They then identify the purpose for reading the text and can explain why the content will be important to know. They are able to filter the reading selection to screen out the trivial points and focus on the most important facts. Using critical thinking skills, they monitor their own understanding of the information by asking themselves questions about what they have read. They use multiple methods to determine the meaning of unknown vocabulary. Finally, they can concisely and succinctly form an overall summary of what they have learned from the text.

Predicting
Predicting requires thinking ahead and, after reading, verifying whether predictions were correct. This method engages students with the text and gets them to pay attention to details that tell them whether their predictions might be coming true. The goal is to help students learn to base their predictions on clues from the text. They should not only state what they predict but also be able to comment on the specifics of the text that lead them to make those predictions.

Summarizing
Through summarizing, students learn to identify the main ideas and differentiate them from the less important information in the text. It helps them remember what they read and retell the central concepts in their own words. As students learn to break down larger chunks of information into more concise sentences, they use analytical thinking skills and hone their critical reading capabilities.

Questioning Techniques
Questioning has immeasurable value in the reading process. Answering questions about a text gives purpose for reading to students and focuses them on reading to learn information. Similarly, generating questions about a text for others to answer enables a student to analyze what is important to learn in the text and glean summarizing skills. Keeping Bloom's Taxonomy in mind, teachers can scaffold students toward increased critical thinking capabilities. Bloom's Taxonomy shows the hierarchy of learning progressing through the following stages:

- Remembering
- Understanding
- Applying
- Analyzing
- Evaluating
- Creating

Clarifying
This is the post-reading phase where students learn to clear up any misunderstandings and unanswered questions. Strategies for clarifying include defining any unknown words, rereading at a slower pace,

reviewing previous segments of the text, referring to their summaries, and skimming future portions of the text.

Sequences of Events in Informational Texts

Analyzing and explaining a set of ideas or events calls for students to follow the logic of an author's text. It's necessary to be able to follow a plot or different concepts presented in an informational text in order to understand its meaning. To reinforce this concept, teachers can have students identify the main idea and supporting points. Successfully doing this demonstrates an understanding of the framework of an argument or the plot of a narrative, for example. It can also help students to recognize patterns in the way an author organizes a text. Students should also be able to make meaningful connections between these ideas.

Good writing is not merely a random collection of sentences. No matter how well written, sentences must relate and coordinate appropriately with one another. If not, the writing seems random, haphazard, and disorganized. Therefore, good writing must be organized, where each sentence fits a larger context and relates to the sentences around it.

Transition Words
The writer should act as a guide, showing the reader how all the sentences fit together. Consider the seat belt example again:

> Seat belts save more lives than any other automobile safety feature. Many studies show that airbags save lives as well. Not all cars have airbags. Many older cars don't. Air bags aren't entirely reliable. Studies show that in 15% of accidents, airbags don't deploy as designed. Seat belt malfunctions are extremely rare.

There's nothing wrong with any of these sentences individually, but together they're disjointed and difficult to follow. The best way for the writer to communicate information is through the use of transition words. Here are examples of transition words and phrases that tie sentences together, enabling a more natural flow:

- To show causality: as a result, therefore, and consequently
- To compare and contrast: however, but, and on the other hand
- To introduce examples: for instance, namely, and including
- To show order of importance: foremost, primarily, secondly, and lastly

NOTE: This is not a complete list of transitions. There are many more that can be used; however, most fit into these or similar categories. The important point is that the words should clearly show the relationship between sentences, supporting information, and the main idea.

Here is an update to the previous example using transition words. These changes make it easier to read and bring clarity to the writer's points:

> Seat belts save more lives than any other automobile safety feature. Many studies show that airbags save lives as well; however, not all cars have airbags. For instance, some older cars don't. Furthermore, air bags aren't entirely reliable. For example, studies show that in 15% of accidents, airbags don't deploy as designed, but, on the other hand, seat belt malfunctions are extremely rare.

Also, be prepared to analyze whether the writer is using the best transition word or phrase for the situation. Take this sentence for example: "As a result, seat belt malfunctions are extremely rare." This sentence doesn't make sense in the context above because the writer is trying to show the contrast between seat belts and airbags, not the causality.

<u>Logical Sequence</u>
Even if the writer includes plenty of information to support their point, the writing is only coherent when the information is in a logical order. First, the writer should introduce the main idea, whether for a paragraph, a section, or the entire piece. Then they should present evidence to support the main idea by using transitional language. This shows the reader how the information relates to the main idea and to the sentences around it. The writer should then take time to interpret the information, making sure necessary connections are obvious to the reader. Finally, the writer can summarize the information in a closing section.

Though most writing follows this pattern, it isn't a set rule. Sometimes writers change the order for effect. For example, the writer can begin with a surprising piece of supporting information to grab the reader's attention, and then transition to the main idea. Thus, if a passage doesn't follow the logical order, don't immediately assume it's wrong. However, most writing usually settles into a logical sequence after a nontraditional beginning.

Introductions and Conclusions

Examining the writer's strategies for introductions and conclusions puts the reader in the right mindset to interpret the rest of the text. Look for methods the writer might use for introductions such as:

- Stating the main point immediately, followed by outlining how the rest of the piece supports this claim.

- Establishing important, smaller pieces of the main idea first, and then grouping these points into a case for the main idea.

- Opening with a quotation, anecdote, question, seeming paradox, or other piece of interesting information, and then using it to lead to the main point.

Whatever method the writer chooses, the introduction should make their intention clear, establish their voice as a credible one, and encourage a person to continue reading.

Conclusions tend to follow a similar pattern. In them, the writer restates their main idea a final time, often after summarizing the smaller pieces of that idea. If the introduction uses a quote or anecdote to grab the reader's attention, the conclusion often makes reference to it again. Whatever way the writer chooses to arrange the conclusion, the final restatement of the main idea should be clear and simple for the reader to interpret. Finally, conclusions shouldn't introduce any new information.

Media and Non-Print Text

In the 21st century, rhetoric is evident in a variety of formats. Blogs, vlogs, videos, news footage, advertisements, and live video fill informational feeds, and readers see many shortened images and snapshot texts a day. It's important to note that the majority of these formats use images to appeal to emotion over factual information. Online visuals spread more quickly and are more easily adopted by consumers as fact than printed formats.

Critical readers should be aware that media and non-print text carries some societal weight to the population. In being inundated with pictures and live footage, readers often feel compelled to skip the task of critical reading analysis and accept truth at literal face value. Authors of non-print media are aware of this fact and frequently capitalize on it.

To critically address non-print media requires that the consumer address additional sources and not exclude printed text in order to reach sound conclusions. While it's tempting for consumers to get swept away in the latest viral media, it's important to remember that creators of such have an agenda, and unless the non-print media in question is backed up with sound supporting evidence, any thesis or message cannot be considered valid or factual. Memes, gifs, and looped video cannot tell the whole, truthful story although they may appeal to opinions with which readers already agree. Sharing such non-print media online can precipitate widespread misunderstanding and invariably does.

When presented with non-print media, critical readers should consider these bits of information as teasers to be investigated for accuracy and veracity. Of course, certain non-print media exists solely for entertainment, but the critical reader should be able to separate out what's generalized for entertainment's sake and what's presented for further verification, before blindly accepting the message. Increasingly, this has become more difficult for readers to do, only because of the onslaught of information to which they are exposed.

If a reader is not to fall prey to strong imagery and non-print media, he or she will need to fact-check. This, of course, requires time and attention on the reader's part, and in current culture, taking the time to fact-check seems counterproductive. However, in order to maintain credibility themselves, readers must be able to evaluate multiple sources of information across media formats and be able to identify the emotional appeal used in the smaller sound bites of non-print media. Readers must view with a discerning eye, listen with a questioning ear, and think with a critical mind.

Consumer, Workplace, and Public Documents

It is important for students to be able to read consumer, workplace, and public documents and understand them without prior knowledge of their content. Structure and content can provide clues to meaning. Knowing how to analyze these texts will help students when they encounter them in everyday life. Some examples of these types of documents are insurance forms, a job application, or a service contract. These documents may contain terminology that readers are unfamiliar with. Teachers can help students to decipher meaning through analysis of the structure and purpose of these documents. They can also help students evaluate key terms and the use of text features like graphics and headers.

While expository in nature, memorandums (memos) are designed to convey basic information in a specific and concise message. Memos have a heading, which includes the information *to, from, date,* and *subject,* and a body, which is either in paragraph form or bullet points that detail what was in the subject line.

Though e-mails often replace memos in the modern workplace, printed memos still have a place. For example, if a supervisor wants to relate information, such as a company-wide policy change, to a large group, posting a memo in a staff lounge or other heavily traveled area is an efficient way to do so.

Posted announcements are useful to convey information to a large group of people. Announcements, however, take on a more informal tone than a memo. Common announcement topics include items for sale, services offered, lost pets, or business openings. Since posted announcements are found in public places, like grocery or hardware stores, they include contact information, purpose, meeting times, and prices, as well as pictures, graphics, and colors to attract the reader's eye.

Classified advertisements are another useful medium to convey information to large groups. Consider using classified advertisements when you want to buy and sell items, or look for services. Classified ads are found in newspapers, or online through *Craigslist*, *eBay*, or similar websites and blogs. While newspapers rely on ads to help fund their publications and often provide only local exposure, online sites provide a statewide or even global platform, thus shipping costs are an important consideration when looking at the cost of the item.

Regardless of the medium, all advertisements offer basic information, such as the item in question, a description, picture, cost, and the seller's contact information. It may also note a willingness to negotiate on the price or offer an option to trade in lieu of a sale. As websites like *Craigslist* and *Buy/Sell/Trade* increase in popularity, more localities offer "safe zones," where purchases and trades are conducted in supervised environments.

Interpreting Informational Texts in their Contexts

Context refers to all the cultural, social, political associations of a text. The way an author was raised and the environment in which they have lived can influence how he or she writes. When a reader knows more about the norms of a culture, such as what is an appropriate greeting among strangers (a hug, a handshake, a nod, etc.), it can allow a deeper understanding when such an event occurs in a text. It's important to take these kinds of associations into consideration when determining things like the author's intended audience and purpose. Teachers can help students to understand context by pointing out the cultural, social, and political aspects of a text, which may be unfamiliar to students, and educating them as to their meaning. An informational text's primary purpose is to convey information about the world. Examples of informational texts are speeches like Abraham Lincoln's *Gettysburg Address* or Martin Luther King's *I Have a Dream* speech or a scientific text like Euclid's *Elements*. The overall goal of these texts is to inform readers, and not to entertain or tell the story of a character.

Craft and Structure of Informational Texts

Interpreting Textual Evidence in Informational Text

Literal and Figurative Meanings
It is important when evaluating informational texts to consider the use of both *literal and figurative meanings*. The words and phrases an author chooses to include in a text must be evaluated. How does the word choice affect the meaning and tone? By recognizing the use of literal and figurative language, a reader can more readily ascertain the message or purpose of a text. Literal word choice is the easiest to analyze as it represents the usual and intended way a word or phrase is used. It is also more common in informational texts because it is used to state facts and definitions. While figurative language is typically associated with fiction and poetry, it can be found in informational texts as well. The reader must determine not only what is meant by the figurative language in context, but also how the author intended it to shape the overall text.

Inference in Informational Text
Inference refers to the reader's ability to understand the unwritten text, i.e., "read between the lines" in terms of an author's intent or message. The strategy asks that a reader not take everything he or she reads at face value but instead, add his or her own interpretation of what the author seems to be trying

to convey. A reader's ability to make inferences relies on his or her ability to think clearly and logically about the text. It does not ask that the reader make wild speculation or guess about the material but demands that he or she be able to come to a sound conclusion about the material.

An author's use of less literal words and phrases requires readers to make more inference when they read. Since inference involves *deduction*—deriving conclusions from ideas assumed to be true—there's more room for interpretation. Still, critical readers who employ inference, if careful in their thinking, can still arrive at the logical, sound conclusions the author intends.

Analyzing and Evaluating Text Structure

Depending on what the author is attempting to accomplish, certain formats or text structures work better than others. For example, a sequence structure might work for narration but not when identifying similarities and differences between dissimilar concepts. Similarly, a comparison-contrast structure is not useful for narration. It's the author's job to put the right information in the correct format.

Readers should be familiar with the five main text structures:

1. *Sequence* structure (sometimes referred to as the order structure) is when the order of events proceed in a predictable order. In many cases, this means the text goes through the plot elements: exposition, rising action, climax, falling action, and resolution. Readers are introduced to characters, setting, and conflict in the exposition. In the rising action, there's an increase in tension and suspense. The climax is the height of tension and the point of no return. Tension decreases during the falling action. In the resolution, any conflicts presented in the exposition are solved, and the story concludes. An informative text that is structured sequentially will often go in order from one step to the next.

2. In the *problem-solution* structure, authors identify a potential problem and suggest a solution. This form of writing is usually divided into two paragraphs and can be found in informational texts. For example, cell phone, cable and satellite providers use this structure in manuals to help customers troubleshoot or identify problems with services or products.

3. When authors want to discuss similarities and differences between separate concepts, they arrange thoughts in a *comparison-contrast* paragraph structure. Venn diagrams are an effective graphic organizer for comparison-contrast structures, because they feature two overlapping circles that can be used to organize similarities and differences. A comparison-contrast essay organizes one paragraph based on similarities and another based on differences. A comparison-contrast essay can also be arranged with the similarities and differences of individual traits addressed within individual paragraphs. Words such as *however*, *but*, and *nevertheless* help signal a contrast in ideas.

4. *Descriptive* writing structure is designed to appeal to your senses. Much like an artist who constructs a painting, good descriptive writing builds an image in the reader's mind by appealing to the five senses: sight, hearing, taste, touch, and smell. However, overly descriptive writing can become tedious; sparse descriptions can make settings and characters seem flat. Good authors strike a balance by applying descriptions only to passages, characters, and settings that are integral to the plot.

5. Passages that use the *cause and effect* structure are simply asking *why* by demonstrating some type of connection between ideas. Words such as *if*, *since*, *because*, *then*, or *consequently* indicate relationship. By switching the order of a complex sentence, the writer can rearrange the emphasis on different clauses. Saying *If Sheryl is late, we'll miss the dance* is different from saying *We'll miss the*

dance if Sheryl is late. One emphasizes Sheryl's tardiness while the other emphasizes missing the dance. Paragraphs can also be arranged in a cause and effect format. Since the format—before and after—is sequential, it is useful when authors wish to discuss the impact of choices. Researchers often apply this paragraph structure to the scientific method.

Text Features

Identifying Information in an Index or Table of Contents
An index is an alphabetical listing of topics, such as people, works, or concepts that appear at the end of expository materials like textbooks, cookbooks, and repair manuals. When these key words are used in paragraphs, they sometimes appear in bold writing to indicate their importance and let the reader know that they're found in the index as well.

Index listings often discard articles like *a*, *an*, and *the*. Additionally, authors will be listed by their last names, not first. Topics may be further divided into subtopics. If you start by looking for the most basic topics first, you can quickly acquire information. For example, when looking for a cookie recipe in a cookbook, first find the word *cookie* in the index and then examine the indented list of cookie-related topics located directly beneath the original heading.

Some textbooks have multiple indexes arranged by different subjects. If, for instance, you're dealing with a weighty literature textbook, you might find one index that lists authors and another devoted to concepts. The lengthier the book, the more likely you are to find this format.

While an index is typically found at the end of a book, a table of contents is found at the beginning to help readers quickly locate information. A table of contents is arranged differently, however, because it provides a chronological listing of each chapter and a corresponding page number. Each entry may also include a description, summary statement, or objective.

When students first receive a textbook, they should take time to preview the table of contents to create a framework for mentally organizing information. By classifying the contents, the reader creates mental schemas and becomes more likely to retain the information longer.

Analyzing Headings and Subheadings
Headings and subheadings are used in writing to organize discussions and allow the reader to find information quickly. Headings show a complete change in thought. Subheadings, which fall below headings, show different aspects of the same topic. For instance, if you saw the title *Government* and the heading *Forms of Government*, you might see the subheadings *Monarchy*, *Oligarchy*, *Democracy*, *Socialism*, and *Totalitarianism*.

As well as providing organization and structure, headings and subheadings also put more white space on a page, which places less strain on the reader's eyes. It's a good idea to skim a document and get familiar with headings and subheadings. Write down the title, headings, and subheadings before you begin reading to provide structure to your notes and thoughts.

Text Features
Text features are used to bring clarity or to affect the meaning of it. Bolding, italics, and underlining are all used to make words stand out. Bolded words are often key concepts and can usually be found in summary statements at the end of chapters and in indexes. Italics can be used to identify words of another language or to add extra emphasis to a word or phrase. Writers will sometime place words in

italics when the word is being referred to as the word itself. Quotation marks or italics can be used for this, as long as there is consistency. Italics are also used to represent a character's thoughts:

> Entering Jessica's room, Jessica's mom stepped over a pile of laundry, a stack of magazines, and a pile of dishes. *My messy daughter*, she thought, shaking her head.

In addition, formatting—such as indentation or bullet points—helps to clearly present content. Writers can come up with their own uses for text features based on what they feel is best. It's important to catch on to the purpose of the text features that the writer uses.

Author's Point of View and Writing Strategies

Determining an Author's Point of View

A *rhetorical strategy*—also referred to as a *rhetorical mode*—is the structural way an author chooses to present his/her argument. Though the terms noted below are similar to the organizational structures noted earlier, these strategies do not imply that the entire text follows the approach. For example, a cause and effect organizational structure is solely that, nothing more. A persuasive text may use cause and effect as a strategy to convey a singular point. Thus, an argument may include several of the strategies as the author strives to convince his or her audience to take action or accept a different point of view. It's important that readers are able to identify an author's thesis and position on the topic in order to be able to identify the careful construction through which the author speaks to the reader. The following are some of the more common rhetorical strategies:

- *Cause and effect*—establishing a logical correlation or causation between two ideas
- *Classification/division*—the grouping of similar items together or division of something into parts
- *Comparison/contrast*—the distinguishing of similarities/differences to expand on an idea
- *Definition*—used to clarify abstract ideas, unfamiliar concepts, or to distinguish one idea from another
- *Description*—use of vivid imagery, active verbs, and clear adjectives to explain ideas
- *Exemplification*—the use of examples to explain an idea
- *Narration*—anecdotes or personal experience to present or expand on a concept
- *Problem/Solution*—presentation of a problem or problems, followed by proposed solution(s)

Rhetorical Strategies and Devices

A *rhetorical device* is the phrasing and presentation of an idea that reinforces and emphasizes a point in an argument. A rhetorical device is often quite memorable. One of the more famous uses of a rhetorical device is in John F. Kennedy's 1961 inaugural address: "Ask not what your country can do for you, ask what you can do for your country." The contrast of ideas presented in the phrasing is an example of the rhetorical device of antimetabole. Some other common examples are provided below, but test takers should be aware that this is not a complete list.

Device	Definition	Example
Allusion	A reference to a famous person, event, or significant literary text as a form of significant comparison	"We are apt to shut our eyes against a painful truth, and listen to the song of that siren till she transforms us into beasts." Patrick Henry
Anaphora	The repetition of the same words at the beginning of successive words, phrases, or clauses, designed to emphasize an idea	"We shall not flag or fail. We shall go on to the end. We shall fight in France, we shall fight on the seas and oceans, we shall fight with growing confidence … we shall fight in the fields and in the streets, we shall fight in the hills. We shall never surrender." Winston Churchill
Understatement	A statement meant to portray a situation as less important than it actually is to create an ironic effect	"The war in the Pacific has not necessarily developed in Japan's favor." Emperor Hirohito, surrendering Japan in World War II
Parallelism	A syntactical similarity in a structure or series of structures used for impact of an idea, making it memorable	"A penny saved is a penny earned." Ben Franklin
Rhetorical question	A question posed that is not answered by the writer though there is a desired response, most often designed to emphasize a point	"Can anyone look at our reduced standing in the world today and say, 'Let's have four more years of this?'" Ronald Reagan

Integration of Knowledge and Ideas in Informational Texts

Integrating Multiple Sources and Formats of Information

Media can be effectively incorporated into instruction before, during, and after students learn a concept. Media messages can be used to introduce a new concept or repeat and reinforce concepts already learned. Teachers should be aware that media messages can be interpreted differently by different students, and it is the teacher's role to help students process the intended concept. Media should be used in conjunction with more traditional instructional methods for optimal effectiveness and critical analysis.

<u>Evaluating Students' Media Presentations</u>
Like peer review in the writing process, students can also benefit from review of their media presentations. Effective review processes should be directed and specific, using questions that help students to identify the intended concepts of a lesson and to make sure the media message is delivered appropriately. Students should be able to identify the purpose of a classmate's presentation, and be clear about the purpose of their own presentations.

<u>Legal Considerations</u>
Teachers are subject to copyright, fair use, and liability laws like any other citizen. Materials used in the classroom should not violate these laws. It is the responsibility of the teacher to know the laws and abide by them in the reproduction and use of any classroom materials. This can be especially challenging with all of the resources readily available on the Internet. Teachers should be aware of and make use of the many free resources afforded to them as educators, such as texts and images in the public domain. Classroom use exemptions do exist for teachers and students to view a movie or perform a play, for example, but there are limitations that teachers should be familiar with before using such materials.

Seminal U.S. Texts

U.S. texts should be evaluated and interpreted by the teacher in advance so that students are receiving the most fair and accurate portrayal of constitutional principles. Political documents can be subjective, so it is important for teachers to provide guidance in order for students to understand the purpose of such texts without bias or political bent.

<u>Declaration of Independence</u>
- Established the intentional separation of the United States from the British empire.

- The document defines the reasons for this separation, which are injustices and abuses inflicted upon the colonies by the king and British government.

- The United States stands as an independent nation with its own core values outlined in the Preamble.

- The Preamble outlines the core beliefs of the new American government: all people are equal and deserve fair representation.

- The Preamble also specifies that when a government has become oppressive and harmful to the people, the people have the right to abolish that government and create a new one.

<u>Articles of Confederation</u>
- This outlines the agreement of the original 13 colonies of the United States on governance and law. The name of the nation is confirmed as the United States of America.

- Specific powers are assigned to the federal and state governments, but the articles had a lack of central leadership.

- People can move unhindered between states; they are all part of the same nation.

- The articles of confederation also establish the sovereignty of each state and confirm that each state has a vote in Congress.

- Congress was given the power to declare war, print money, and enter treaties. Federal government dictates foreign relations.

The Constitution
- The Constitution lays out the fundamental laws of the United States and lists the basic rights of the people.

- The U.S. Constitution was heavily influenced by the British government itself, as well as legal documents such as the Magna Carta and the British Bill of Rights.

- The Constitution serves as the defining framework for the government in which other laws and amendments are measured against.

- The Constitution is composed of the Preamble, the closing endorsement, and seven distinct articles.

- The articles establish the amendment process, create checks and balances, create a court system, and more.

Bill of Rights
- The Bill of Rights is the first ten amendments to the constitution. These are very direct statements outlining the individual rights of the people.

- In addition to outlining the core rights of the people, the Bill of Rights establishes a clear line of protection for the rights by ensuring that the law of the land is bound to acknowledge and uphold these rights for each person. An example of this can be seen in the Fourth Amendment.

- The Fourth Amendment is the freedom from unlawful search and seizure. Protections like this serve to maintain civil liberties from government abuses. Defending the individual from oppression is a recurring theme in American law, heavily influenced by British government and abuses suffered during British rule.

Federalist Papers
- The Federalist Papers are written as letters that were published in the newspaper during the 1780s to promote the ratification of the Constitution.

- The Papers are made of 85 individual letters written by Alexander Hamilton, John Jay, and James Madison, who wrote the letters under the shared pseudonym of Publius.

- The style is inherently persuasive. The authors argue that the Constitution would both preserve the Union and give power to the federal government to act in the best interest of the whole nation.

- The goal was also to quell fears of states' losing power.

Lincoln's First Inaugural Address
- Due to the fragile state of the union at the time, Lincoln's initial address to the nation was to try and keep the southern states from fracturing and prevent civil war.

- Lincoln cited previous statements that he made, ensuring the South that though he was Republican, (the party at the time which opposed slavery) his goal was not to take their property (slaves). Lincoln's diction is assuring in order to keep the states together.

- It must be recognized that Lincoln's primary intention was to preserve the union and avert war. The drive to end slavery become a key motivation for the union (officially) after the war was started and the Emancipation Proclamation was issued.

Gettysburg Address
- The address was used to dedicate a national cemetery commemorating those who died fighting in the Civil War.

- Lincoln's first words invoke the original ambition of United States' founders to establish liberty and justice for all. The war is nothing less than a fight for the fate of this ideal.

- He emphasizes that all men are created equal as expressed in the Declaration of Independence. This is a direct contradiction to Confederate ideas surrounding slavery.

- It states that the war is being fought for nothing less than "a new birth of freedom," for the government developed and led by all of its people.

Emancipation Proclamation
- This was the executive order Abraham Lincoln issued to free all slaves from bondage.

- The Emancipation Proclamation would inspire and lead to the 13th Amendment to the U.S. Constitution, which eliminated the purchase and sale of African Americans; this amendment simultaneously prohibits the slavery and forced servitude of all persons. The exception to this rule is when labor is used as punishment for crimes.

- This Emancipation Proclamation helped reinforce the principle that all people are equal and share common inalienable rights that cannot be taken away or infringed upon.

- The Emancipation Proclamation also made the abolishment of slavery a key objective in the Civil War.

Letter from Birmingham Jail
- These letters outline Dr. Martin Luther King Jr.'s reasons behind his activism in Birmingham, one of which is his defining beliefs that injustice at any location is a threat to the freedom and justice everywhere.

- Dr. King also outlines the methodology used in his mission. He chiefly emphasizes the importance of non-violence in the effort to effect real change and establish a sense of unity for all peoples.

- Dr. King also lists nine criticisms that play a role in his strategy and thoughts on activism. One of his monumental stances is that he intends to carry on the Civil Rights movement with or without the support of the church. This is particularly significant given that King was also a Protestant minister.

Analyzing the Foundational U.S. Documents

Teachers must familiarize themselves with foundational U.S. documents such as The Declaration of Independence, The U.S. Constitution, and The Bill of Rights to engage students with the past. Each should be evaluated for their place in history as well as their significance today. Careful evaluation of these documents can aid teachers in interpreting their meaning and significance. This will help teach students to understand the overall purpose of each document and any language that may be unfamiliar. Documents should be evaluated for author, purpose, context, and audience. The following documents have been briefly evaluated in this manner:

Document	Author	Purpose	Context	Audience
U.S. Constitution	James Madison and other Founding Fathers	Create government, divide power between states and federal government, protect personal liberty	Written in 1787 at the Constitutional Convention in Philadelphia	All citizens of the United States
The Declaration of Independence	Thomas Jefferson and other Founding Fathers	The U.S. wanted to declare independence from Britain	Written in July 1776 for the Continental Congress	The King of England, US citizens, other foreign nations

Text Complexity

Evaluate Text Complexity

Texts used in the classroom should be evaluated for their complexity or level of challenge to ensure they are appropriate for students' reading levels and understanding. Teachers should match students to texts based on their knowledge, experience, and motivation. Text types should be selected from a wide range of topics and cultural backgrounds. There are three main criteria for evaluating texts: Qualitative Dimensions, Quantitative Dimensions, and Reader and Task Considerations. Qualitative Dimensions are those that can be measured by a reader. They involve discerning meaning and purpose of the text and the conventions in the language used. Quantitative Dimensions are those that can only be measured by a computer. They include word length, frequency, and cohesion. Reader and Task Considerations are those variables that are unique to individual readers, including the reader's level of knowledge and experience and the purpose of the task. The following table explains the quantitative tools and measures for evaluating text complexity:

Qualitative Dimensions	Quantitative Dimensions	Reader and Task Considerations
Measured by attentive reader	Measured by computer	Specific to individual readers
Meaning, purpose, language conventionality	Word length, frequency, text cohesion	Knowledge level, experiences, purpose of task

Levels of Text Complexity

The following levels of text complexity are based on the Lexile scale. Lexiles are a numeric measure of text complexity used in the Common Core standards. Lexiles are like a thermometer reading for the difficulty of a text. They are determined by sentence length and the difficulty of the vocabulary. Teachers should familiarize themselves with this scale in order to accurately match students to texts and evaluate student reading levels.

Grade	Mid-Year Lexile Levels of Middle 50% of Students	Text Demand of Common Core Stretch-Level Texts
K	–	–
1	Up to 300 L	190L to 530L
2	140L–500L	420L to 650L
3	330L–700L	520L to 820L
4	445L–810L	740L to 940L
5	656L–910L	830L to 1010L

Reader Variables and Task Variables

Teachers should use quantitative, qualitative, and reader/task considerations in order to match students with appropriate reading materials and assignments. This requires careful observation and evaluation of students throughout the school year in an effort to meet their changing needs. Additionally, teachers must be aware of the texts available to readers and evaluate their readability for students. They should also plan tasks accordingly for students of all reading levels. It is important for teachers to be aware of the challenges a text presents, and to support readers of different abilities. When evaluating a reader, considerations such as the following should be made:

- Reading and Cognitive Skills
- Prior Knowledge and Experience
- Motivation and Engagement
- Task concerns

Active Reading
It has been shown that the teacher who employs multiple reading strategies in a variety of reading situations has the most success in fostering critical thinkers. Teachers should strive to make reading an active, observable process. *Active reading* involves reading with a purpose and determination to not only understand, but evaluate text using critical reading skills. Critical reading skills need to be fostered in a way that allows students to read and retain information and then gain interactive feedback experience with peers and with an instructor. Employing multiple reading strategies, either through assigned, independent reading with follow up or through a shared experience, aids in active reading.

The following are some of the reading strategies that should be utilized:

- Modeling prediction
- Modeling inference
- Asking students to connect text to self, the world, and to other text
- Asking students to visualize what they read (playing the "video" in their head)
- Asking students to partner in their reading experiences
- Helping students determine the importance of ideas in what they read
- Modeling the critical thinking process
- Modeling analyzation
- Modeling summarization

Another form of instruction is *discipline-based inquiry*, which encourages students to analyze writing models in a particular mode to better grasp the characteristics of that style. For example, before assigning students a persuasive writing assignment, an instructor would first give several samples of persuasive passages to students and ask them to read the texts carefully, paying attention to components such as diction—what kind of emotional or connotative language the writer uses to subtly influence readers' opinion, supporting arguments—how the writer integrates objective data to support a subjective argument, and organization—how the writer presents the information and argument. By focusing students' attention on a specific writing mode, the instructor allows students to use their analytical and observation skills to formulate an idea about the prominent characteristics of a particular mode of writing.

In *Self-Regulated Strategy Development* (SRSD), instructors progressively instill independent skills in students by first prompting students for their prior knowledge about a subject, building on that background knowledge, instructing them more deeply in strategies related to the learning objective, and then practicing the strategy enough times so that it becomes an embedded habit in students' learning process.

Finally, encouraging students to write with one another in a collaborative setting is a good way to enhance revision, editing, and publishing skills by learning, discussing, and writing for each other. By giving constructive feedback to their peers, students learn how to recognize and apply standards of effective writing, and they also become more skilled at troubleshooting and making corrections when problems occur in the writing process.

Practice Questions

1. Read the following poem. Which option best expresses the symbolic meaning of the "road" and the overall theme?

Two roads diverged in a yellow wood,
And sorry I could not travel both
And be one traveler, long I stood
And looked down one as far as I could
To where it bent in the undergrowth;   5
Then took the other, as just as fair,
And having perhaps the better claim,
Because it was grassy and wanted wear;
Though as for that the passing there
Had worn them really about the same,   10
And both that morning equally lay
In leaves no step had trodden black.
Oh, I kept the first for another day!
Yet knowing how way leads on to way,
I doubted if I should ever come back.   15
I shall be telling this with a sigh
Somewhere ages and ages hence:
Two roads diverged in a wood, and I—
I took the one less traveled by,
And that has made all the difference.   20

Robert Frost, "The Road Not Taken"

    a. A divergent spot where the traveler had to choose the correct path to his destination
    b. A choice between good and evil that the traveler needs to make
    c. The traveler's struggle between his lost love and his future prospects
    d. Life's journey and the choices with which humans are faced

2. Which option best exemplifies an author's use of *alliteration* and *personification*?
    a. Her mood hung about her like a weary cape, very dull from wear.
    b. It shuddered, swayed, shook, and screamed its way into dust under hot flames.
    c. The house was a starch sentry, warning visitors away.
    d. At its shoreline, visitors swore they heard the siren call of the cliffs above.

3. Read the following poem. Which option best depicts the rhyme scheme?

> A slumber did my spirit seal;
> I had no human fears:
> She seemed a thing that could not feel
> The touch of earthly years.
>
> William Wordsworth, "A Slumber Did My Spirit Seal"

   a. BAC BAC
   b. ABAB
   c. ABBA
   d. AB CD AB

4. Read the following poem. Which option describes its corresponding meter?

> Half a league, half a league
> Half a league onward,
> All in the valley of Death
> Rode the six hundred.
> 'Forward, the Light Brigade!
> Charge for the guns!' he said:
> Into the valley of Death
> Rode the six hundred.
>
> Alfred Lord Tennyson "The Charge of the Light Brigade"

   a. Iambic (unstressed/stressed syllables)
   b. Anapest (unstressed/unstressed/stressed syllables)
   c. Spondee (stressed/stressed syllables)
   d. Dactyl (stressed/unstressed/unstressed syllables)

5. This work, published in 1922, was a modernist piece that was banned both in the United States and overseas for meeting the criteria of obscenity. Taking place in a single day (June 16th, 1904), the novel contains eighteen episodes reflecting the activities of character Leopold Bloom in Dublin, Ireland. Originally written as to portray an Odysseus figure for adults, the structure of the work is often viewed as convoluted and chaotic, as its author utilized the stream of consciousness technique. Its literary reception was vastly polarized and remains so to this day, although modern critics tend to hail the novel as addressing the vast panoramic of futility within contemporary history.

The above passage describes which famous literary work?
   a. James Joyce's *Ulysses*
   b. Anne Sexton's poem "45 Mercy Street"
   c. F. Scott Fitzgerald's *Tender is the Night*
   d. George Eliot's *Middlemarch: A Study of Provincial Life*

Question 6 is based on the following passage:

In 1889, Jerome K. Jerome wrote a humorous account of a boating holiday. Originally intended as a chapter in a serious travel guide, the work became a prime example of a comic novel. Read the passage below, noting the word/words in italics. Answer the question that follows.

I felt rather hurt about this at first; it seemed somehow to be a sort of slight. Why hadn't I got housemaid's knee? Why this invidious reservation? After a while, however, less grasping feelings prevailed. I reflected that I had every other known malady in the pharmacology, and I grew less selfish, and determined to do without housemaid's knee. Gout, in its most malignant stage, it would appear, had seized me without my being aware of it; and *zymosis* I had evidently been suffering with from boyhood. There were no more diseases after *zymosis*, so I concluded there was nothing else the matter with me.—Jerome K. Jerome, *Three Men in a Boat*

6. Which definition best fits the word *zymosis*?
   a. Discontent
   b. An infectious disease
   c. Poverty
   d. Bad luck

7. Read the following poem. Which option best describes the use of the spider?

   > The spider as an artist
   > Has never been employed
   > Though his surpassing merit
   > Is freely certified
   > By every broom and Bridget
   > Throughout a Christian land.
   > Neglected son of genius,
   > I take thee by the hand—
   >
   > Emily Dickinson, "Cobwebs"

   a. Idiom
   b. Haiku
   c. ABBA rhyming convention
   d. Simile

8. Which option best defines a *fable*?
   a. A melancholy poem lamenting its subject's death
   b. An oral tradition influenced by culture
   c. A story with events that occur in threes and in sevens
   d. A short story with animals, fantastic creatures, or other forces within nature

9. Which phrase best completes the definition of a *memoir*?
   a. A historical account of a person's life written by one who has intimate knowledge of the person's life
   b. A historical account of a person's life written by the person himself or herself
   c. A fictional account about a famous person
   d. A nonfictional account about a famous person without factual reference

Read the excerpt below called "To Waken an Old Lady," a poem by William Carlos Williams;
Questions 10 – 12 are based on the following poem:

> Old age is
> a flight of small
> cheeping birds
> skimming
> bare trees
> above a snow glaze.
> Gaining and failing
> they are buffeted
> by a dark wind—
> But what?
> On harsh weedstalks
> the flock has rested,
> the snow
> is covered with broken
> seedhusks
> and the wind tempered
> by a shrill
> piping of plenty.

10. This poem uses which of the following literary techniques typical of its time period?
    a. Meter
    b. Anaphora
    c. Imagery
    d. Synecdoche

11. This poem comes out of which of the following literary periods?
    a. Romanticism
    b. Modernism
    c. Postmodernism
    d. Confessional poetry

12. Which of the following provides the best analysis of the poem?
    a. The poem acts as an extended metaphor of old age. Its juxtaposed imagery suggests the frailty of life ("Gaining and failing / they are buffeted / by a dark wind") alongside the fullness of life and its "piping of plenty."
    b. The poem describes a flock of birds and their relationship with nature. They rest "On harsh weedstalks" and are "buffeted / by a dark wind." The poem concludes suggesting that their greatest joy as well as their greatest strife is nature itself.
    c. The poem is an ode to the wind. Although the poem starts off comparing old age to birds, we see the poem calling upon the wind at the end in order to make sense of the world. The wind is ultimately in control in the poem—it is the driving force of the poem.
    d. This poem is about writing poetry. Old age signifies the poet, while the "small / cheeping birds" signifies the poet's words. The conclusion of the poem describes the wind as the creative process of writing a poem, and the "piping of plenty" is what the author gets in writing a fulfilling, lengthy poem.

13. Which of the following describes the organizational pattern of chronological or sequence order?
    a. Text organized by describing a dilemma and a possible solution
    b. Text organized by observing the consequences of an action
    c. Text organized by the timing of events or actions
    d. Text organized by analyzing the relative placement of an object or event

14. Which of the following is an example of a rhetorical strategy?
    a. Cause and effect
    b. Antimetabole
    c. Individual vs. Self
    d. Ad hominem

Questions 15 – 18 are based on the following passage:

This article discusses the famous poet and playwright William Shakespeare.

People who argue that William Shakespeare is not responsible for the plays attributed to his name are known as anti-Stratfordians (from the name of Shakespeare's birthplace, Stratford-upon-Avon). The most common anti-Stratfordian claim is that William Shakespeare simply was not educated enough or from a high enough social class to have written plays overflowing with references to such a wide range of subjects like history, the classics, religion, and international culture. William Shakespeare was the son of a glove-maker, he only had a basic grade school education, and he never set foot outside of England—so how could he have produced plays of such sophistication and imagination? How could he have written in such detail about historical figures and events, or about different cultures and locations around Europe? According to anti-Stratfordians, the depth of knowledge contained in Shakespeare's plays suggests a well-traveled writer from a wealthy background with a university education, not a countryside writer like Shakespeare. But in fact, there is not much substance to such speculation, and most anti-Stratfordian arguments can be refuted with a little background about Shakespeare's time and upbringing.

First of all, those who doubt Shakespeare's authorship often point to his common birth and brief education as stumbling blocks to his writerly genius. Although it is true that Shakespeare did not come from a noble class, his father was a very *successful* glove-maker and his mother was from a very wealthy land owning family—so while Shakespeare may have had a country upbringing, he was certainly from a well-off family and would have been educated accordingly. Also, even though he did not attend university, grade school education in Shakespeare's time was actually quite rigorous and exposed students to classic drama through writers like Seneca and Ovid. It is not unreasonable to believe that Shakespeare received a very solid foundation in poetry and literature from his early schooling.

Next, anti-Stratfordians tend to question how Shakespeare could write so extensively about countries and cultures he had never visited before (for instance, several of his most famous works like *Romeo and Juliet* and *The Merchant of Venice* were set in Italy, on the opposite side of Europe!). But again, this criticism does not hold up under scrutiny. For one thing, Shakespeare was living in London, a bustling metropolis of international trade, the most populous city in England, and a political and cultural hub of Europe. In the daily crowds of people, Shakespeare would certainly have been able to meet travelers from other countries and hear firsthand accounts of life in their home country. And, in addition to the influx of information from world travelers, this was also the age of the printing press, a jump in technology that made it possible to print and circulate books much more easily than in the past. This also allowed for a freer flow of information across different countries, allowing people to read about life and ideas from throughout Europe. One needn't travel the continent in order to learn and write about its culture.

15. Which sentence contains the author's thesis?
   a. People who argue that William Shakespeare is not responsible for the plays attributed to his name are known as anti-Stratfordians.
   b. But in fact, there is not much substance to such speculation, and most anti-Stratfordian arguments can be refuted with a little background about Shakespeare's time and upbringing.
   c. It is not unreasonable to believe that Shakespeare received a very solid foundation in poetry and literature from his early schooling.
   d. Next, anti-Stratfordians tend to question how Shakespeare could write so extensively about countries and cultures he had never visited before.

16. In the first paragraph, "How could he have written in such detail about historical figures and events, or about different cultures and locations around Europe?" is an example of which of the following?
   a. Hyperbole
   b. Onomatopoeia
   c. Rhetorical question
   d. Appeal to authority

17. How does the author respond to the claim that Shakespeare was not well-educated because he did not attend university?
   a. By insisting upon Shakespeare's natural genius.
   b. By explaining grade school curriculum in Shakespeare's time.
   c. By comparing Shakespeare with other uneducated writers of his time.
   d. By pointing out that Shakespeare's wealthy parents probably paid for private tutors.

18. The word "bustling" in the third paragraph most nearly means which of the following?
   a. Busy
   b. Foreign
   c. Expensive
   d. Undeveloped

19. Which poem belongs to the metaphysical literary movement?
   a. Emily Dickinson's "If I Should Die"
   b. Elizabeth Barrett Browning's "A Child Asleep"
   c. Andrew Marvell's "To His Coy Mistress"
   d. Sylvia Plath's "The Bell Jar"

20. Which word serves as the best example of the poetic device, *onomatopoeia*?
   a. Crackle
   b. Eat
   c. Provide
   d. Walking

21. Which term best defines a *sonnet*?
    a. A Japanese love poem
    b. An eight-line stanza or poem
    c. A fourteen-line poem written in iambic pentameter
    d. A ceremonious, lyric poem

22. Which literary school of thought developed out of structuralism in the twentieth century?
    a. Deconstruction
    b. Post-Structuralism
    c. Marxism
    d. Both A and B

Questions 23 – 28 are based on the following passage:

The following is an excerpt from Kate Chopin's "The Story of an Hour"

> Knowing that Mrs. Mallard was afflicted with heart trouble, great care was taken to break to her as gently as possible the news of her husband's death.
>
> It was her sister Josephine who told her, in broken sentences; veiled hints that revealed in half concealing. Her husband's friend Richards was there, too, near her. It was he who had been in the newspaper office when intelligence of the railroad disaster was received, with Brently Mallard's name leading the list of "killed." He had only taken the time to assure himself of its truth by a second telegram, and had hastened to forestall any less careful, less tender friend in bearing the sad message.
>
> She did not hear the story as many women have heard the same, with a paralyzed inability to accept its significance. She wept at once, with sudden, wild abandonment, in her sister's arms. When the storm of grief had spent itself she went away to her room alone. She would have no one follow her.
>
> There stood, facing the open window, a comfortable, roomy armchair. Into this she sank, pressed down by a physical exhaustion that haunted her body and seemed to reach into her soul.
>
> She could see in the open square before her house the tops of trees that were all aquiver with the new spring life. The delicious breath of rain was in the air. In the street below a peddler was crying his wares. The notes of a distant song which some one was singing reached her faintly, and countless sparrows were twittering in the eaves.
>
> There were patches of blue sky showing here and there through the clouds that had met and piled one above the other in the west facing her window.
>
> She sat with her head thrown back upon the cushion of the chair, quite motionless, except when a sob came up into her throat and shook her, as a child who has cried itself to sleep continues to sob in its dreams.
>
> She was young, with a fair, calm face, whose lines bespoke repression and even a certain strength. But now here was a dull stare in her eyes, whose gaze was fixed away off yonder on one of those patches of blue sky. It was not a glance of reflection, but rather indicated a suspension of intelligent thought.

There was something coming to her and she was waiting for it, fearfully. What was it? She did not know; it was too subtle and elusive to name. But she felt it, creeping out of the sky, reaching toward her through the sounds, the scents, and color that filled the air.

Now her bosom rose and fell tumultuously. She was beginning to recognize this thing that was approaching to possess her, and she was striving to beat it back with her will—as powerless as her two white slender hands would have been. When she abandoned herself a little whispered word escaped her slightly parted lips. She said it over and over under her breath: "free, free, free!" The vacant stare and the look of terror that had followed it went from her eyes. They stayed keen and bright. Her pulses beat fast, and the coursing blood warmed and relaxed every inch of her body.

She did not stop to ask if it were or were not a monstrous joy that held her. A clear and exalted perception enabled her to dismiss the suggestion as trivial. She knew that she would weep again when she saw the kind, tender hands folded in death; the face that had never looked save with love upon her, fixed and gray and dead. But she saw beyond that bitter moment a long procession of years to come that would belong to her absolutely. And she opened and spread her arms out to them in welcome.

23. What point of view is the above passage told in?
    a. First person
    b. Second person
    c. Third person omniscient
    d. Third person limited

24. What kind of irony are we presented with in this story?
    a. The way Mrs. Mallard reacted to her husband's death.
    b. The way in which Mr. Mallard died.
    c. The way in which the news of her husband's death was presented to Mrs. Mallard.
    d. The way in which nature is compared with death in the story.

25. Kate Chopin is the author of *The Awakening*. *The Awakening* and this excerpt from "The Story of an Hour" have which of the following themes in common?
    a. Horrors of war and soldiers' deaths
    b. Liberation from marriage and cultural limitations
    c. Terminal illness and loneliness
    d. Family life and friendship

26. What is the best summary of the passage above?
    a. Mr. Mallard, a soldier during World War I, is killed by the enemy and leaves his wife widowed.
    b. Mrs. Mallard understands the value of friendship when her friends show up for her after her husband's death.
    c. Mrs. Mallard combats mental illness daily and will perhaps be sent to a mental institution soon.
    d. Mrs. Mallard, a newly widowed woman, finds unexpected relief in her husband's death.
    d. Calmly

Question 27 is based on the following passage:

In 2015, 28 countries, including Estonia, Portugal, Slovenia, and Latvia, scored significantly higher than the United States on standardized high school math tests. In the 1960s, the United

States consistently ranked first in the world. Today, the United States spends more than $800 billion dollars on education, which exceeds the next highest country by more than $600 billion dollars. The United States also leads the world in spending per school-aged child by an enormous margin.

27. If these statements above are factual, which of the following statements must be correct?
    a. Outspending other countries on education has benefits beyond standardized math tests.
    b. The United States' education system is corrupt and broken.
    c. The standardized math tests are not representative of American academic prowess.
    d. Spending more money does not guarantee success on standardized math tests.

28. Which phrase below best defines *inference*?
    a. Reading between the lines
    b. Skimming a text for context clues
    c. Writing notes or questions that need answers during the reading experience
    d. Summarizing the text

Questions 29 – 31 are based on the following passage:

George Washington emerged out of the American Revolution as an unlikely champion of liberty. On June 14, 1775, the Second Continental Congress created the Continental Army, and John Adams, serving in the Congress, nominated Washington to be its first commander. Washington fought under the British during the French and Indian War, and his experience and prestige proved instrumental to the American war effort. Washington provided invaluable leadership, training, and strategy during the Revolutionary War. He emerged from the war as the embodiment of liberty and freedom from tyranny.

After vanquishing the heavily favored British forces, Washington could have pronounced himself as the autocratic leader of the former colonies without any opposition, but he famously refused and returned to his Mount Vernon plantation. His restraint proved his commitment to the fledgling state's republicanism. Washington was later unanimously elected as the first American president. But it is Washington's farewell address that cemented his legacy as a visionary worthy of study.

In 1796, President Washington issued his farewell address by public letter. Washington enlisted his good friend, Alexander Hamilton, in drafting his most famous address. The letter expressed Washington's faith in the Constitution and rule of law. He encouraged his fellow Americans to put aside partisan differences and establish a national union. Washington warned Americans against meddling in foreign affairs and entering military alliances. Additionally, he stated his opposition to national political parties, which he considered partisan and counterproductive.

Americans would be wise to remember Washington's farewell, especially during presidential elections when politics hits a fever pitch. They might want to question the political institutions that were not planned by the Founding Fathers, such as the nomination process and political parties themselves.

29. Which of the following statements is logically based on the information contained in the passage above?

    a. George Washington's background as a wealthy landholder directly led to his faith in equality, liberty, and democracy.

    b. George Washington would have opposed America's involvement in the Second World War.

    c. George Washington would not have been able to write as great a farewell address without the assistance of Alexander Hamilton.

    d. George Washington would probably not approve of modern political parties.

30. Which of the following statements is the best description of the author's purpose in writing this passage about George Washington?

    a. To inform American voters about a Founding Father's sage advice on a contemporary issue and explain its applicability to modern times

    b. To introduce George Washington to readers as a historical figure worthy of study

    c. To note that George Washington was more than a famous military hero

    d. To convince readers that George Washington is a hero of republicanism and liberty

31. In which of the following materials would the author be the most likely to include this passage?

    a. A history textbook

    b. An obituary

    c. A fictional story

    d. A newspaper editorial

Questions 32 – 36 are based on the following passage:

The following is from a historical essay written on Leif Erikson:

> Christopher Columbus is often credited for discovering America. This is incorrect. First, it is impossible to "discover" something where people already live; however, Christopher Columbus did explore places in the New World that were previously untouched by Europe, so the term "explorer" would be more accurate. Another correction must be made, as well: Christopher Columbus was not the first European explorer to reach the present day Americas! Rather, it was Leif Erikson who first came to the New World and contacted the natives, nearly five hundred years before Christopher Columbus.

> Leif Erikson, the son of Erik the Red (a famous Viking outlaw and explorer in his own right), was born in either 970 or 980, depending on which historian you seek. His own family, though, did not raise Leif, which was a Viking tradition. Instead, one of Erik's prisoners taught Leif reading and writing, languages, sailing, and weaponry. At age 12, Leif was considered a man and returned to his family. He killed a man during a dispute shortly after his return, and the council banished the Erikson clan to Greenland.

> In 999, Leif left Greenland and traveled to Norway where he would serve as a guard to King Olaf Tryggvason. It was there that he became a convert to Christianity. Leif later tried to return home with the intention of taking supplies and spreading Christianity to Greenland, however his ship was blown off course and he arrived in a strange new land: present day Newfoundland, Canada.

> When he finally returned to his adopted homeland Greenland, Leif consulted with a merchant who had also seen the shores of this previously unknown land we now know as Canada. The son of the legendary Viking explorer then gathered a crew of 35 men and set sail. Leif became the

first European to touch foot in the New World as he explored present-day Baffin Island and Labrador, Canada. His crew called the land Vinland since it was plentiful with grapes.

During their time in present-day Newfoundland, Leif's expedition made contact with the natives whom they referred to as Skraelings (which translates to "wretched ones" in Norse). There are several secondhand accounts of their meetings. Some contemporaries described trade between the peoples. Other accounts describe clashes where the Skraelings defeated the Viking explorers with long spears, while still others claim the Vikings dominated the natives. Regardless of the circumstances, it seems that the Vikings made contact of some kind. This happened around 1000, nearly five hundred years before Columbus famously sailed the ocean blue.

Eventually, in 1003, Leif set sail for home and arrived at Greenland with a ship full of timber.

In 1020, seventeen years later, the legendary Viking died. Many believe that Leif Erikson should receive more credit for his contributions in exploring the New World.

32. Which of the following best describes how the author generally presents the information?
    a. Chronological order
    b. Comparison-contrast
    c. Cause-effect
    d. Conclusion-premises

33. Which of the following is an opinion, rather than historical fact, expressed by the author?
    a. Leif Erikson was definitely the son of Erik the Red; however, historians debate the year of his birth.
    b. Leif Erikson's crew called the land Vinland since it was plentiful with grapes.
    c. Leif Erikson deserves more credit for his contributions in exploring the New World.
    d. Leif Erikson explored the Americas nearly five hundred years before Christopher Columbus.

34. Which of the following most accurately describes the author's main conclusion?
    a. Leif Erikson is a legendary Viking explorer.
    b. Leif Erikson deserves more credit for exploring America hundreds of years before Columbus.
    c. Spreading Christianity motivated Leif Erikson's expeditions more than any other factor.
    d. Leif Erikson contacted the natives nearly five hundred years before Columbus.

35. Which of the following best describes the author's intent in the passage?
    a. To entertain
    b. To inform
    c. To alert
    d. To suggest

36. Which of the following can be logically inferred from the passage?
    a. The Vikings disliked exploring the New World.
    b. Leif Erikson's banishment from Iceland led to his exploration of present-day Canada.
    c. Leif Erikson never shared his stories of exploration with the King of Norway.
    d. Historians have difficulty definitively pinpointing events in the Vikings' history.

Questions 37 – 42 are based on the following passage:

This excerpt is an adaptation from Charles Dickens' speech in Birmingham in England on December 30, 1853 on behalf of the Birmingham and Midland Institute.

My Good Friends—When I first imparted to the committee of the projected Institute my particular wish that on one of the evenings of my readings here the main body of my audience should be composed of working men and their families, I was animated by two desires; first, by the wish to have the great pleasure of meeting you face to face at this Christmas time, and accompany you myself through one of my little Christmas books; and second, by the wish to have an opportunity of stating publicly in your presence, and in the presence of the committee, my earnest hope that the Institute will, from the beginning, recognise one great principle—strong in reason and justice—which I believe to be essential to the very life of such an Institution. It is, that the working man shall, from the first unto the last, have a share in the management of an Institution which is designed for his benefit, and which calls itself by his name.

I have no fear here of being misunderstood—of being supposed to mean too much in this. If there ever was a time when any one class could of itself do much for its own good, and for the welfare of society—which I greatly doubt—that time is unquestionably past. It is in the fusion of different classes, without confusion; in the bringing together of employers and employed; in the creating of a better common understanding among those whose interests are identical, who depend upon each other, who are vitally essential to each other, and who never can be in unnatural antagonism without deplorable results, that one of the chief principles of a Mechanics' Institution should consist. In this world a great deal of the bitterness among us arises from an imperfect understanding of one another. Erect in Birmingham a great Educational Institution, properly educational; educational of the feelings as well as of the reason; to which all orders of Birmingham men contribute; in which all orders of Birmingham men meet; wherein all orders of Birmingham men are faithfully represented—and you will erect a Temple of Concord here which will be a model edifice to the whole of England.

Contemplating as I do the existence of the Artisans' Committee, which not long ago considered the establishment of the Institute so sensibly, and supported it so heartily, I earnestly entreat the gentlemen—earnest I know in the good work, and who are now among us,—by all means to avoid the great shortcoming of similar institutions; and in asking the working man for his confidence, to set him the great example and give him theirs in return. You will judge for yourselves if I promise too much for the working man, when I say that he will stand by such an enterprise with the utmost of his patience, his perseverance, sense, and support; that I am sure he will need no charitable aid or condescending patronage; but will readily and cheerfully pay for the advantages which it confers; that he will prepare himself in individual cases where he feels that the adverse circumstances around him have rendered it necessary; in a word, that he will feel his responsibility like an honest man, and will most honestly and manfully discharge it. I now proceed to the pleasant task to which I assure you I have looked forward for a long time.

37. Which word is most closely synonymous with the word "patronage" as it appears in the following statement?

"that I am sure he will need no charitable aid or condescending patronage"

a. Auspices
b. Aberration
c. Acerbic
d. Adulation

38. Which term is most closely aligned with the definition of the term "working man" as it is defined in the following passage?

"You will judge for yourselves if I promise too much for the working man, when I say that he will stand by such an enterprise with the utmost of his patience, his perseverance, sense, and support"

a. Plebian
b. Viscount
c. Entrepreneur
d. Bourgeois

39. Which of the following statements most closely correlates with the definition of the term "working man" as it is defined in Question 38?
a. A working man is not someone who works for institutions or corporations, but someone who is well versed in the workings of the soul
b. A working man is someone who is probably not involved in social activities because the physical demand for work is too high
c. Working man is someone who works for wages among the middle class.
d. The working man has historically taken to the field, to the factory, and now to the screen

40. Based upon the contextual evidence provided in the passage above, what is the meaning of the term "enterprise" in the third paragraph?
a. Company
b. Courage
c. Game
d. Cause

41. The speaker addresses his audience as My Good Friends—what kind of credibility does this salutation give to the speaker?
a. The speaker is an employer addressing his employees, so the salutation is a way for the boss to bridge the gap between himself and his employees. .
b. The speaker's salutation is one from an entertainer to his audience and uses the friendly language to connect to his audience before a serious speech.
c. The salutation gives the serious speech that follows a somber tone, as it is used ironically.
d. The speech is one from a politician to the public, so the salutation is used to grab the audience's attention.

42. According to the aforementioned passage, what is the speaker's second desire for his time in front of the audience?
    a. To read a Christmas story
    b. For the working man to have a say in his institution which is designed for his benefit
    c. To have an opportunity to stand in their presence
    d. For the life of the institution to be essential to the audience as a whole

Questions 43 – 47 are based on the following passage:

When researchers and engineers undertake a large-scale scientific project, they may end up making discoveries and developing technologies that have far wider uses than originally intended. This is especially true in NASA, one of the most influential and innovative scientific organizations in America. NASA spinoff technology refers to innovations originally developed for NASA space projects that are now used in a wide range of different commercial fields. Many consumers are unaware that products they are buying are based on NASA research! Spinoff technology proves that it is worthwhile to invest in science research because it could enrich people's lives in unexpected ways.

The first spinoff technology worth mentioning is baby food. In space, where astronauts have limited access to fresh food and fewer options about their daily meals, malnutrition is a serious concern. Consequently, NASA researchers were looking for ways to enhance the nutritional value of astronauts' food. Scientists found that a certain type of algae could be added to food, improving the food's neurological benefits. When experts in the commercial food industry learned of this algae's potential to boost brain health, they were quick to begin their own research. The nutritional substance from algae then developed into a product called life's DHA, which can be found in over 90% of infant food sold in America.

Another intriguing example of a spinoff technology can be found in fashion. People who are always dropping their sunglasses may have invested in a pair of sunglasses with scratch resistant lenses—that is, it's impossible to scratch the glass, even if the glasses are dropped on an abrasive surface. This innovation is incredibly advantageous for people who are clumsy, but most shoppers don't know that this technology was originally developed by NASA. Scientists first created scratch resistant glass to help protect costly and crucial equipment from getting scratched in space, especially the helmet visors in space suits. However, sunglasses companies later realized that this technology could be profitable for their products, and they licensed the technology from NASA.

43. What is the main purpose of this article?
    a. To advise consumers to do more research before making a purchase
    b. To persuade readers to support NASA research
    c. To tell a narrative about the history of space technology
    d. To define and describe instances of spinoff technology

44. What is the organizational structure of this article?
    a. A general definition followed by more specific examples
    b. A general opinion followed by supporting arguments
    c. An important moment in history followed by chronological details
    d. A popular misconception followed by counterevidence

45. Why did NASA scientists research algae?
   a. They already knew algae was healthy for babies.
   b. They were interested in how to grow food in space.
   c. They were looking for ways to add health benefits to food.
   d. They hoped to use it to protect expensive research equipment.

46. Why does the author mention space suit helmets?
   a. To give an example of astronaut fashion
   b. To explain where sunglasses got their shape
   c. To explain how astronauts protect their eyes
   d. To give an example of valuable space equipment

47. Which statement would the author probably NOT agree with?
   a. Consumers don't always know the history of the products they are buying.
   b. Sometimes new innovations have unexpected applications.
   c. It is difficult to make money from scientific research.
   d. Space equipment is often very expensive.

Questions 48 – 50 are based on the following passage:

1   Although many Missourians know that Harry S. Truman and Walt Disney hailed from their great state, probably far fewer know that it was also home to the remarkable George Washington Carver. (48) <u>As a child, George was driven to learn, and he loved painting.</u> At the end of the Civil War, Moses Carver, the slave owner who owned George's parents, decided to keep George and his brother and raise them on his farm.

2   He even went on to study art while in college but was encouraged to pursue botany instead. He spent much of his life helping others (49) <u>by showing them better ways to farm, his ideas improved agricultural productivity</u> in many countries. One of his most notable contributions to the newly emerging class of Negro farmers was to teach them the negative effects of agriculture monoculture, i.e. growing the same crops in the same fields year after year, depleting the soil of much needed nutrients, resulting in a lesser yielding crop.

3   Carver was an innovator, always thinking of new and better way to do things, and is most famous for his over three hundred uses for the peanut. Toward the end of his career, Carver returned to his first love of art. Through his artwork, he hoped to inspire people to see the beauty around them and to do great things themselves. (50) <u>Because Carver died</u>, he left his money to help fund ongoing agricultural research. Today, people still visit and study at the George Washington Carver foundation at Tuskegee Institute.

48. Which of the following would be the best choice for this sentence?
   a. (No change)
   b. Move to the end of the first paragraph.
   c. Move to the beginning of the first paragraph.
   d. Move to the end of the second paragraph.

49. Which of the following would be the best choice for this sentence?
   a. (No change)
   b. by showing them better ways to farm his ideas improved agricultural productivity
   c. by showing them better ways to farm . . . his ideas improved agricultural productivity
   d. by showing them better ways to farm; his ideas improved agricultural productivity

50. Which of the following would be the best choice for this sentence?
   a. (No change)
   b. Although Carver died,
   c. When Carver died,
   d. Finally Carver died,

Answer Explanations

1. D: Choice *D* correctly summarizes Frost's theme of life's journey and the choices one makes. While Choice *A* can be seen as an interpretation, it is a literal one and is incorrect. Literal is not symbolic. Choice *B* presents the idea of good and evil as a theme, and the poem does not specify this struggle for the traveler. Choice *C* is a similarly incorrect answer. Love is not the theme.

2. B: Only Choice *B* uses both repetitive beginning sounds (alliteration) and personification—the portrayal of a building as a human crumbling under a fire. Choice *A* is a simile and does not utilize alliteration or the use of consistent consonant sounds for effect. Choice *C* is a metaphor and does not utilize alliteration. Choice *D* describes neither alliteration nor personification.

3. B: The correct answer is ABAB. Choice *A* is not a valid rhyme scheme. Choice *C* would require the second and third lines to rhyme, so it is incorrect. Choice *D* would require the first and fifth lines rhyme, then the second and sixth. This is also incorrect as the passage only contains four lines.

4. D: The correct answer is dactyl. If read with the combination of stressed and unstressed syllables as Tennyson intended and as the poem naturally flows, the reader will stumble upon the stressed/unstressed/unstressed rhythmic, dactyl meter similar to a waltz beat. Choices *A*, *B*, and *C* describe meters that do not follow the dactyl pattern.

5. A: The correct answer is *A* as it is the only option that utilizes stream of consciousness technique in a novel format. Choice *B* is a poem by poet Anne Sexton, not a novel. Although Ms. Sexton's works were often criticized for their intimate content, this answer does not meet the question's criteria. Choices *C* and *D* are both incorrect. Both are novels, but not of the appropriate time period, country, or literary content.

6. B: The correct answer is an infectious disease. By reading context, all other options can be eliminated since the author restates zymosis as disease.

7. D: The correct answer is simile. Choice *A* is incorrect because the poem does not contain an idiom. Choice *B* is incorrect since the poem is not haiku. Choice *C* is incorrect as it does not use the ABBA rhyming convention.

8. D: The correct answer is a short story with animals, fantastic creatures, or other forces within nature. Choice *A* defines an elegy. Choice *B* partially alludes to folklore. Choice *C* defines a fairytale.

9. A: The correct answer is a historical account of a person's life written by one who has intimate knowledge of the person's life. Choice *B* is not applicable since it is the definition of an autobiography. Choice *C* strictly refers to fiction and is not applicable to nonfiction. Choice *D* indicates that a memoir is not based on historical fact. In many instances, it is.

10. C: The poem uses imagery. William Carlos Williams is considered a Modernist poet who relied heavily on imagery to bring poetry to life. Poets like William Carlos Williams, Ezra Pound, and Marianne Moore wrote imagist poems typical of their time period. The poem is not metrical, but written in free verse, so Choice *A* is incorrect. Anaphora, Choice *B*, is a repetition of words at the beginning of a succession of lines. Synecdoche, Choice *D*, refers to a part of something that represents a whole.

11. B: This poem comes from the Modernist period. Modernism is a literary movement featuring writers like William Carlos Williams, Ezra Pound, T.S. Eliot, Marianne Moore, and Wallace Stevens. The poetry is a reaction to traditional metrical poetry and its outdated language. Modernists rely on heavy imagery and sometimes short, terse stanzas to create the impact of disjointedness with the self and language.

12. A: The poem acts as an extended metaphor of old age. Its juxtaposed imagery suggests the frailty of life ("Gaining and failing / they are buffeted / by a dark wind") alongside the fullness of life and its "piping of plenty." The other choices may have some aspects that are true of an effective analysis; however, the most important thing to recognize here is that the poem starts off very clearly as an extended metaphor.

13. C: The correct answer is text organized by the timing of events or actions. Chronological or sequence order is the organizational pattern that structures text to show the passage of time or movement through steps in a certain order. Choice *A* demonstrates the problem/solution structure. Choice *B* defines the cause/effect pattern. Choice *D* represents the spatial order structure.

14. A: The correct answer is cause and effect. A writer may use cause and effect as a strategy to illustrate a point in order to convince an audience. Choice *B* is a rhetorical device, not a strategy. Choice *C* refers to a narrative conflict, and Choice *D* is a logical fallacy.

15. B: But in fact, there is not much substance to such speculation, and most anti-Stratfordian arguments can be refuted with a little background about Shakespeare's time and upbringing. The thesis is a statement that contains the author's topic and main idea. The main purpose of this article is to use historical evidence to provide counterarguments to anti-Stratfordians. Choice *A* is simply a definition; Choice *C* is a supporting detail, not a main idea; and Choice *D* represents an idea of anti-Stratfordians, not the author's opinion.

16. C: Rhetorical question. This requires readers to be familiar with different types of rhetorical devices. A rhetorical question is a question that is asked not to obtain an answer but to encourage readers to more deeply consider an issue.

17. B: By explaining grade school curriculum in Shakespeare's time. This question asks readers to refer to the organizational structure of the article and demonstrate understanding of how the author provides details to support their argument. This particular detail can be found in the second paragraph: "even though he did not attend university, grade school education in Shakespeare's time was actually quite rigorous."

18. A: Busy. This is a vocabulary question that can be answered using context clues. Other sentences in the paragraph describe London as "the most populous city in England" filled with "crowds of people," giving an image of a busy city full of people. Choice *B* is incorrect because London was in Shakespeare's home country, not a foreign one. Choice *C* is not mentioned in the passage. Choice *D* is not a good answer choice because the passage describes how London was a popular and important city, probably not an underdeveloped one.

19. C: The correct answer is Andrew Marvell's "To His Coy Mistress." Emily Dickinson, Elizabeth Barrett Browning, and Sylvia Plath all belonged to different literary movements and contexts.

20. A: The correct answer is *crackle* as it is the only option that reflects the sound that the action would make. The other options do not.

21. C: The correct answer is a fourteen-line poem written in iambic pentameter. Choice *A* is incorrect as it incorrectly alludes to the haiku form. Choice *B* defines the octave poetic structure. Choice *D* defines what a poetic ode is.

22. D: The correct answer is that both Deconstruction and Post-structuralism developed in response to the Structuralism movement of the twentieth century. Choices *A* and *B* are incomplete answers as they do not complete both literary movements which encapsulate the response to Structuralism. Choice *C* is incorrect as Marxism was a response to the writings of Karl Marx and not in direct response to Structuralism.

23. C: The point of view is told in third person omniscient. We know this because the story starts out with us knowing something that the character does not know: that her husband has died. Mrs. Mallard eventually comes to know this, but we as readers know this information before it is broken to her. In third person limited, Choice *D*, we would only see and know what Mrs. Mallard herself knew, and we would find out the news of her husband's death when she found out the news, not before.

24. A: The way Mrs. Mallard reacted to her husband's death. The irony in this story is called situational irony, which means the situation that takes place is different than what the audience anticipated. At the beginning of the story, we see Mrs. Mallard react with a burst of grief to her husband's death. However, once she's alone, she begins to contemplate her future and says the word "free" over and over. This is quite a different reaction from Mrs. Mallard than what readers expected from the first of the story.

25. B: Liberation from marriage and cultural limitations. The other answer choices may be touched upon in one or both of the texts, but they are not the central themes of both texts. *The Awakening* is the story of a woman who awakens slowly to her desire to live a life true to herself. She craves freedom from convention and in search of this, creates conflict with those around her. "The Story of an Hour" is also about craving freedom from convention (from marriage), and is an instant awakening to this desire instead of a progressive one.

26. D: Mrs. Mallard, a newly widowed woman, finds unexpected relief in her husband's death. A summary is a brief explanation of the main point of a story. The story mostly focuses on Mrs. Mallard and her reaction to her husband's death, especially in the room when she's alone and contemplating the present and future. All of the other answer choices except Choice *C* are briefly mentioned in the story; however, they are not the main focus of the story.

27. D: Outspending other countries on education could have other benefits, but there is no reference to this in the passage, so Choice *A* is incorrect. Choice *B* is incorrect because the author does not mention corruption. Choice *C* is incorrect because there is nothing in the passage stating that the tests are not genuinely representative. Choice *D* is accurate because spending more money has not brought success. The United States already spends the most money, and the country is not excelling on these tests. Choice *D* is the correct answer.

28. A: Inferring is reading between the lines. Choice *B* describes the skimming technique. Choice *C* describes a questioning technique readers should employ, and Choice *D* is a simple statement regarding summary. It's an incomplete answer and not applicable to inference.

29. D: Although Washington is from a wealthy background, the passage does not say that his wealth led to his republican ideals, so Choice *A* is not supported. Choice *B* also does not follow from the passage. Washington's warning against meddling in foreign affairs does not mean that he would oppose wars of every kind, so Choice *B* is wrong. Choice *C* is also unjustified since the author does not indicate that

Alexander Hamilton's assistance was absolutely necessary. Choice *D* is correct because the farewell address clearly opposes political parties and partisanship. The author then notes that presidential elections often hit a fever pitch of partisanship. Thus, it is follows that George Washington would not approve of modern political parties and their involvement in presidential elections.

30. A: The author finishes the passage by applying Washington's farewell address to modern politics, so the purpose probably includes this application. Choice *B* is wrong because George Washington is already a well-established historical figure; furthermore, the passage does not seek to introduce him. Choice *C* is wrong because the author is not fighting a common perception that Washington was merely a military hero. Choice *D* is wrong because the author is not convincing readers. Persuasion does not correspond to the passage. Choice *A* states the primary purpose.

31. D: Choice *A* is wrong because the last paragraph is not appropriate for a history textbook. Choice *B* is false because the piece is not a notice or announcement of Washington's death. Choice *C* is clearly false because it is not fiction, but a historical writing. Choice *D* is correct. The passage is most likely to appear in a newspaper editorial because it cites information relevant and applicable to the present day, a popular format in editorials.

32. D: The passage does not proceed in chronological order since it begins by pointing out Leif Erikson's explorations in America so Choice *A* does not work. Although the author compares and contrasts Erikson with Christopher Columbus, this is not the main way the information is presented; therefore, Choice *B* does not work. Neither does Choice *C* because there is no mention of or reference to cause and effect in the passage. However, the passage does offer a conclusion (Leif Erikson deserves more credit) and premises (first European to set foot in the New World and first to contact the natives) to substantiate Erikson's historical importance. Thus, Choice *D* is correct.

33. C: Choice *A* is wrong because it describes facts: Leif Erikson was the son of Erik the Red and historians debate Leif's date of birth. These are not opinions. Choice *B* is wrong; that Erikson called the land Vinland is a verifiable fact as is Choice *D* because he did contact the natives almost 500 years before Columbus. Choice *C* is the correct answer because it is the author's opinion that Erikson deserves more credit. That, in fact, is his conclusion in the piece, but another person could argue that Columbus or another explorer deserves more credit for opening up the New World to exploration. Rather than being an incontrovertible fact, it is a subjective value claim.

34. B: Choice *A* is wrong because the author aims to go beyond describing Erikson as a mere legendary Viking. Choice *C* is wrong because the author does not focus on Erikson's motivations, let alone name the spreading of Christianity as his primary objective. Choice *D* is wrong because it is a premise that Erikson contacted the natives 500 years before Columbus, which is simply a part of supporting the author's conclusion. Choice *B* is correct because, as stated in the previous answer, it accurately identifies the author's statement that Erikson deserves more credit than he has received for being the first European to explore the New World.

35. B: Choice *A* is wrong because the author is not in any way trying to entertain the reader. Choice *D* is wrong because he goes beyond a mere suggestion; "suggest" is too vague. Although the author is certainly trying to alert the readers of Leif Erikson's unheralded accomplishments, the nature of the writing does not indicate the author would be satisfied with the reader merely knowing of Erikson's exploration (Choice *C*). Rather, the author would want the reader to be informed about it, which is more substantial (Choice *B*).

36. D: Choice *A* is wrong because the author never addresses the Vikings' state of mind or emotions. Choice *B* is wrong because the author does not elaborate on Erikson's exile and whether he would have become an explorer if not for his banishment. Choice *C* is wrong because there is not enough information to support this premise. It is unclear whether Erikson informed the King of Norway of his finding. Although it is true that the King did not send a follow-up expedition, he could have simply chosen not to expend the resources after receiving Erikson's news. It is not possible to logically infer whether Erikson told him. Choice *D* is correct because there are two examples—Leif Erikson's date of birth and what happened during the encounter with the natives—of historians having trouble pinning down important dates in Viking history.

37. A: The word *patronage* most nearly means *auspices*, which means *protection* or *support*. Choice *B*, *aberration*, means *deformity* and does not make sense within the context of the sentence. Choice *C*, *acerbic,* means *bitter* and also does not make sense in the sentence. Choice *D*, *adulation*, is a positive word meaning *praise*, and thus does not fit with the word *condescending* in the sentence.

38. D: *Working man* is most closely aligned with Choice *D*, *bourgeois.* In the context of the speech, the word *bourgeois* means *working* or *middle class*. Choice *A*, *plebian*, does suggest *common people*; however, this is a term that is specific to ancient Rome. Choice *B*, *viscount*, is a European title used to describe a specific degree of nobility. Choice *C*, *entrepreneur*, is a person who operates their own business.

39. C: In the context of the speech, the term *working man* most closely correlates with Choice *C*, *working man is someone who works for wages among the middle class.* Choice *A* is not mentioned in the passage and is off-topic. Choice *B* may be true in some cases, but it does not reflect the sentiment described for the term *working man* in the passage. Choice *D* may also be arguably true. However, it is not given as a definition but as *acts* of the working man, and the topics of *field, factory,* and *screen* are not mentioned in the passage.

40. D: *Enterprise* most closely means *cause*. Choices *A, B,* and *C* are all related to the term *enterprise*. However, Dickens speaks of a *cause* here, not a company, courage, or a game. *He will stand by such an enterprise* is a call to stand by a cause to enable the working man to have a certain autonomy over his own economic standing. The very first paragraph ends with the statement that the working man *shall...have a share in the management of an institution which is designed for his benefit.*

41. B: The speaker's salutation is one from an entertainer to his audience and uses the friendly language to connect to his audience before a serious speech. Recall in the first paragraph that the speaker is there to "accompany [the audience] . . . through one of my little Christmas books," making him an author there to entertain the crowd with his own writing. The speech preceding the reading is the passage itself, and, as the tone indicates, a serious speech addressing the "working man." Although the passage speaks of employers and employees, the speaker himself is not an employer of the audience, so Choice *A* is incorrect. Choice *C* is also incorrect, as the salutation is not used ironically, but sincerely, as the speech addresses the wellbeing of the crowd. Choice *D* is incorrect because the speech is not given by a politician, but a writer.

42. B: For the working man to have a say in his institution which is designed for his benefit. Choice *A* is incorrect because that is the speaker's *first* desire, not his second. Choices *C* and *D* are tricky because the language of both of these is mentioned after the word *second*. However, the speaker doesn't get to the second wish until the next sentence. Choices *C* and *D* are merely prepositions preparing for the statement of the main clause, Choice *B*.

43. D: To define and describe instances of spinoff technology. This is an example of a purpose question—*why* did the author write this? The article contains facts, definitions, and other objective information without telling a story or arguing an opinion. In this case, the purpose of the article is to inform the reader. The only answer choice that is related to giving information is Choice *D*: to define and describe.

44. A: A general definition followed by more specific examples. This organization question asks readers to analyze the structure of the essay. The topic of the essay is about spinoff technology; the first paragraph gives a general definition of the concept, while the following two paragraphs offer more detailed examples to help illustrate this idea.

45. C: They were looking for ways to add health benefits to food. This reading comprehension question can be answered based on the second paragraph—scientists were concerned about astronauts' nutrition and began researching useful nutritional supplements. Choice *A* in particular is incorrect because it reverses the order of discovery (first NASA identified algae for astronaut use, and then it was further developed for use in baby food).

46. D: To give an example of valuable space equipment. This purpose question requires readers to understand the relevance of the given detail. In this case, the author mentions "costly and crucial equipment" before mentioning space suit visors, which are given as an example of something that is very valuable. Choice *A* is incorrect because fashion is only related to sunglasses, not to NASA equipment. Choice *B* can be eliminated because it is simply not mentioned in the passage. While *C* seems like it could be a true statement, it is also not relevant to what is being explained by the author.

47. C: It is difficult to make money from scientific research. The article gives several examples of how businesses have been able to capitalize on NASA research, so it is unlikely that the author would agree with this statement. Evidence for the other answer choices can be found in the article: for Choice *A*, the author mentions that "many consumers are unaware that products they are buying are based on NASA research"; *B* is a general definition of spinoff technology; and *D* is mentioned in the final paragraph.

48. B: The best place for this sentence given all the answer choices is at the end of the first paragraph. Choice *A* is incorrect; the passage is told in chronological order, and leaving the sentence as-is defies that order, since we haven't been introduced to who raised Carver. Choice *C* is incorrect because this sentence is not an introductory sentence. It does not provide the main topic of the paragraph. Choice *D* is incorrect because again, it defies chronological order. By the end of paragraph two we have already gotten to Carver as an adult, so this sentence would not make sense here.

49. D: Out of these choices, a semicolon would be the best fit because there is an independent clause on either side of the semicolon, and the two sentences closely relate to each other. Choice *A* is incorrect because putting a comma between two independent clauses (i.e. complete sentences) creates a comma splice. Choice *B* is incorrect; omitting punctuation here creates a run-on sentence. Choice *C* is incorrect because an ellipses (. . .) is used to designate an omission in the text.

50. C: The correct choice is the subordinating conjunction, "When." We should look at the clues around the phrase to see what fits best. Carver left his money "when he died." Choice *A*, "Because," could perhaps be correct, but "When" is the more appropriate word to use here. Choice *B* is incorrect; "Although" denotes a contrast, and there is no contrast here. Choice *D* is incorrect because "Finally" indicates something at the very end of the list or series, and there is no series at this point in the text.

Subtest II: Language, Linguistics, and Literacy

Human Language Structures

Nature of Human Language

Language arts educators often seem to be in the position of teaching the "right" way to use English, particularly in lessons about grammar and vocabulary. However, all it takes is back-to-back viewings of speeches by the queen of England and the president of the United States or side-by-side readings of a contemporary poem and one written in the 1600s to come to the conclusion that there is no single, fixed, correct form of spoken or written English. Instead, language varies and evolves across different regions and time periods. It also varies between cultural groups depending on factors such as race, ethnicity, age, and socioeconomic status. Students should come away from a language arts class with more than a strictly prescriptive view of language; they should have an appreciation for its rich diversity.

It is important to understand some key terms in discussing linguistic variety.

Language is a tool for communication. It may be spoken, unspoken—as with body language—written, or codified in other ways. Language is symbolic in the sense that it can describe objects, ideas, and events that are not actually present, have not actually occurred, or only exist in the mind of the speaker. All languages are governed by systematic rules of grammar and semantics. These rules allow speakers to manipulate a finite number of elements, such as sounds or written symbols, to create an infinite number of meanings.

A *dialect* is a distinct variety of a language in terms of patterns of grammar, vocabulary, and/or *phonology*—the sounds used by its speakers—that distinguish it from other forms of that language. Two dialects are not considered separate languages if they are *mutually intelligible*—if speakers of each dialect are able to understand one another. A dialect is not a subordinate version of a language. Examples of English dialects include Scottish English and American Southern English.

By definition, *Standard English* is a dialect. It is one variety of English with its own usage of grammar, vocabulary, and pronunciation. Given that Standard English is taught in schools and used in places like government, journalism, and other professional workplaces, it is often elevated above other English dialects. Linguistically, though, there is nothing that makes Standard English more correct or advanced than other dialects.

A *pidgin* is formed when speakers of different languages begin utilizing a simplified mixture of elements from both languages to communicate with each other. In North America, pidgins occurred when Africans were brought to European colonies as slaves, leading to a mixture of African and European languages. Historically, pidgins also sprung up in areas of international trade. A pidgin is communication born of necessity and lacks the full complexity or standardized rules that govern a language.

When a pidgin becomes widely used and is taught to children as their native language, it becomes a *Creole*. An example is Haitian Creole, a language based on French and including elements of West African languages.

An *accent* is a unique speech pattern, particularly in terms of tone or intonation. Speakers from different regions tend to have different accents, as do learners of English from different native languages. In some cases, accents are mutually intelligible, but in other cases, speakers with different accents might have some difficulty in understanding one another.

Colloquial language is language that is used conversationally or familiarly—e.g., "What's up?"—in contrast to formal, professional, or academic language—"How are you this evening?"

Vernacular refers to the native, everyday language of a place. Historically, for instance, Bibles and religious services across Europe were primarily offered in Latin, even centuries after the fall of the Roman Empire. After the revolution of the printing press and the widespread availability of vernacular translations of the Bible in the fifteenth and sixteenth centuries, everyday citizens were able to study from Bibles in their own language without needing specialized training in Latin.

A *regionalism* is a word or expression used in a particular region. In the United States, for instance, examples of regionalisms might be *soda*, *pop*, or *Coke*—terms that vary in popularity according to region.

Jargon is vocabulary used within a specialized field, such as computer programming or mechanics. Jargon may consist of specialized words or of everyday words that have a different meaning in this specialized context.

Slang refers to non-standard expressions that are not used in elevated speech and writing. Slang creates linguistic in-groups and out-groups of people, those who can understand the slang terms and those who can't. Slang is often tied to a specific time period. For example, "groovy" and "far out" are connected to the 1970s, and "as if!" and "4-1-1-" are connected to the 1990s.

Understanding Dialect and its Appropriateness
Certain forms of language are viewed differently depending on the context. Lessons learned in the classroom have a real-life application to a student's future, so he or she should know where, when, and how to utilize different forms of language.

Awareness of dialect can help students as readers. Many writers of literary fiction and nonfiction utilize dialect and colloquialisms to add verisimilitude to their writing. This is especially true for authors who focus on a particular region or cultural group in their works, also known as *regionalism* or *local color literature*. Examples include Zora Neale Hurston's *Their Eyes Were Watching God* and the short stories of Kate Chopin. Students can be asked to consider how the speech patterns in a text affect a reader's understanding of the characters—how the pattern reflects a character's background and place in society. They might consider a reader's impression of the region—how similar or different it is from the reader's region or what can be inferred about the region based on how people speak. In some cases, unfamiliar dialect may be very difficult for readers to understand on the page but becomes much more intelligible when read aloud—as in the reading of Shakespeare.

Word Analysis

It is imperative that educators understand the five basic components of reading education. If there is any deficit in any one of these following components, a child is likely to experience reading difficulty:

- Phonemic Awareness
- Phonics
- Fluency
- Vocabulary
- Comprehension

Phonemic Awareness

A phoneme is the smallest unit of sound in a given language and is one aspect under the umbrella of skills associated with phonological awareness. A child demonstrates phonemic awareness when identifying rhymes, recognizing alliterations, and isolating specific sounds inside a word or a set of words. Students who demonstrate basic phonemic awareness will eventually also be able to independently and appropriately blend together a variety of phonemes.

Some classroom strategies to strengthen phonemic awareness may include:

- Introduction to nursery rhymes and word play
- Speech discrimination techniques to train the ear to hear more accurately
- Repeated instruction connecting sounds to letters and blending sounds
- Use of visual images coupled with corresponding sounds and words
- Teaching speech sounds through direct instruction
- Comparing known to unfamiliar words
- Practicing pronunciation of newly introduced letters, letter combinations, and words
- Practicing word decoding
- Differentiating similar sounding words

Inflection Derivation and Compounding

Inflection is the modification of a word to show different grammatical categories such as tense, case, number, and other aspects. This is done by changing a given word's prefix, suffix, or infix to alter the word's meaning. For example, changing the suffix of the word *cling*, you can make it *clung* and *clang*, expressing different cases. It's important to note that inflection retains the original meaning of the word; only the way in which it is used in the sentences changes.

Derivation is when a new prefix or suffix is added to an existing word to create a new word. Unlike inflection, this process actually does change the meaning of the new word. For example, consider when the suffix *ness* is added to the word *slow* to make *slowness*. Both words are connected with slow: not moving fast. However, slowness describes the quality of not moving fast while slow *is* the act of moving without speed. The terms are related but different.

Compounding involves the binding of two or more words to form a single word with a new meaning. The words are usually unrelated but brought together for a specific term such as *footrace* or *sleepwalk*. These new words are called compound words. Compound words can be formed by combining a noun and a verb, like the previous examples, or by combining two nouns like *snowstorm*. Compounds can also be formed using adjectives, adverbs, and propositions. Some compound words utilize a dash to connect the word or phrase such as: *environmentally-friendly*.

Phonological and Phonemic Awareness Instruction

Age-appropriate and developmentally appropriate instruction for phonological and phonemic awareness is key to helping students strengthen their reading and writing skills. Phonological and phonemic awareness, or PPA, instruction works to enhance correct speech, improve understanding and application of accurate letter-to-sound correspondence, and strengthen spelling skills. Since skill-building involving phonemes is not a natural process but needs to be taught, PPA instruction is especially important for students who have limited access and exposure to reading materials and who lack familial encouragement to read. Strategies that educators can implement include leading word and sound games, focusing on phoneme skill-building activities, and ensuring all activities focus on the fun, playful nature of words and sounds instead of rote memorization and drilling techniques.

Phonics

Phonics is the ability to apply letter-sound relationships and letter patterns in order to accurately pronounce written words. Students with strong phonics skills are able to recognize familiar written words with relative ease and quickly decipher or "decode" unfamiliar words. As one of the foundational skills for reading readiness, phonics essentially enables young readers to translate printed words into recognizable speech. If students lack proficiency in phonics, their ability to read fluently and to increase vocabulary will be limited, which consequently leads to reading comprehension difficulties.

Emergent readers benefit from explicit word decoding instruction that focuses on letter-sound relationships. This includes practicing sounding out words and identifying exceptions to the letter-sound relationships. A multi-sensory approach to word decoding instruction has also been found to be beneficial. By addressing a wide variety of learning styles and providing visual and hands-on instruction, educators help to bridge the gap between guided word decoding and it as an automatic process.

Morphology

By analyzing and understanding Latin, Greek, and Anglo-Saxon word roots, prefixes, and suffixes one can better understand word meanings. Of course, people can always look words up if a dictionary or thesaurus if available, but meaning can often be gleaned on the spot if the writer learns to dissect and examine words.

A word can consist of the following:

- root
- root + suffix
- prefix + root
- prefix + root + suffix

For example, if someone was unfamiliar with the word *submarine* they could break the word into its parts.

- prefix + root
- sub + marine

It can be determined that *sub* means *below* as in *subway* and *subpar*. Additionally, one can determine that *marine* refers to *the sea* as in *marine life*. Thus, it can be figured that *submarine* refers to something below the water.

Roots

Roots are the basic components of words. Many roots can stand alone as individual words, but others must be combined with a prefix or suffix to be a word. For example, *calc* is a root but it needs a suffix to be an actual word (*calcium*).

Prefixes

A *prefix* is a word, letter, or number that is placed before another. It adjusts or qualifies the root word's meaning. When written alone, prefixes are followed by a dash to indicate that the root word follows. Some of the most common prefixes are the following:

Prefix	Meaning	Example
dis-	not or opposite of	disabled
in-, im-, il-, ir-	not	illiterate
re-	again	return
un-	not	unpredictable
anti-	against	antibacterial
fore-	before	forefront
mis-	wrongly	misunderstand
non-	not	nonsense
over-	more than normal	overabundance
pre-	before	preheat
super-	above	superman

Suffixes

A suffix is a letter or group of letters added at the end of a word to form another word. The word created from the root and suffix is either a different tense of the same root (*help + ed = helped*) or a new word (*help + ful = helpful*). When written alone, suffixes are preceded by a dash to indicate that the root word comes before.

Some of the most common prefixes are the following:

Suffix	Meaning	Example
Ed	makes a verb past tense	Wash*ed*
Ing	makes a verb a present participle verb	Wash*ing*
Ly	to make characteristic of	Love*ly*
s/es	to make more than one	chair*s*, box*es*
Able	can be done	Deplor*able*
Al	having characteristics of	Comic*al*
Est	comparative	Great*est*
Ful	full of	Wonder*ful*
Ism	belief in	Commun*ism*
Less	without	Faith*less*
Ment	action or process	Accomplish*ment*
Ness	state of	Happi*ness*
ize, ise	to render, to make	steril*ize*, advert*ise*
cede/ceed/sede	go	con*cede*, pro*ceed*, super*sede*

Here are some helpful tips:

- When adding a suffix that starts with a vowel (for example, -*ed*) to a one-syllable root whose vowel has a short sound and ends in a consonant (for example, *stun*), double the final consonant of the root (*n*).

    stun + ed = stun*n*ed

    Exception: If the past tense verb ends in *x* such as *box*, do not double the *x*.

    box + ed = boxed

- If adding a suffix that starts with a vowel (-*er*) to a multi-syllable word ending in a consonant (*begin*), double the consonant (*n*).

    begin + er = begin*n*er

- If a short vowel is followed by two or more consonants in a word such as *i+t+c+h = itch,* do <u>not</u> double the last consonant.

    itch + ed = itched

- If adding a suffix that starts with a vowel (-*ing*) to a word ending in *e* (for example, *name*), that word's final *e* is generally (but not always) dropped.

    name + ing = naming
    exception: manage + able = manag*e*able

- If adding a suffix that starts with a consonant (-*ness*) to a word ending in *e* (*complete*), the *e* generally (but not always) remains.

    complete + ness = completeness
    exception: judge + ment = judgment

- There is great diversity on handling words that end in *y*. For words ending in a vowel + y, nothing changes in the original word.

    play + ed = played

- For words ending in a consonant + *y*, change the *y* to *i* when adding any suffix except for *–ing*.

    marry + ed = married
    marry + ing = marrying

Syntax, Semantics, and Pragmatics

Syntax

With its origins from the Greek word, "syntaxis," which means arrangement, *syntax* is the study of phrase and sentence formation. The study of syntax focuses on the ways in which specific words can be combined to create coherent meaning. For example: the simple rearrangement of the words, "I can run," is different from the question, "Can I run?" which is also different from the meaningless "Run I can."

The following methods can be used to teach syntax:

- Proper Syntax Modeling: Students don't need to be corrected for improper syntax. Instead, they should be shown ways to rephrase what they said with proper syntax. If a student says, "Run I can," then the teacher should say, "Oh, you can run how fast?" This puts syntax in place with conversational skills.

- Open-Ended Sentences: Students can complete open-ended sentences with proper syntax both orally and in written format, or they can correct sentences that have improper syntax so that they make sense.

- Listening for Syntax: Syntax is auditory. Students can often hear a syntax error before they can see it in writing. Teachers should have students use word cards or word magnets to arrange and rearrange simple sentences and read them aloud to check for syntax.

- Repetition: Syntax can be practiced by using songs, poems, and rhymes for repetitive automation.

Semantics

Semantics is the branch of linguistics that addresses meanings. Morphemes, words, phrases, and sentences all carry distinct meanings. The way these individual parts are arranged can have a significant effect on meaning. In order to construct language, students must be able to use semantics to arrange and rearrange words to achieve the particular meaning they are striving for. Activities that teach semantics revolve around teaching the arrangement of word parts (morphology) and root words, and then the teaching of vocabulary. Moving from vocabulary words into studying sentences and sentence structure leads students to learn how to use context clues to determine meaning and to understand anomalies such as metaphors, idioms, and allusions. There are five types of semantic relationships that are critical to understand:

- *Hyponyms* refer to a relationship between words where general words have multiple more-specific words (hyponyms) that fall into the same category (e.g., horse: mare, stallion, foal, Appaloosa, Clydesdale).

- *Meronyms* refer to a relationship between words where a whole word has multiple parts (meronyms) that comprise it (e.g., horse: tail, mane, hooves, ears).

- *Synonyms* refer to words that have the same meaning as another word (e.g., instructor/teacher/educator, canine/dog, feline/cat, herbivore/vegetarian).

- *Antonyms* refer to words that have the opposite meaning as another word (e.g., true/false, up/down, in/out, right/wrong).

- *Homonyms* refer to words that are spelled the same (homographs) or sound the same (homophones) but mean different things (e.g., there/their/they're, two/too/to, principal/principle, plain/plane, (kitchen) sink/ sink (down as in water)).

Pragmatics

Pragmatics is the study of what words mean in certain situations. It helps to understand the intentions and interpretations of intentions through words used in human interaction. Different listeners and different situations call for different language and intonations of language. When people engage in a conversation, it is usually to convey a certain message, and the message (even using the same words) can change depending on the setting and the audience. The more fluent the speaker, the more success she or he will have in conveying the intended message.

The following methods can be used to teach pragmatics:

- When students state something incorrectly, a response can be given to what they intended to say in the first place. For instance, if a student says, "That's how it didn't happen." Then the teacher might say, "Of course, that's not how it happened." Instead of putting students on defense by being corrected, this method puts them at ease and helps them learn.

- Role-playing conversations with different people in different situations can help teach pragmatics. For example, pretend playing can be used where a situation remains the same but the audience changes, or the audience stays the same but the situations change. This can be followed with a discussion about how language and intonations change too.

- Different ways to convey a message can be used, such as asking vs. persuading, or giving direct vs. indirect requests and polite vs. impolite messages.

- Various non-verbal signals can be used to see how they change pragmatics. For example, students can be encouraged to use mismatched words and facial expressions, such as angry words while smiling or happy words while pretending to cry.

Acquisition and Development of Language and Literacy

Cognitive, Affective, and Sociocultural Factors on Language Acquisition

Planning Instruction Responsive to Students' Individual and Group Needs

It can be difficult as a teacher to be mindful of the varying individual and group identities present in the classroom. Every adult has internalized beliefs that he or she has learned through experience or was taught as a child. To encourage cultural understanding and dismantle stereotypes, an essential part of the curriculum should be devoted to teaching students tolerance of themselves and others.

One thing teachers should keep in mind is that although students may share similar group identities—race, nationality, socioeconomic status—they also contain differing individual identities. They may have different religions, different ancestry, or different languages. These differences will present themselves in everything the students do, from curricular activities, such as reading and writing, to social interaction in speaking and listening.

To incorporate cultural awareness into classroom instruction, the teacher must first express interest in the cultural backgrounds of his or her students. If the instructor is closed off against certain identities, the students will echo these viewpoints, being reserved in expression and also harboring the same reservations towards cultures different than their own. Therefore, the first step in planning instructions that tailors to the cultural needs of the students is to be interested in their identities. This can be done in many ways, but one sure way that a teacher can show he or she cares is by engaging in diversity activities, such as introduction cards or online questionnaires that students can fill out about themselves. These may include the following categories:

- Where they or their ancestors are from
- Their age
- Their primary and secondary languages, if applicable
- Their religious or spiritual beliefs
- Their race
- Their gender, what they identify as
- Any other information they feel comfortable introducing to the class

These are only a few examples of the information that can be gathered on index cards or questionnaires. Teachers can have the students go around the room and introduce themselves, while displaying curiosity about the backgrounds of their classmates. The information may then be kept throughout the year for reference and will also help the teacher collect a sort of census on the different cultural backgrounds their students possess.

Another proven way to show interest in the students and instill a sense of cultural awareness in the classroom is to assign a family survey project in which the students report on their heritage, the special customs or holidays that they practice in their home, the languages they speak, or anything they wish to share about their families and identities. These projects can be completed on PowerPoint presentations, poster boards, or video interviews, and students should be encouraged to bring items of cultural significance to share with their classmates.

The knowledge gained from these sorts of activities will greatly help the teacher to create a curriculum of instruction that encourages tolerance. For example, in reading about historic events involving horrendous crimes against a certain race or culture, teachers should try to read texts that contain both perspectives—e.g., texts from German, American, and Jewish voices related to the Holocaust. Discussions such as these can be taught in very compassionate and empathetic ways, while still recognizing the horrors of the crimes committed. Students can also consider historical and contemporary texts to see how perspectives have evolved on significant cultural issues throughout history.

It is also important to create a curriculum in which all students see themselves, their race, their genders, and their religions represented in their studies. The curriculum should not to focus on the achievements of one particular group, such as only teaching history related to Christian Caucasian culture. Further, teachers should be ready and willing to alter the curriculum to respond to the needs of the students.

To instill a sense of tolerance in the classroom, students can complete worksheets on the kinds of behavior and diction that are acceptable when they encounter differences in cultures or belief systems. They can create a play or scene where they write out such an encounter and how they would approach it to build understanding between people from different backgrounds. Monitoring the interactions between the students and pointing out any situation or comment that unintentionally conveys intolerance will help make them more aware. Students should be educated on stereotypes. Most importantly, teachers should always lead by example by being as open and impartial as possible.

Strategies for Creating a Safe Environment
There are countless different strategies for creating a culturally-safe environment in which reading, writing, speaking, and listening can take place. First, the classroom should be clean and orderly to minimize distractions. It should reflect cultural diversity or impartiality. The classroom should be arranged with resources readily available and easily accessible so that a teacher never has to turn his or her back on their students. Secondly, the classroom should be arranged in a way that makes interaction with fellow students easy. The classroom environment also must convey a sense of emotional safety where students feel comfortable expressing themselves without fear of bullying or prejudice. This means teachers should be modeling respectful behavior for students, establishing rules of respectful interaction between students, and addressing any instances of disrespectful speech or behavior. Once the classroom has been set up safely, the following strategies are effective ways to incorporate cultural awareness into the curriculum:

Reading

- Choosing texts that reflect multicultural perspectives and include different cultures

- Clarifying that chosen texts may contain culturally and racially-sensitive language and pointing out the intolerance in such texts—e.g., the excessive use of racial slurs in Mark Twain's *Huckleberry Finn* and what they suggested of cultural intolerance at the time

- Trying not to choose texts that talk about an entire race or religion in general, but specific aspects of the race or religion to avoid sweeping generalizations or stereotypes about a group— e.g., choosing books on certain Native American tribes, rather than books solely on Native Americans, texts that offer specifics about a particular religion

- Choosing texts that are both fun and serious, such as texts on cultural festivities and fun, as well as those about wars and hardships

- Choosing texts that are historically accurate and up-to-date

- If allowing students to choose their own books, encouraging them to explore texts that are culturally different than their own

Writing

- Requiring that students complete a project, such as a presentation or examination of a famous figure, who represents a culture or religion or philosophy that differs from their own

- Monitoring student writing, checking for the presence of stereotypes and intolerance, and holding one-on-one conferences with students whenever concerns arise

- Instructing students on the appropriate vocabulary, diction, and phrasing when writing on culturally or racially sensitive subjects

- Encouraging students to write together via collaborative discussion boards, blogs, or group projects

- Assigning students to groups with varying cultural, religious, racial, or socioeconomic backgrounds

- Having students write on personal experiences where they have encountered intolerance against themselves or others

Speaking

- Holding frequent group discussions in which students can learn how to converse with people of different backgrounds, which may include inviting guest speakers

- Arranging chairs in circles or allowing students to remain at their desks in a way that demonstrates equality among all participants

- Monitoring student behavior during such discussions, calling attention to any inappropriate dialogue, use of stereotypes, or displays of intolerance the moment they occur

- Leading by example by treating all races, religions, cultures, genders and gender identities with tolerance and respect

- Beginning every discussion with a reminder to be accepting and tolerant of differing perspectives and beliefs and asserting that offensive language or behavior will not be tolerated

Listening

- Encouraging active listening by allowing students to take notes and ask questions

- Asking students to summarize what they heard

- Discouraging interruptions or non-verbal negative responses, such as eye-rolls, sighs, or noises of disgust, to reduce disrespectful behavior during discussion

- Allowing enough time for all students to speak so that others may listen and giving everyone an equal amount of time to speak without letting any one person dominate discussion

When an instructor is knowledgeable in a subject, demonstrates passion for the work, and creates an environment of respect, students will learn a great deal from him or her as a mentor, both in real-world situations and in academics.

Influence of a First Language on a Subsequent Language

For the vast majority of people, native language acquisition comes about naturally in childhood. From the time they are born, babies are usually surrounded by the language use of their parents or caregivers. The human brain is hardwired to learn language, meaning that babies do not have to put conscious effort into unraveling the intricacies of grammar or pronunciation; it is something that happens automatically as they are exposed to language. Furthermore, caregivers do not have to formally teach first language skills to babies.

First language acquisition in infancy and early childhood passes through several predictable stages. Babies begin by crying to express a range of emotions like hunger or discomfort. By the time they are two months old, they then begin cooing to convey other emotions, such as happiness and satisfaction. In later months, infants start to experiment with different sounds like babbling and gurgling by repeating simple syllables like "goo goo goo" and "ma ma ma" and show signs of comprehending certain full words. A baby's first word often occurs around one year of age, and for the next six months, the baby can conduct simple communication through one-word expressions like "Daddy," "milk," and "cat."

After they reach eighteen months, young children begin to use two- and three-word utterances to express more complex meaning, such as "Mommy go?" "Don't want to!" and "Where juice?" By the time they are two and a half years old, toddlers enter the telegraphic stage of language where they begin using the grammatical structure of their native language, although not without some problems. A common error is "I goed to school," instead of "I went to school." However, even though young children do make mistakes in their language usage, it is nevertheless remarkable that they achieve functional mastery of a language in such a short amount of time, generally without any formal instruction.

Although acquisition of a first language is largely a natural process of childhood development, *second language acquisition* in older children or adults is quite different. This is partially linked to the critical period hypothesis, which states that language acquisition only occurs readily and naturally during the first few years of life; language acquisition that happens later, perhaps after puberty, is much more difficult and less successful. Children who are not exposed to any language before the age of five or so will have extreme difficulty learning a language later. This seems to indicate that the brain is primed to learn language from birth, but this readiness quickly diminishes after the critical period has been passed.

Although scientists continue to debate the exact significance of a critical period on second language development, learning a second language later in life clearly presents different challenges than learning a first language. In linguistics, *L1* refers to a speaker's native language and *L2* refers to a second language.

L2 acquisition follows different stages from that of L1. L2 acquisition begins with *preproduction*, also known as the *silent stage*, during which the learner is exposed to the new language, but lacks the skills to communicate and may only use body language or other non-verbal expressions. During the early production stage, the L2 learner begins using simple expressions and has limited comprehension ability.

Next is *speech emergence*—the low-intermediate stage. At this point, the language learner can form simple sentences although he or she makes frequent errors in grammar and usage. L2 learners then pass to *intermediate fluency*, where they begin to gain skills in academic or idiomatic language, demonstrate a much higher level of comprehension, and make fewer mistakes in their expressions.

Finally, the learner reaches *advanced fluency*, exhibiting near-native expressive and comprehensive skills. It is worth noting that even with near-native skills, after many years of advanced fluency, L2 learners may continue to speak with a different accent or use certain idiosyncratic expressions that are markedly different from native speakers. Nevertheless, they are certainly fluent.

In 2013, the Census Bureau reported that one in five Americans are speaking a language other than English at home, so language arts instructors will encounter a mixture of native speakers and second language learners in the classroom. In both cases, though, certain goals and strategies remain the same. The purpose of a language arts class is not to teach students language from scratch, but rather to further develop their preexisting knowledge and increase their awareness of how to use language for more effective and meaningful communication.

For both native and non-native English speakers, the exposure to written and spoken language that they receive outside of school impacts their future performance in school. In a notable 1995 study, researchers observed children in low- and high-income families and found that those in high-income households were exposed to 30 million more words during their childhood than those from families on welfare. When researchers followed up on these children in third grade, those who had been exposed to more words early on showed greater success in measures of reading comprehension and vocabulary.

Academic Literacy

Evaluating the Effectiveness of Specific Strategies
New research on teaching strategies is emerging all the time, and it is important for instructors to stay abreast of new developments while evaluating when and how to implement any changes in their classroom. Instructors should also consider the pros and cons of different approaches to teaching.

In terms of encouraging students to seek outside language resources (noted the section above), the effectiveness differs greatly depending on students' background and home life. Students who must work after school to support themselves or their families may not have much time to stop by the public library or to read for leisure; in this case, instructors need to maximize in-class instruction time. According to another strategy, the three-tier approach, tier two words are most important in a language arts classroom. However, some L2 students in the early production or intermediate fluency stages may lack basic tier one skills and struggle with understanding more advanced academic vocabulary.

Also, the integrated approach to learning vocabulary in a group of related words calls on instructors to present words as they are actually used in context, which might involve using some tier three words related to specific fields of study. Is it more effective to focus only on having a broad base of general vocabulary or to spend some time building skills in different specialized areas? This question might be answered differently depending on the needs of students in class.

As they experiment with the effectiveness of new methods of instruction, educators can also move beyond outdated learning practices. Assignments such as getting a list of words to look up in the dictionary are not generally considered effective methods. As discussed earlier, words contain a multitude of meanings that take on importance dependent on context; simply memorizing words outside of context, then, does not provide long-term benefits to students' productive language skills.

Instructor-centered models of learning have also been overturned by more recent pedagogical research. While instructors are a valuable resource of providing information and modeling language use for students, educators simply supply the input while students still need a chance to produce output. This means giving students ample opportunity to practice and apply new vocabulary, calling on students' prior knowledge when introducing new vocabulary, and demonstrating how students can use language skills outside of the classroom.

<u>Semantic Mapping, Word Analogies, and Cohesion Analysis</u>
Recalling information can seem daunting, particularly during a test, an essay, or even conversation. The best remedy for this is to develop methods that will make it easier to pinpoint and remember key information easier. One method is to use semantic mapping. This process relies on creating a visual web of sequential or relevant information. Simply write down key details in notes, circle them, and then draw a line connecting the individual details with other relevant information. Another variation would be to write down a central theme or idea and then branch off to facts surrounding it.

Word analogies can also be a useful trigger for mental recall. Humans naturally associate keywords with specific information. If there's a specific individual, location, or trivia that needs to be recalled, begin by defining key words associated with them. Then create a phrase that uses the key word. For example: *Buddha followed the Eightfold Path, the Eightfold path was developed by the Buddha.* The analogy can be simple, complex, even repetitive—whatever helps to associate keywords with information.

Cohesion analysis will help break information down so that it can be processed and remembered a lot easier. Break apart the core components of a text or even a sentence into sections. This can also help with the formation of word analogies. Basically, cohesion analysis will enable the distinction of details to create a logical understanding of why facts are the way they are, as well as the components of the needed information.

Research Strategies and Reference Materials

The CSET tests will assess educational candidates' familiarity with common research-based strategies for reading instruction. This will require potential teachers to be knowledgeable in current practices as well as able to evaluate the effectiveness of those practices as applicable to reading tasks and apply them to reading instruction challenges.

As this is a widely varied topic across educational levels, student abilities, and many reading comprehension skills, the potential test taker is advised to read further on the subject. Many online resources are available, but some additional works to consider include:

- McGregor, Tanny. *Comprehension Connections: Bridges to Strategic Reading*. Portsmouth, New Hampshire: Heinemann, 2007.

- Miller, Brett, Cutting, Laurie E., McCardle, Peggy. *Unraveling Reading Comprehension*. Baltimore, Maryland: Paul H. Brooks Publishing Co., Inc. 2013.

- Tovani, Cris. *I Read it, but I Don't Get it: Comprehension Strategies for Adolescent Readers*. Portland, ME: Stenhouse Publishing, 2000.

- Wilhelm, Jeffrey D. *Improving Comprehension with Think-Aloud Strategies*. New York, New York: Scholastic Inc., 2001.

A potential educator needs to be aware that teaching reading comprehension involves developing skills beyond mere word recognition. It involves being able to teach critical thinking skills and being able to teach students how to process unfamiliar material based on prior knowledge. It involves getting students involved in what they read, based on their interests, and their ability to relate to the material. It involves encouraging students to ask questions and explore.

In demonstrating one's ability to use common research-based strategies for reading instruction, a potential test taker should be able to show his or her awareness of theory regarding how to activate students' prior knowledge, how to model meta-cognitive practices, and how to employ multiple reading strategies for a variety of situations for the most comprehensive student experience.

Activating Prior Knowledge

Activating students' prior knowledge—sometimes referred to as *schemas*—means being able to get students to ascertain what they already know, so they can apply it to their reading. A common strategy to use prior to reading is a K-W-L chart, a graphic organizer which has students determine what they already know about a topic, what they want to know, and what they learned after reading. Graphic organizers are a great way of integrating knowledge and ideas. Having students complete the K section before reading is a tangible way to activate their schemas.

It is important students make connections and relate reading passages to their own experiences— referred to as *text to self*, to their world knowledge— referred to as *text to world*, and to other texts— referred to as *text to text*. The ability to make these connections helps students better understand what they have read.

Potential teachers should be able to model asking questions during the reading experience and model the finding of those answers, based on prior knowledge. Having students read, then write about the connections they make to the text will increase reading comprehension skills. Of course, teaching students to activate and use their schema as it applies to their reading is a skill that should be taught over time. Encourage students to ask how text passages relate to what they already know within their own lives, how those passages relate to what they already know about the world, and how those passages relate to other things they've read. Doing so will result in more critical thinkers and, in turn, more critical readers.

Reference Materials

A college-level dictionary will be the most useful and authoritative source for word meanings, origins, and forms. Rhyming dictionaries list all possible rhymes for a word, which can be useful in poetry or songwriting, and for younger students learning to read. Bilingual dictionaries define word meaning and pronunciation in more than one language. They are useful for English Language Learners and native English speaking students who are learning a new language. A glossary is a list of specialized terms and their definitions. It is typically found in the back of a text for readers to better understand the material covered in the text. A thesaurus contains synonyms for words and can be helpful for any writer who is looking to broaden their vocabulary.

Reference materials can be an asset to any classroom. Teachers should be aware of their options for general and specialized reference books, both in print and online, and familiarize themselves with how to use these resources. Dictionaries can be invaluable in the classroom in teaching students word pronunciations, definitions, origins, and alphabetical order. Reference texts can be useful in aiding research and to supplement classroom instruction. Teachers can model search techniques and how to use reference materials in the different stages of the students' writing process.

Knowledge of Academic Words and Phrases

As the early stages of both L1 and L2 acquisition show, learners need language input before they can achieve language output. Providing students with a variety of language resources, both formally and informally, can give them valuable exposure to new means of expression. In class, this exposure can include daily assignments, a classroom library, or a bulletin board with news for students. Educators can also get students in the habit of accessing resources outside of the classroom such as visiting the school or public library, watching, reading, or listening to the news, or reading informally from magazines, blogs, or other sources of interest.

This exposure also relates to two different forms of vocabulary acquisition—through incidental learning or direct instruction. *Incidental learning* occurs when students naturally encounter new vocabulary in context during daily life whereas *direct instruction* occurs through structured lessons and assignments in an academic setting.

In vocabulary development in particular, when it comes to direct instruction, there are several approaches to teaching new words to students.

One is the *three-tier approach*, which states that vocabulary can be classified into three levels as shown in the graphic below. These tiers are known as: conversational (tier 1), academic (tier 2), and domain-specific language (tier 3).

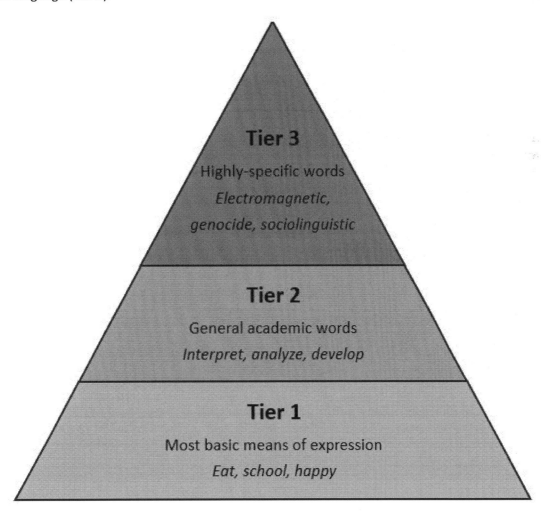

Tier 3
Highly-specific words
Electromagnetic, genocide, sociolinguistic

Tier 2
General academic words
Interpret, analyze, develop

Tier 1
Most basic means of expression
Eat, school, happy

Tier three words should be taught within the subjects that they are directly related to rather than in a language arts class. Instead, language arts instruction should focus on tier two words that are broadly applicable to a range of subjects and, therefore, more practical for students.

Another theory of vocabulary development is learning language through chunks or groups of related words. By learning words in context along with other connected words, students are better able to connect vocabulary to areas of prior knowledge and more effectively store new words in their long-term memory. Students also gain a more complete set of tools with which to form new expressions, rather than simply learning new words in isolation. Learning in *semantic chunks*—clusters of five to ten words forming a connected phrase or sentence—is particularly useful for L2 learners in gaining familiarity with how to manipulate vocabulary and combine words to build meaning.

Vocabulary learning can also be conducted through a variety of media, combining visual, auditory, and active cues. One strategy is known as the *total physical response*, where students learn to associate a word with a certain physical reaction. For example, in response to the word *circumference*, students might use their finger to draw a circle in the air. Students can also watch videos related to the vocabulary topic they are learning about or look at visual representations of new words through a picture dictionary. By activating different styles of learning, instructors can provide students with more opportunities to acquire new language skills.

Greek, Latin, and Anglo-Saxon Roots and Affixes

Understanding the meaning of a part of a word can aid in understanding the meaning of the entire word. Knowledge of Greek, Latin, and Anglo-Saxon roots and affixes can help students to decode the meaning of unfamiliar words and build vocabulary. Some example follow:

Greek Root	Meaning	Latin Root	Meaning	Anglo-Saxon Root	Meaning
cosm	universe	bene	good	ber	carry
dec	ten	clar	clear	kno	skill
macro	large	ject	throw	tru	faithful
poli	city	mot	move	ward	guard

Words are made up of roots, prefixes, and suffixes. Here are some examples:

Root	Meaning	Example Words
multi	Many	multicolored, multitask
loc	Place	location, relocate, local
port	Carry	transport, export
semi	Half	semicircle, semiannual
sect	Cut	intersect, dissect
aqua	Water	aquarium, aquatic

Prefix	Meaning	Suffix	Meaning
anti–	against	-able	can be done
inter–	between	-less	without
un–	not	-ment	action or process

Cognitive Elements of Reading and Writing Processes

Both reading and writing rely on decoding and encoding processes respectively. When reading through the written text, you must absorb and interpret the information that's being presented. This can be done by identifying keywords and stylistic choices throughout the text that illuminates the theme. The genre of the writing can actually reveal much about the content and how it should be interpreted.

Fiction uses distinct conventions such as symbolism, allegory, metaphor, and other artistic styles to convey meaning. The decoding method for this genre is to identify the symbolism and artistic pattern, then analyze this content for meaning. Sometimes this means linking the content with real events or symbols outside of the text. Constructing a concrete meaning for fiction writing involves combining these different allusions and symbols into an interwoven understanding of the text as a whole. All of the symbols and metaphors serve to create an overarching message within the narrative and make the text more comprehensive.

Writing fiction relies on encoding (or inserting information into) the theme and plot points within the narrative. This relies on using dialogue and storytelling to either directly or subliminally touch on relevant topics. The use of simile and metaphor can also create meaning within the work.

Interpreting nonfiction is very different than fiction. This is because the text does not use the same artistic conventions. While non-fiction can be well written and even use descriptions like metaphors and similes, the information is presented in a far more direct manner. Rather than striving to be symbolic, nonfiction writers want to be clear and direct about their views or topic. Facts and argument take the place of symbolism and allusion. Instead of decoding symbolic references or specific word choices, the key is to focus on the significance of the information presented and how the writer expresses said information.

Non-fiction conventions are less artistic, focusing more on persuading and/or educating the reader in a straightforward way. Style can vary, but the core purpose of the writing is to outline facts and opinions. Facts are delivered straightforward and in detail. If the text in question is argumentative, there will be a distinctive stance throughout the text.

Non-fiction persuasive works follow a central view or thesis, followed by proof used to support the writer's perspective, and then analysis to elucidate why the evidence strengthens the argument. To decode persuasive non-fiction, examine the evidence, analysis, and other details to form an opinion on the content presented.

Metacognitive Strategies

Metacognitive strategies ask the student to decode text passages. In part, they require the student to preview text, be able to recognize unfamiliar words, then use context clues to define them for greater understanding. In addition, meta-cognitive strategies in the classroom employ skills such as being able to decode imagery, being able to predict, and being able to summarize. If a student can define unfamiliar vocabulary, make sense of an author's use of imagery, preview text prior to reading predict outcomes during reading, and summarize the material, he or she is achieving effective reading comprehension. When approaching reading instruction, the teacher who encourages students to use phrases such as *I'm noticing*, *I'm thinking*, and *I'm wondering* is teaching a meta-cognitive type strategy.

Pre-Reading Strategies

Pre-reading strategies are important, yet often overlooked. Non-critical readers will often begin reading without taking the time to review factors that will help them understand the text. Skipping pre-reading strategies may result in a reader having to re-address a text passage more times than is necessary. Some pre-reading strategies include the following:

- Previewing the text for clues
- Skimming the text for content
- Scanning for unfamiliar words in context
- Formulating questions on sight
- Making predictions
- Recognizing needed prior knowledge

Before reading a text passage, a reader can enhance his or her ability to comprehend material by *previewing the text for clues*. This may mean making careful note of any titles, headings, graphics, notes, introductions, important summaries, and conclusions. It can involve a reader making physical notes regarding these elements or highlighting anything he or she thinks is important before reading. Often, a reader will be able to gain information just from these elements alone. Of course, close reading is required in order to fill in the details. A reader needs to be able to ask what he or she is reading about and what a passage is trying to say. The answers to these general questions can often be answered in previewing the text itself.

It's helpful to use pre-reading clues to determine the main idea and organization. First, any titles, sub-headings, chapter headings should be read, and the test taker should make note of the author's credentials if any are listed. It's important to deduce what these clues may indicate as it pertains to the focus of the text and how it's organized.

During pre-reading, readers should also take special note of how text features contribute to the central idea or thesis of the passage. Is there an index? Is there a glossary? What headings, footnotes, or other visuals are included and how do they relate to the details within the passage? Again, this is where any pre-reading notes come in handy, since a test taker should be able to relate supporting details to these textual features.

Next, a reader should *skim* the text for general ideas and content. This technique does not involve close reading; rather, it involves looking for important words within the passage itself. These words may have something to do with the author's theme. They may have to do with structure—for example, words such as *first, next, therefore,* and *last.* Skimming helps a reader understand the overall structure of a passage and, in turn, this helps him or her understand the author's theme or message.

From there, a reader should quickly *scan* the text for any unfamiliar words. When reading a print text, highlighting these words or making other marginal notation is helpful when going back to read text critically. A reader should look at the words surrounding any unfamiliar ones to see what contextual clues unfamiliar words carry. Being able to define unfamiliar terms through contextual meaning is a critical skill in reading comprehension.

A reader should also *formulate any questions* he or she might have before conducting close reading. Questions such as "What is the author trying to tell me?" or "Is the author trying to persuade my thinking?" are important to a reader's ability to engage critically with the text. Questions will focus a reader's attention on what is important in terms of idea and what is supporting detail.

Along with formulating questions, it is helpful to make predictions of what the answers to these questions and others will be. *Making predictions* involves using information from the text and personal experiences to make a thoughtful guess as to what will happen in the story and what outcomes can be expected.

Last, a reader should recognize that authors assume readers bring a *prior knowledge* set to the reading experience. Not all readers have the same experience, but authors seek to communicate with their readers. In turn, readers should strive to interact with the author of a particular passage by asking themselves what the passage demands they know during reading. This is also known as making a text-to-self connection. If a passage is informational in nature, a reader should ask "What do I know about this topic from other experiences I've had or other works I've read?" If a reader can relate to the content, he or she will better understand it.

All of the above pre-reading strategies will help the reader prepare for a closer reading experience. They will engage a reader in active interaction with the text by helping to focus the reader's full attention on the details that he or she will encounter during the next round or two of critical, closer reading.

Strategies During Reading
After pre-reading, a test taker can employ a variety of other reading strategies while conducting one or more closer readings. These strategies include the following:

- Clarifying during a close read
- Questioning during a close read
- Organizing the main ideas and supporting details
- Summarizing the text effectively

A reader needs to be able to *clarify* what he or she is reading. This strategy demands a reader think about how and what he or she is reading. This thinking should occur during and after the act of reading. For example, a reader may encounter one or more unfamiliar ideas during reading, then be asked to apply thoughts about those unfamiliar concepts after reading when answering test questions.

Questioning during a critical read is closely related to clarifying. A reader must be able to ask questions in general about what he or she is reading and questions regarding the author's supporting ideas. Questioning also involves a reader's ability to self-question. When closely reading a passage, it's not enough to simply try and understand the author. A reader must consider critical thinking questions to ensure he or she is comprehending intent. It's advisable, when conducting a close read, to write out margin notes and questions during the experience. These questions can be addressed later in the thinking process after reading and during the phase where a reader addresses the test questions. A reader who is successful in reading comprehension will iteratively question what he or she reads, search text for clarification, then answer any questions that arise.

A reader should *organize* main ideas and supporting details cognitively as he or she reads, as it will help the reader understand the larger structure at work. The use of quick annotations or marks to indicate what the main idea is and how the details function to support it can be helpful. Understanding the structure of a text passage is sometimes critical to answering questions about an author's approach, theme, messages, and supporting detail. This strategy is most effective when reading informational or nonfiction text. Texts that try to convince readers of a particular idea, that present a theory, or that try to explain difficult concepts are easier to understand when a reader can identify the overarching structure at work.

Post-Reading Strategies

After completing a text, a reader should be able to *summarize* the author's theme and supporting details in order to fully understand the passage. Being able to effectively restate the author's message, sub-themes, and pertinent, supporting ideas will help a reader gain an advantage when addressing standardized test questions.

A reader should also evaluate the strength of the predictions that were made in the pre-reading stage. Using textual evidence, predictions should be compared to the actual events in the story to see if the two were similar or not. Employing all of these strategies will lead to fuller, more insightful reading comprehension.

Grammatical Structures of English

Sentence Construction

Sentence Types

There are four ways in which we can structure sentences: simple, compound, complex, and compound-complex. Sentences can be composed of just one clause or many clauses joined together.

When a sentence is composed of just one clause (an independent clause), we call it a simple sentence. Simple sentences do not necessarily have to be short sentences. They just require one independent clause with a subject and a predicate. For example:

Thomas marched over to Andrew's house.

Jonah and Mary constructed a simplified version of the Eiffel Tower with Legos.

When a sentence has two or more independent clauses we call it a compound sentence. The clauses are connected by a comma and a coordinating conjunction—*and, but, or, nor, for*—or by a semicolon. Compound sentences do not have dependent clauses. For example:

We went to the fireworks stand, and we bought enough fireworks to last all night.

The children sat on the grass, and then we lit the fireworks one at a time.

When a sentence has just one independent clause and includes one or more dependent clauses, we call it a complex sentence:

Because she slept well and drank coffee, Sarah was quite productive at work.

Although Will had coffee, he made mistakes while using the photocopier.

When a sentence has two or more independent clauses and at least one dependent clause, we call it a compound-complex sentence:

It may come as a surprise, but I found the tickets, and you can go to the show.

Jade is the girl who dove from the high-dive, and she stunned the audience silent.

Sentence Fragments

Remember that a complete sentence must have both a subject and a verb. Complete sentences consist of at least one independent clause. Incomplete sentences are called sentence fragments. A sentence fragment is a common error in writing. Sentence fragments can be independent clauses that start with subordinating words, such as *but, as, so that,* or *because,* or they could simply be missing a subject or verb.

You can correct a fragment error by adding the fragment to a nearby sentence or by adding or removing words to make it an independent clause. For example:

> Dogs are my favorite animals. Because cats are too independent. (Incorrect; the word because creates a sentence fragment)

> Dogs are my favorite animals because cats are too independent. (Correct; the fragment becomes a dependent clause.)

> Dogs are my favorite animals. Cats are too independent. (Correct; the fragment becomes a simple sentence.)

Run-On Sentences

Another common mistake in writing is the run-on sentence. A run-on is created when two or more independent clauses are joined without the use of a conjunction, a semicolon, a colon, or a dash. We don't want to use commas where periods belong. Here is an example of a run-on sentence:

> Making wedding cakes can take many hours I am very impatient, I want to see them completed right away.

There are a variety of ways to correct a run-on sentence. The method you choose will depend on the context of the sentence and how it fits with neighboring sentences:

> Making wedding cakes can take many hours. I am very impatient. I want to see them completed right away. (Use periods to create more than one sentence.)

> Making wedding cakes can take many hours; I am very impatient—I want to see them completed right away. (Correct the sentence using a semicolon, colon, or dash.)

> Making wedding cakes can take many hours and I am very impatient, so I want to see them completed right away. (Correct the sentence using coordinating conjunctions.)

> I am very impatient because I would rather see completed wedding cakes right away than wait for it to take many hours. (Correct the sentence by revising.)

Dangling and Misplaced Modifiers

A modifier is a word or phrase meant to describe or clarify another word in the sentence. When a sentence has a modifier but is missing the word it describes or clarifies, it's an error called a dangling modifier. We can fix the sentence by revising to include the word that is being modified. Consider the following examples with the modifier italicized:

> *Having walked five miles*, this bench will be the place to rest. (Incorrect; this version of the sentence implies that the bench walked the miles, not the person.)

Having walked five miles, Matt will rest on this bench. (Correct; in this version, *having walked five miles* correctly modifies *Matt*, who did the walking.)

Since midnight, my dreams have been pleasant and comforting. (Incorrect; in this version, the adverb clause *since midnight* cannot modify the noun *dreams*.)

Since midnight, I have had pleasant and comforting dreams. (Correct; in this version, *since midnight* modifies the verb *have had*, telling us when the dreams occurred.)

Sometimes the modifier is not located close enough to the word it modifies for the sentence to be clearly understood. In this case, we call the error a misplaced modifier. Here is an example with the modifier italicized and the modified word in underlined.

We gave the hot <u>cocoa</u> to the children *that was filled with marshmallows.* (Incorrect; this sentence implies that the children are what are filled with marshmallows.)

We gave the hot <u>*cocoa*</u> *that was filled with marshmallows* to the children. (Correct; here, the cocoa is filled with marshmallows. The modifier is near the word it modifies.)

Parallelism and Subordination
Parallelism
To be grammatically correct we must use articles, prepositions, infinitives, and introductory words for dependent clauses consistently throughout a sentence. This is called parallelism. We use parallelism when we are matching parts of speech, phrases, or clauses with another part of the sentence. Being inconsistent creates confusion. Consider the following example.

Incorrect: Be ready for running and to ride a bike during the triathlon.

Correct: Be ready to run and to ride a bike during the triathlon.

Correct: Be ready for running and for riding a bike during the triathlon.

In the incorrect example, the gerund *running* does not match with the infinitive *to ride*. Either both should be infinitives or both should be gerunds.

Subordination
Sometimes we have unequal pieces of information in a sentence where one piece is more important than the other. We need to show that one piece of information is subordinate to the other. We can make the more important piece an independent clause and connect the other piece by making it a dependent clause. Consider this example:

Central thought: Kittens can always find their mother.

Subordinate: Kittens are blind at birth.

Complex Sentence: Despite being blind at birth, kittens can always find their mother.

The sentence "Kittens are blind at birth" is made subordinate to the sentence "Kittens can always find their mother" by placing the word "Despite" at the beginning and removing the subject, thus turning an independent clause ("kittens are blind at birth") into a subordinate phrase ("Despite being blind at birth").

<u>Clauses</u>
Clauses are groups of words within a sentence that have both a subject and a verb. We can distinguish a clause from a phrase because phrases do not have both a subject and a verb. There are several types of clauses; clauses can be independent or dependent and can serve as a noun, an adjective, or an adverb.

An *independent clause* could stand alone as its own sentence if the rest of the sentence were not there. For example:

> *The party is on Tuesday* after the volleyball game is over.

> *I am excited to go to the party* because my best friend will be there.

A *dependent clause*, or subordinating clause, is the part of the sentence that gives supportive information but cannot create a proper sentence by itself. However, it will still have both a subject and a verb; otherwise, it is a phrase. In the example above, *after the volleyball game is over* and *because my best friend will be there* are dependent because they begin with the conjunctions *after* and *because*, and a proper sentence does not begin with a conjunction.

Noun clauses are groups of words that collectively form a noun. Look for the opening words *whether, which, what, that, who, how,* or *why.* For example:

> I had fun cooking *what we had for dinner last night.*

> I'm going to track down *whoever ate my sandwich.*

Adjective clauses collectively form an adjective that modifies a noun or pronoun in the sentence. If you can remove the adjective clause and the leftovers create a standalone sentence, then the clause should be set off with commas, parentheses, or dashes. If you can remove the clause it is called nonrestrictive. If it can't be removed without ruining the sentence then it is called restrictive and does not get set off with commas.

> Jenna, *who hates to get wet,* fell into the pool. (Nonrestrictive)

> The girl *who hates to get wet* fell into the pool. (Restrictive; the clause tells us which girl, and if removed there is confusion)

Adverbial clauses serve as an adverb in the sentence, modifying a verb, adjective, or other adverb. Look for the opening words *after, before, as, as if, although, because, if, since, so, so that, when, where, while,* or *unless.*

> She lost her wallet after she left the theme park.

> Her earring fell through the crack before she could catch it.

<u>Phrases</u>
A phrase is a group of words that go together but do not include both a subject and a verb. We use them to add information, explain something, or make the sentence easier for the reader to understand. Unlike clauses, phrases cannot ever stand alone as their own sentence if the rest of the sentence were not there. They do not form complete thoughts. There are noun phrases, prepositional phrases, verbal phrases, appositive phrases, and absolute phrases. Let's look at each of these.

Noun phrases: A noun phrase is a group of words built around a noun or pronoun that serves as a unit to form a noun in the sentence. Consider the following examples. The phrase is built around the underlined word. The entire phrase can be replaced by a noun or pronoun to test whether or not it is a noun phrase.

> I like the chocolate chip ice cream. (I like it.)

> I know all the shortest routes. (I know them.)

> I met the best supporting actress. (I met her.)

Prepositional phrases: These are phrases that begin with a preposition and end with a noun or pronoun. We use them as a unit to form the adjective or adverb in the sentence. Prepositional phrases that introduce a sentence are called introductory prepositional phrases and are set off with commas.

> I found the Frisbee *on the roof peak.* (Adverb; where it was found)

> The girl *with the bright red hair* was prom queen. (Adjective; which girl)

> *Before the sequel,* we wanted to watch the first movie. (Introductory phrase)

Verbal phrases: Some phrases look like verbs but do not serve as the verb in the sentence. These are called verbal phrases. There are three types: participial phrases, gerund phrases, and infinitive phrases.

Participial phrases start with a participle and modify nouns or pronouns; therefore, they act as the adjective in the sentence.

> *Beaten by the sun,* we searched for shade to sit in. (Modifies the pronoun *we*)

> The hikers, *being eaten by mosquitoes,* longed for repellant. (Modifies the noun *hikers*)

Gerund phrases often look like participles because they end in *-ing*, but they serve as the noun, not the adjective, in the sentence. Like any noun, we can use them as the subject or as the object of a verb or preposition in the sentence.

> *Eating green salad* is the best way to lose weight. (Subject)

> Sumo wrestlers are famous for *eating large quantities of food.* (Object)

Infinitive phrases often look like verbs because they start with the word *to,* but they serve as an adjective, adverb, or noun.

> *To survive the chill* is the goal of the Polar Bear Plunge. (Noun)

> A hot tub is at the scene *to warm up after the jump.* (Adverb)

> The jumpers have hot cocoa *to drink right away.* (Adjective)

Appositive phrases: We can use any of the above types of phrases to rename nouns or pronouns, and we call this an appositive phrase. Appositive phrases usually appear either just before or just after the noun or pronoun they are renaming. Appositive phrases are essential when the noun or pronoun is too general, and they are nonessential when they just add information.

The two famous brothers Orville and Wilbur Wright invented the airplane. (Essential)

Sarah Calysta, *my great grandmother,* is my namesake. (Nonessential)

Absolute phrases: When a participle comes after a noun and forms a phrase that is not otherwise part of the sentence, it's called an absolute phrase. Absolute phrases are not complete thoughts and cannot stand alone because they do not have a subject and a verb. They are not essential to the sentence in that they do not explain or add additional meaning to any other part of the sentence.

The engine roaring, Jada closed her eyes and waited for the plane to take off.

The microphone crackling, the flight attendant announced the delayed arrival.

Parts of Speech

Collective Nouns
Collective nouns can use a singular or plural verb depending on their function in the sentence. If the collective noun is acting as a unit, then a singular verb is needed. Otherwise, it's necessary to use a plural verb.

The staff is required to meet every third Friday of the month.

The *staff* is meeting as a collective unit, so a singular verb is needed.

The staff are getting in their cars to go home.

The staff get into their cars separately, so a plural verb is needed.

Plural Nouns with Singular Meaning
Certain nouns end in *s*, like a plural noun, but have singular meaning, such as *mathematics, news,* and *civics*. These nouns should use a singular verb.

The news is on at 8:00 tonight.

Nouns that are single things, but have two parts, are considered plural and should use a plural verb, such as *scissors, pants,* and *tweezers.*

My favorite pants are in the washing machine.

There Is and There Are
There cannot be a subject, so verb agreement should be based on a word that comes after the verb.

There is a hole in the road.

The subject in this sentence is *hole*, which is singular, so the verb should be singular (*is*).

There are kids playing kickball in the street.

The subject in this sentence is *kids*, which is plural, so the verb should be plural (*are*).

Adjectives

An adjective modifies a noun, making it more precise or giving more information about it. Adjectives answer these questions: What kind? Which one?

> I just bought a *red* car.

> I don't like *cold* weather.

One special type of word that modifies a noun is a *determiner.* In fact, some grammarians classify determiners as a separate part of speech because whereas adjectives simply describe additional qualities of a noun, a determiner is often a necessary part of a noun phrase, without which the phrase is grammatically incomplete. A determiner indicates whether a noun is definite or indefinite, and can identify which noun is being discussed. It also introduces context to the noun in terms of quantity and possession. The most commonly-used determiners are articles—a, an, the.

> I ordered *a* pizza.

> She lives in *the* city.

Possessive pronouns discussed above, such as *my, your,* and *our,* are also determiners, along with *demonstratives*—this, that—and *quantifiers*—much, many, some. These determiners can take the place of an article.

> Are you using *this* chair?

> I need *some* coffee!

Adverbs

Adverbs modify verbs, adjectives, and other adverbs. Words that end in –ly are usually adverbs. Adverbs answer these questions: When? Where? In what manner? To what degree?

> She talks *quickly*.

> The mountains are *incredibly* beautiful!

> The students arrived *early*.

> Please take your phone call *outside*.

Prepositions

Prepositions show the relationship between different elements in a phrase or sentence and connect nouns or pronouns to other words in the sentence. Some examples of prepositions are words such as *after, at, behind, by, during, from, in, on, to,* and *with*.

> Let's go *to* class.

> Starry Night was painted *by* Vincent van Gogh *in* 1889.

Pronouns

Pronouns function as substitutes for nouns or noun phrases. Pronouns are often used to avoid constant repetition of a noun or to simplify sentences. *Personal pronouns* are used for people. Some pronouns are *subject pronouns*; they are used to replace the subject in a sentence—I, we, he, she, they.

> Is *he* your friend?

> *We* work together.

English Verb System

Modals

Auxiliary (helping) verbs are forms of the words *have, do,* and *be,* as well as other auxiliary verbs called *modals.* Modals and semi-modals (modal phrases) express ability, possibility, permission, or obligation. Modals and semi-modal examples are *can/could/be able to, may/might, shall/should, must/have to,* and *will/would.* "I *should* go to the store."

Complements

A *complement* completes the meaning of an expression. A complement can be a pronoun, noun, or adjective. A verb complement refers to the direct object or indirect object in the sentence. An object complement gives more information about the direct object:

> The magician got the kids excited.

Kids is the direct object, and *excited* is the object complement.

A *subject complement* comes after a linking verb. It is typically an adjective or noun that gives more information about the subject:

> The king was noble and spared the thief's life.

Noble describes the *king* and follows the linking verb *was.*

Verb Phrases

Verb phrases include all of the words in a verb group, even if they are not directly adjacent to each other:

> I *should have woken up* earlier this morning.

> The company **is** now *offering* membership discounts for new enrollers.

This sentence's verb phrase is *is offering.* Even though they are separated by the word *now,* they function together as a single verb phrase.

Conventions of English Orthography

Orthography refers to the spelling conventions of a language. Knowing the conventions of English orthography can aid in the teaching of spelling. It can help students learn spelling rules and recognize spelling patterns through strategies like word walls and dividing words into syllables. Attention should be paid to exceptions to the rules and breaks in spelling patterns. Students should be encouraged to recognize spelling patterns in their daily reading and writing activities.

Spelling might or might not be important to some, or maybe it just doesn't come naturally, but those who are willing to discover some new ideas and consider their benefits can learn to spell better and improve their writing. Misspellings reduce a writer's credibility and can create misunderstandings. Spell checkers built into word processors are not a substitute for accuracy. They are neither foolproof nor without error. In addition, a writer's misspelling of one word may also be a word. For example, a writer intending to spell *herd* might accidentally type *s* instead of *d* and unintentionally spell *hers*. Since *her*s is a word, it would not be marked as a misspelling by a spell checker. In short, use spell check, but don't rely on it.

Guidelines for Spelling

Saying and listening to a word serves as the beginning of knowing how to spell it. Keep these subsequent guidelines in mind, remembering there are often exceptions because the English language is replete with them.

Guideline #1: Syllables must have at least one vowel. In fact, every syllable in every English word has a vowel.

- d*o*g
- h*a*yst*a*ck
- *a*nsw*e*r*i*ng
- *a*bstent*iou*s
- s*i*mpl*e*

Guideline #2: The long and short of it. When the vowel has a short vowel sound as in *mad* or *bed,* only the single vowel is needed. If the word has a long vowel sound, add another vowel, either alongside it or separated by a consonant: bed/*bead*; mad/*made.* When the second vowel is separated by two spaces—*madder*—it does not affect the first vowel's sound.

Guideline #3: Suffixes. Refer to the examples listed above.

Guideline #4: Which comes first; the *i* or the *e*? Remember the saying, "*I* before *e* except after *c* or when sounding as *a* as in *neighbor* or *weigh*." Keep in mind that these are only guidelines and that there are always exceptions to every rule.

Guideline #5: Vowels in the right order. Another helpful rhyme is, "When two vowels go walking, the first one does the talking." When two vowels are in a row, the first one often has a long vowel sound and the other is silent. An example is *team*.

If you have difficulty spelling words, determine a strategy to help. Work on spelling by playing word games like Scrabble or Words with Friends. Consider using phonics, which is sounding words out by slowly and surely stating each syllable. Try repeating and memorizing spellings as well as picturing words in your head. Try making up silly memory aids. See what works best.

Homophones

Homophones are two or more words that have no particular relationship to one another except their identical pronunciations. Homophones make spelling English words fun and challenging like these:

Common Homophones		
affect, effect	cell, sell	it's, its
allot, a lot	do, due, dew	knew, new
barbecue, barbeque	dual, duel	libel, liable
bite, byte	eminent, imminent	principal, principle
brake, break	flew, flu, flue	their, there, they're
capital, capitol	gauge, gage	to, too, two
cash, cache	holy, wholly	yoke, yolk

Irregular Plurals

Irregular plurals are words that aren't made plural the usual way.

- Most nouns are made plural by adding –*s* (book*s*, television*s*, skyscraper*s*).

- Most nouns ending in *ch, sh, s, x,* or *z* are made plural by adding –*es* (church*es*, marsh*es*).

- Most nouns ending in a vowel + *y* are made plural by adding –*s* (day*s*, toy*s*).

- Most nouns ending in a consonant + *y,* are made plural by the -*y* becoming -*ies* (baby becomes *babies*).

- Most nouns ending in an *o* are made plural by adding –*s* (piano*s*, photo*s*).

- Some nouns ending in an *o*, though, may be made plural by adding –*es* (example: potato*es*, volcano*es*), and, of note, there is no known rhyme or reason for this!

- Most nouns ending in an *f* or *fe* are made plural by the -*f* or -*fe* becoming -*ves*! (example: wolf becomes *wolves*).

- Some words function as both the singular and plural form of the word (fish, deer).

- Other exceptions include *man* becomes *men, mouse* becomes *mice, goose* becomes *geese,* and *foot* becomes *feet.*

Contractions

The basic rule for making *contractions* is one area of spelling that is pretty straightforward: combine the two words by inserting an apostrophe (') in the space where a letter is omitted. For example, to combine *you* and *are*, drop the *a* and put the apostrophe in its place: *you're.*

> he + is = he's
> you + all = y'all (informal but often misspelled)

Note that *it's*, when spelled with an apostrophe, is always the contraction for *it is*. The possessive form of the word is written without an apostrophe as *its.*

Correcting Misspelled Words

A good place to start looking at commonly misspelled words here is with the word *misspelled*. While it looks peculiar, look at it this way: *mis* (the prefix meaning *wrongly*) + *spelled* = *misspelled*.

Let's look at some commonly misspelled words and see where writers often go wrong with them.

Commonly Misspelled Words					
accept	benign	existence	jewelry	parallel	separate
acceptable	bicycle	experience	judgment	pastime	sergeant
accidentally	brief	extraordinary	library	permissible	similar
accommodate	business	familiar	license	perseverance	supersede
accompany	calendar	February	maintenance	personnel	surprise
acknowledgement	campaign	fiery	maneuver	persuade	symmetry
acquaintance	candidate	finally	mathematics	possess	temperature
acquire	category	forehead	mattress	precede	tragedy
address	cemetery	foreign	millennium	prevalent	transferred
aesthetic	changeable	foremost	miniature	privilege	truly
aisle	committee	forfeit	mischievous	pronunciation	usage
altogether	conceive	glamorous	misspell	protein	valuable
amateur	congratulations	government	mortgage	publicly	vengeance
apparent	courtesy	grateful	necessary	questionnaire	villain
appropriate	deceive	handkerchief	neither	recede	Wednesday
arctic	desperate	harass	nickel	receive	weird
asphalt	discipline	hygiene	niece	recommend	
associate	disappoint	hypocrisy	ninety	referral	
attendance	dissatisfied	ignorance	noticeable	relevant	
auxiliary	eligible	incredible	obedience	restaurant	
available	embarrass	intelligence	occasion	rhetoric	
balloon	especially	intercede	occurrence	rhythm	
believe	exaggerate	interest	omitted	schedule	
beneficial	exceed	irresistible	operate	sentence	

Practice Test

1. What is the structure of the following sentence?

   The restaurant is unconventional because it serves both Chicago style pizza and New York style pizza.

   a. Simple
   b. Compound
   c. Complex
   d. Compound-complex

2. The following sentence contains what kind of error?

   This summer, I'm planning to travel to Italy, take a Mediterranean cruise, going to Pompeii, and eat a lot of Italian food.

   a. Parallelism
   b. Sentence fragment
   c. Misplaced modifier
   d. Subject-verb agreement

3. The following sentence contains what kind of error?

   Forgetting that he was supposed to meet his girlfriend for dinner, Anita was mad when Fred showed up late.

   a. Parallelism
   b. Run-on sentence
   c. Misplaced modifier
   d. Subject-verb agreement

4. The following sentence contains what kind of error?

   Some workers use all their sick leave, other workers cash out their leave.

   a. Parallelism
   b. Comma splice
   c. Sentence fragment
   d. Subject-verb agreement

5. A student writes the following in an essay:

> *Protestors filled the streets of the city. Because they were dissatisfied with the government's leadership.*

Which of the following is an appropriately-punctuated correction for this sentence?

a. Protestors filled the streets of the city, because they were dissatisfied with the government's leadership.
b. Protesters, filled the streets of the city, because they were dissatisfied with the government's leadership.
c. Because they were dissatisfied with the government's leadership protestors filled the streets of the city.
d. Protestors filled the streets of the city because they were dissatisfied with the government's leadership.

6. What is the part of speech of the underlined word in the sentence?
   We need to come up with a fresh <u>approach</u> to this problem.

a. Noun
b. Verb
c. Adverb
d. Adjective

7. What is the part of speech of the underlined word in the sentence?
   Investigators conducted an <u>exhaustive</u> inquiry into the accusations of corruption.

a. Noun
b. Verb
c. Adverb
d. Adjective

8. The underlined portion of the sentence is an example of which sentence component?
   New students should report <u>to the student center</u>.

a. Dependent clause
b. Adverbial phrase
c. Adjective clause
d. Noun phrase

9. What is the noun phrase in the following sentence?
   Charlotte's new German shepherd puppy is energetic.

a. Puppy
b. Charlotte
c. German shepherd puppy
d. Charlotte's new German shepherd puppy

10. Which word choices will correctly complete the sentence?

Increasing the price of bus fares has had a greater [affect / effect] on ridership [then / than] expected.

a. affect; then
b. affect; than
c. effect; then
d. effect; than

11. While studying vocabulary, a student notices that the words *circumference*, *circumnavigate*, and *circumstance* all begin with the prefix *circum–*. The student uses her knowledge of affixes to infer that all of these words share what related meaning?

a. Around, surrounding
b. Travel, transport
c. Size, measurement
d. Area, location

12. A student wants to rewrite the following sentence:

Entrepreneurs use their ideas to make money.

He wants to use the word *money* as a verb, but he isn't sure which word ending to use. What is the appropriate suffix to add to *money* to complete the following sentence?

Entrepreneurs _____ their ideas.

a. –ize
b. –ical
c. –en
d. –ful

13. A student reads the following sentence:

A hundred years ago, automobiles were rare, but now cars are ubiquitous.

However, she doesn't know what the word *ubiquitous* means. Which key context clue is essential to decipher the word's meaning?

a. Ago
b. Cars
c. Now
d. Rare

14. A local newspaper is looking for writers for a student column. A student would like to submit his article to the newspaper, but he isn't sure how to format his article according to journalistic standards. What resource should he use?

a. A thesaurus
b. A dictionary
c. A style guide
d. A grammar book

15. A student encounters the word *aficionado* and wants to learn more about it. It doesn't sound like other English words he knows, so the student is curious to identify the word's origin. What resource should he consult?
    a. A thesaurus
    b. A dictionary
    c. A style guide
    d. A grammar book

16. Which domain is likely to be used by a website run by a nonprofit group?
    a. .com
    b. .edu
    c. .org
    d. .gov

17. Several generations ago, immigrants and locals in a region developed a simplified mixture of their two languages in order to carry out basic communication tasks. However, usage of this mixed language increased, and later generations passed it down to their children as their first language. These children are now speaking what kind of language?
    a. A pidgin
    b. A Creole
    c. A jargon
    d. A regionalism

18. Which of the following is true of Standard English?
    a. It is one dialect of English.
    b. It is the original form of English.
    c. It is the most complex form of English.
    d. It is the form that follows grammatical rules.

19. A teacher notices that, when students are talking to each other between classes, they are using their own unique vocabulary words and expressions to talk about their daily lives. When the teacher hears these non-standard words that are specific to one age or cultural group, what type of language is she listening to?
    a. Slang
    b. Jargon
    c. Dialect
    d. Vernacular

20. A teacher wants to counsel a student about using the word *ain't* in a research paper for a high school English class. What advice should the teacher give?
    a. *Ain't* is not in the dictionary, so it isn't a word.
    b. Because the student isn't in college yet, *ain't* is an appropriate expression for a high school writer.
    c. *Ain't* is incorrect English and should not be part of a serious student's vocabulary because it sounds uneducated.
    d. *Ain't* is a colloquial expression, and while it may be appropriate in a conversational setting, it is not standard in academic writing.

21. Which of the following is true of first language acquisition?
    a. Children need some instruction from parents or caregivers to learn a first language.
    b. Children first begin forming complete words when they are about two years old.
    c. Children experiment with the sounds of a language before they form words.
    d. Children have no language comprehension before they can speak.

22. Which of the following is true of second language acquisition?
    a. Students learn best through memorization of new vocabulary words.
    b. Second language acquisition follows the same stages as first language acquisition.
    c. Advanced fluency is achieved when the speaker has no accent in his or her second language.
    d. Second language learners experience a preproduction stage, during which they are unable to produce verbal expressions.

23. Which of the following would NOT be a recommended vocabulary teaching strategy?
    a. Focusing on specialized academic jargon that students will encounter in college
    b. Creating a word map to understand the connection between vocabulary terms
    c. Accessing prior knowledge when introducing a new area of vocabulary
    d. Providing examples of how to use terms inside and outside of class

24. Which of the following is an example of incidental learning in vocabulary development?
    a. After reading a story in class, the teacher provides students with a list of keywords to know from the text.
    b. While reading a novel for class, a student encounters an unfamiliar word and looks it up in the dictionary.
    c. As part of a writing assignment, students are instructed to utilize certain academic words and expressions in their essay.
    d. After getting back the results of a vocabulary exam, students are assigned to make personal study guides based on the words that they missed on the test.

25. A teacher is considering integrating some media sources like television and the Internet into his classroom, but he is unsure of how effective it will be. Which of the following is true about media literacy in language development?
    a. Instruction should focus only on professional media sources such as scientific journals and mainstream news publications to emphasize Standard English skills.
    b. In the twenty-first century, every student has access to and proficiency in using the Internet, so it is unnecessary to spend time on building skills in class.
    c. Students should explore media resources in their personal areas of interest to develop regular language habits in an enjoyable way.
    d. The Internet serves as a huge distraction for students and should not be part of instruction.

26. Compared to other students, twelve-year-old Dave is somewhat of an oddity at six feet, two inches (tallness runs in his family). The parentheses here indicate what?
    a. The information within is essential to the paragraph.
    b. The information, though relevant, carries less emphasis.
    c. The information is redundant and should be eliminated.
    d. The information belongs elsewhere.

27. The student at a high school, after witnessing some wrongdoing on behalf of others, needed to talk to several _____ based on his _____ .
    a. principals; principles
    b. principles; principals
    c. princapals; princaples
    d. princaples; princapals

28. Each patient, having gone through rehabilitative therapy, needed _____ file returned to the nursing station.
    a. their
    b. there
    c. his or her
    d. the people's

29. A man decided not to take his family to the zoo after hearing about a bomb threat on the news. The man believed the threat to be real and _____ .
    a. eminent
    b. imminent
    c. emanate
    d. amanita

30. Which of the following is punctuated correctly?
    a. Martha expertly read and analyzed a copy of *Taming of the Shrew*: she presented her findings to the class.
    b. Martha expertly read and analyzed a copy of *Taming of the Shrew*, she presented her findings to the class.
    c. Martha expertly read and analyzed a copy of *Taming of the Shrew*; she presented her findings to the class.
    d. Martha expertly read and analyzed a copy of *Taming of the Shrew* she presented her findings to the class.

31. Which of the following exemplifies a compound sentence?
    a. Tod and Elissa went to the movies, got some dessert, and slept.
    b. Though Tod and Elissa decided to go to the movies, Marge stayed home.
    c. Tod and Elissa decided to go to the movies, and Marge read a book.
    d. Tod and Elissa went to the movies while Marge slept.

32. The professor's engaging lecture, though not his best, ran over thirty minutes late. Which of the following words in this preceding sentence functions as a verb?
    a. Engaging
    b. Though
    c. Ran
    d. Over

33. Dave arrived at work almost thirty minutes late. His boss, who was irritated, lectured him. Dave was inconsolable the rest of the shift. Which of the following words in this preceding passage function as an adverb?

    a. Arrived

    b. Almost

    c. Irritated

    d. Rest

34. Which of the following is capitalized correctly?

    a. History 220 is taught by one of my favorite professors. He used to teach an entry-level sociology class but decided he likes teaching Advanced History better.

    b. History 220, taught by Mr. Hart, the Professor, focuses on the conflicts that transformed America: The Revolution, The Civil War, The Korean War, World War I, World War II, and Vietnam.

    c. In particular, he likes to discuss how Yankee ingenuity helped overcome the British army and navy, the world's most formidable world power at the time.

    d. Mr. Hart is scheduled to retire in the summer of 2018. President Williams already said he'll be in charge of retirement party planning.

35. Which of the following passages best displays clarity, fluency, and parallelism?

    a. Ernest Hemingway is probably the most noteworthy of expatriate authors. Hemingway's concise writing style, void of emotion and stream of consciousness, had a lasting impact, one which resonates to this very day. In Hemingway's novels, much like in American cinema, the hero acts without thinking, is living in the moment, and is repressing physical and emotional pain.

    b. Ernest Hemingway is probably the most noteworthy of expatriate authors since his concise writing style is void of emotion and stream of consciousness and has had a lasting impact on Americans which has resonated to this very day, and Hemingway's novels are much like in American cinema. The hero acts. He doesn't think. He lives in the moment. He represses physical and emotional pain.

    c. Ernest Hemingway is probably the most noteworthy of authors. His concise writing style, void of emotion and consciousness, had a lasting impact, one which resonates to this very day. In Hemingway's novels, much like in American cinema, the hero acts without thinking, lives in the moment, and represses physical and emotional pain.

    d. Ernest Hemingway is probably the most noteworthy of expatriate authors. His concise writing style, void of emotion and stream of consciousness, had a lasting impact, one which resonates to this very day. In Hemingway's novels, much like in American cinema, the hero acts without thinking, lives in the moment, and represses physical and emotional pain.

36. Which of the following is punctuated correctly?

    a. After reading *Frankenstein*, Daisy turned to her sister and said, "You told me this book wasn't 'all that bad.' You scare me as much as the book!"

    b. After reading "Frankenstein," Daisy turned to her sister and said, "You told me this book wasn't 'all that bad.' You scare me as much as the book!"

    c. After reading *Frankenstein*, Daisy turned to her sister and said, 'You told me this book wasn't "all that bad." You scare me as much as the book!'

    d. After reading *Frankenstein*, Daisy turned to her sister, and said "You told me this book wasn't 'all that bad'. You scare me as much as the book!"

37. Which of the following subject-verb examples is correct?
    a. Each of the members of the chess club, who have been successful before on their own, struggled to unite as a team.
    b. Everyone who has ever owned a pet and hasn't had help knows it's difficult.
    c. Neither of the boys, after a long day of slumber, have cleaned their bedrooms.
    d. One of the very applauded and commended lecturers are coming to our campus!

38. Sara, who is never late, showed up today ten minutes after Mr. Gray's class had begun. Her hair was a tangled mess, and she looked distraught. Everybody wondered what had happened.

Which of the following words from the preceding passage is an adjective?
    a. Never
    b. After
    c. Mess
    d. Distraught

39. When giving a presentation, one should have three to five bullet points per slide. It is impossible for a presenter to memorize an entire speech, but if you can memorize the main ideas connected to the bullet points, then your speech will be more natural and fluid.

The point(s) of view represented in this passage is/are:
    a. First person only
    b. Third person only
    c. Second person and third person
    d. First person and third person

40. Even though Ralph knew it was wrong to steal, he had still taken a grape from the vegetable stand. He stood there, befuddled, wrestling with his _____ , trying decide whether to put it back or pop it in his mouth.
    a. Conscious
    b. Conscience
    c. Consensus
    d. Census

41. Which of the following demonstrates a simple sentence?
    a. Ted loves to rock climb even though he tore his rotator cuff.
    b. Ted, who is not yet sixty, still easily fishes and camps, too.
    c. Ted loves the outdoors, but, strangely enough, his wife is a homebody.
    d. Ted will also be retired soon; nevertheless, he likes to stay busy.

42. Which of the following examples displays correct use of the possessive?
    a. The womens' portfolios are available for the teacher's review.
    b. A well-trained dog always returns to it's master.
    c. The visitor center is a good place to start the tour.
    d. The businesses' clients had a great time at the convention.

43. An antibiotic is prescribed to eliminate bacterial infections; someone who is antisocial ignores society and laws. Based on these two definitions, the Latin prefix *anti-* would most likely mean:
   a. Reduce
   b. Revolt
   c. Oppose
   d. Without

44. *Conform* means to adjust one's behavior to better fit in with social norms. Inform means to communicate new knowledge to another. Based on these definitions, the Latin suffix *-form* most likely means:
   a. Match
   b. Relay
   c. Negate
   d. Shape

45. Every week, Cindy volunteers time at the local shelter. She always has a smile on her face, and she always talks to others with kindness and patience. Considering that her current job is very taxing, that two of her three children are still in diapers, and that her husband, Steve, the old curmudgeon, is the opposite of her in temperament, it's amazing that no one has ever seen her angry.

Based on the context in this passage, the best substitute for *curmudgeon* would be:
   a. Stingy
   b. Surly
   c. Scared
   d. Shy

46. Most mammals in the New World have prehensile tails while most in Africa do not. Almost all primatologists would agree that animals in places like South America evolved this way to deal with denser vegetation. By moving to a loftier position, animals could avoid predators and move through foliage, unimpeded. On the other hand, it would be less advantageous for a mammal to have a prehensile tail on the African plains. On the long expanses of African savannah, movement is critical for survival, but mammals there would rely on other appendages.

Based on this passage, the best word describing what a *prehensile tail* can do would be:
   a. Grasp
   b. Punch
   c. Move
   d. Walk

47. We went on vacation this summer to Arizona. Mom had always wanted to see the Grand Canyon. Dad, on the other hand, wanted to see Saguaro National Park and Hoover Dam. Other than the flat tire our car got, it was a fantastic time.

The point(s) of view represented in this passage is/are:
   a. First person only
   b. Third person only
   c. Second person and third person
   d. First person and third person

48. Which of the following exemplifies a complex sentence?
    a. To make your fruit last longer, keep it out of the sunlight.
    b. Make sure to clock out after your shift is through.
    c. Making a good fire requires using the proper wood and stacking it properly.
    d. Whenever possible, make sure to yield to oncoming traffic.

49. The people of Scotland are known not only for their unique _____ but also the taxing _____ they make to villages nestled high in the mountains.
    a. Ascents; accents
    b. Accents; ascents
    c. accents; assents
    d. Assents; accents

50. Which sentence below does not contain an error in comma usage for dates?
    a. My niece arrives from Australia on Monday, February 4, 2016.
    b. My cousin's wedding this Saturday June 9, conflicts with my best friend's birthday party.
    c. The project is due on Tuesday, May, 17, 2016.
    d. I can't get a flight home until Thursday September 21.

Answers and Explanations

1. C: A complex sentence joins an independent or main clause with a dependent or subordinate clause. In this case, the main clause is "The restaurant is unconventional." This is a clause with one subject-verb combination that can stand alone as a grammatically-complete sentence. The dependent clause is "because it serves both Chicago style pizza and New York style pizza." This clause begins with the subordinating conjunction *because* and also consists of only one subject-verb combination. *A* is incorrect because a simple sentence consists of only one verb-subject combination—one independent clause. *B* is incorrect because a compound sentence contains two independent clauses connected by a conjunction. *D* is incorrect because a complex-compound sentence consists of two or more independent clauses and one or more dependent clauses.

2. A: Parallelism refers to consistent use of sentence structure or word form. In this case, the list within the sentence does not utilize parallelism; three of the verbs appear in their base form—*travel, take*, and *eat*—but one appears as a gerund—*going*. A parallel version of this sentence would be "This summer, I'm planning to travel to Italy, take a Mediterranean cruise, go to Pompeii, and eat a lot of Italian food." *B* is incorrect because this description is a complete sentence. *C* is incorrect as a misplaced modifier is a modifier that is not located appropriately in relation to the word or words they modify. *D* is incorrect because subject-verb agreement refers to the appropriate conjugation of a verb in relation to its subject.

3. C: In this sentence, the modifier is the phrase "Forgetting that he was supposed to meet his girlfriend for dinner." This phrase offers information about Fred's actions, but the noun that immediately follows it is Anita, creating some confusion about the "do-er" of the phrase. A more appropriate sentence arrangement would be "Forgetting that he was supposed to meet his girlfriend for dinner, Fred made Anita mad when he showed up late." *A* is incorrect as parallelism refers to the consistent use of sentence structure and verb tense, and this sentence is appropriately consistent. *B* is incorrect as a run-on sentence does not contain appropriate punctuation for the number of independent clauses presented, which is not true of this description. *D* is incorrect because subject-verb agreement refers to the appropriate conjugation of a verb relative to the subject, and all verbs have been properly conjugated.

4. B: A comma splice occurs when a comma is used to join two independent clauses together without the additional use of an appropriate conjunction. One way to remedy this problem is to replace the comma with a semicolon. Another solution is to add a conjunction: "Some workers use all their sick leave, but other workers cash out their leave." *A* is incorrect as parallelism refers to the consistent use of sentence structure and verb tense; all tenses and structures in this sentence are consistent. *C* is incorrect because a sentence fragment is a phrase or clause that cannot stand alone—this sentence contains two independent clauses. *D* is incorrect because subject-verb agreement refers to the proper conjugation of a verb relative to the subject, and all verbs have been properly conjugated.

5. D: The problem in the original passage is that the second sentence is a dependent clause that cannot stand alone as a sentence; it must be attached to the main clause found in the first sentence. Because the main clause comes first, it does not need to be separated by a comma. However, if the dependent clause came first, then a comma would be necessary, which is why Choice *C* is incorrect. *A* and *B* also insert unnecessary commas into the sentence.

6. A: A noun refers to a person, place, thing, or idea. Although the word *approach* can also be used as a verb, in the sentence it functions as a noun within the noun phrase "a fresh approach," so *B* is incorrect. An adverb is a word or phrase that provides additional information of the verb, but because the verb is *need* and not *approach*, then *C* is false. An adjective is a word that describes a noun, used here as the word *fresh*, but it is not the noun itself. Thus, *D* is also incorrect.

7. D: An adjective modifies a noun, answering the question "Which one?" or "What kind?" In this sentence, the word *exhaustive* is an adjective that modifies the noun investigation. Another clue that this word is an adjective is the suffix *–ive*, which means "having the quality of." The nouns in this sentence are investigators, inquiry, accusations, and corruption; therefore, A is incorrect. The verb in this sentence is conducted because this was the action taken by the subject the investigators; therefore, B is incorrect. C is incorrect because an adverb is a word or phrase that provides additional information about the verb, expressing how, when, where, or in what manner.

8. B: In this case, the phrase functions as an adverb modifying the verb *report*, so *B* is the correct answer. "To the student center" does not consist of a subject-verb combination, so it is not a clause; thus, Choices *A* and *C* can be eliminated. This group of words is a phrase. Phrases are classified by either the controlling word in the phrase or its function in the sentence. *D* is incorrect because a noun phrase is a series of words that describe or modify a noun.

9. D: A noun phrase consists of the noun and all of its modifiers. In this case, the subject of the sentence is the noun *puppy*, but it is preceded by several modifiers—adjectives that give more information about what kind of puppy, which are also part of the noun phrase. Thus, *A* is incorrect. Charlotte is the owner of the puppy and a modifier of the puppy, so *B* is false. *C* is incorrect because it contains some, but not all, of the modifiers pertaining to the puppy. *D* is correct because it contains all of them.

10. D: In this sentence, the first answer choice requires a noun meaning *impact* or *influence*, so *effect* is the correct answer. For the second answer choice, the sentence is drawing a comparison. *Than* shows a comparative relationship whereas *then* shows sequence or consequence. *A* and *C* can be eliminated because they contain the choice *then*. *B* is incorrect because *affect* is a verb while this sentence requires a noun.

11. A: The affix *circum–* originates from Latin and means *around or surrounding*. It is also related to other round words, such as circle and circus. The rest of the choices do not relate to the affix *circum–* and are therefore incorrect.

12. A: Only two of these suffixes, *–ize* and *–en*, can be used to form verbs, so *B* and *D* are incorrect. Those choices create adjectives. The suffix *–ize* means "to convert or turn into." The suffix *–en* means "to become." Because this sentence is about converting ideas into money, money + *–ize* or *monetize* is the most appropriate word to complete the sentence, so *C* is incorrect.

13. D: Students can use context clues to make a careful guess about the meaning of unfamiliar words. Although all of the words in a sentence can help contribute to the overall sentence, in this case, the adjective that pairs with *ubiquitous* gives the most important hint to the student—cars were first *rare*, but now they are *ubiquitous*. The inversion of *rare* is what gives meaning to the rest of the sentence and *ubiquitous* means "existing everywhere" or "not rare." *A* is incorrect because *ago* only indicates a time frame. *B* is incorrect because *cars* does not indicate a contrasting relationship to the word *ubiquitous* to provide a good context clue. *C* is incorrect because it also only indicates a time frame, but used together with *rare*, it provides the contrasting relationship needed to identify the meaning of the unknown word.

14. C: A style guide offers advice about proper formatting, punctuation, and usage when writing for a specific field, such as journalism or scientific research. The other resources would not offer similar information. A dictionary is useful for looking up definitions; a thesaurus is useful for looking up synonyms and antonyms. A grammar book is useful for looking up specific grammar topics. Thus, Choices *A*, *C*, and *D* are incorrect.

15. B: A word's origin is also known as its *etymology*. In addition to offering a detailed list of a word's various meanings, a dictionary also provides information about a word's history, such as when it first came into use, what language it originated from, and how its meaning may have changed over time. A thesaurus is for identifying synonyms and antonyms, so *A* is incorrect. A style guide provides formatting, punctuation, and syntactical advice for a specific field, and a grammar book is related to the appropriate placement of words and punctuation, which does not provide any insight into a word's meaning. Therefore, Choices *A*, *C*, and *D* are incorrect.

16. C: The .org domain on websites is generally used by nonprofit groups or community organizations. A government website uses .gov, and .edu is used for educational institutions. Private companies and businesses use .com, so Choices *A*, *B*, and *D* are incorrect.

17. B: A utilitarian combination of two or more languages that springs up where different linguistic groups overlap is known as a pidgin; it is used for communication tasks but not as a first language. However, when that pidgin becomes entrenched in the culture and is then taught to children as their first, native language, it is known as a Creole. *C* and *D* are not correct because they both refer to vocabulary, not to entire languages. Jargon is the vocabulary of a specific field or industry, and regionalisms are the vocabulary of a specific place.

18. A: A dialect of a language refers to one version of that language that follows specific patterns of grammar, spelling, pronunciation, and vocabulary. In this sense, then, Standard English is simply one of many different dialects of English. Standard English is not the original form of English because the language has evolved considerably over the past several centuries and will most likely continue to do so in the future. Also, there is nothing that makes Standard English more complex or grammatical than other dialects of English. Although other dialects may deviate from the grammar used in Standard English, these dialects still follow their own predictable rules and patterns of grammar.

19. A: Slang refers to non-standard expressions that are not used in elevated speech and writing. Slang tends to be specific to one group or time period and is commonly used within groups of young people during their conversations with each other. Jargon refers to the language used in a specialized field. The vernacular is the native language of a local area, and a dialect is one form of a language in a certain region. Thus, *B*, *C*, and *D* are incorrect.

20. D: Colloquial language is that which is used conversationally or informally, in contrast to professional or academic language. While *ain't* is common in conversational English, it is a non-standard expression in academic writing. For college-bound students, high school should introduce them to the expectations of a college classroom, so *B* is not the best answer. Teachers should also avoid placing moral or social value on certain patterns of speech. Rather than teaching students that their familiar speech patterns are bad, teachers should help students learn when and how to use appropriate forms of expression, so *C* is wrong. *Ain't* is in the dictionary, so *A* is incorrect, both in the reason for counseling and in the factual sense.

21. C: In the babbling stage, children repeat simple syllables that will later form the building blocks of their first words, such as ma-ma and da-da. *A* is not a correct answer because children learn their first language simply by being exposed to it, without any formal instruction required. *B* is also incorrect because most children utter their first word by about one year old. Babies demonstrate understanding of language before they are able to actually form words themselves, so *D* is not correct.

22. D: This is the first stage of L2 acquisition, before the learner is ready to communicate in the target language. Both L1 and L2 acquisition clearly follow different stages, so *B* is incorrect. The final stage of L2 development, advanced fluency, does not require the speaker to have a native accent; rather, it refers to the stage at which the speaker encounters no difficulty in expression or comprehension in both conversational and academic settings; thus, *C* is incorrect. L2 learners benefit from a variety of instruction techniques, and students require both input—such as studying new vocabulary words—and output—actually using those words in productive language tasks—in order to develop new skills; therefore, *A* is also incorrect.

23. A: Although it is useful to introduce students to concepts they might encounter in a college classroom, making jargon the focus of instruction at the expense of vocabulary with more widely-applicable usage will not meet the needs of the majority of students in class. The other strategies are all appropriate ways to have students integrate new vocabulary into their existing knowledge structures and their everyday lives.

24. B: Incidental learning contrasts with direct instruction, wherein instructors direct students in the precise meaning of new vocabulary or call students' attention to important vocabulary skills in a given lesson. In incidental learning, students learn new vocabulary as they encounter unfamiliar terms during other learning tasks. In this case, *B* is the correct answer because the student uses a reading assignment as an opportunity to learn a new word. In all of the other answer choices, the instructor is the one guiding the students' attention towards specific vocabulary words.

25. C: Students should explore media resources in their personal areas of interest to develop regular language habits in an enjoyable way. Multimedia resources are a powerful educational resource and should be integrated into class instruction when possible, making *D* a poor answer choice. *B* is incorrect because it cannot be assumed that every student has regular access to the internet, and even students who do have home internet access may still need guidance in how to use it to find learning resources. *A* is incorrect because though it is useful to introduce students to academic and professional media sources, the diversity of media available means that these do not need to be the sole emphasis of instruction. Rather, it can be useful to help students explore areas of their own interest and build skills in how to apply language development concepts—e.g., reading comprehension skills, using context to learn new words, keeping a journal of new words and expressions, or formulating a reading response— both inside and outside of the classroom.

26. B: Parentheses indicate that the information contained within carries less weight or importance than the surrounding text. The word *essential* makes Choice *A* false. The information, though relevant, is not essential, and the paragraph could survive without it. For Choice *C*, the information is not repeated at any point, and, therefore, is not redundant. For Choice *D*, the information is placed next to his height, which is relevant. Placing it anywhere else would make it out of place.

27. A: *Principals* are the leaders of a school. *Principles* indicate values, morals, or ideology. For Choice *B*, the words are reversed. For Choices *C* and *D*, both answers are misspelled, regardless of position.

28. C: *His* or *her* is correct. *Each* indicates the need for a singular pronoun, and because the charts belong to the patients, they must be possessive as well. To indicate that the group of patients could include males and females, *his* and *her* must be included. For Choice *A*, *there* is plural. For Choice *B*, *there* is an adverb, not a pronoun. For Choice *D*, *the people's* is collective plural, not singular.

29. B: *Imminent* means impending or happening soon. The man fears going to the zoo because a bomb might soon be detonated. For Choice *A*, *eminent* means of a high rank or status. For Choice *C*, *emanate* means to originate from. For Choice *D*, *amanita* is a type of fungus.

30. C: Semicolons can function as conjunctions. When used thus, they take the place of *and*, joining two independent clauses together. Choice *A* is incorrect because colons introduce lists or a final, emphasized idea. The independent clauses in this example carry equal emphasis. Choice *B* is an example of a run-on sentence. Commas may not be used to join two independent clauses. Choice *D* is also a run-on sentence. There's not punctuation of any type to indicate two separate clauses that can stand on their own.

31. C: This answer includes two independent clauses that could stand on their own. To test this, try separating each sentence and putting a period at the end. For Choice *C*, since each clause includes its own noun and verb, they each could stand independently of one another. For Choice *A*, there are two nouns, Tod and Elissa, and three verbs: went, got, and slept. This sentence cannot be separated into independent clauses. Choice *B* begins with a subordinate conjunction, making one sentence rely on the other. The same goes for Choice *D*; *while Marge slept* is a dependent clause.

32. C: *Ran* functions as a verb and is conjugated with the noun *lecture*. For Choice *A*, *engaging* acts as a gerund and an adjective, describing what type of lecture. For Choice *B*, *though* can act as a conjunction or adverb, but not a verb. For Choice *D*, *over* is an adverb that describes *ran*.

33. B: Adverbs describe verbs or adjectives. In this instance, *almost* describes *arrived*, the verb. Adverbs answer questions like *how* or *where* and here *almost* describes *how* he arrived. For *A*, *arrived* is a past-tense verb. For *C*, *irritated* functions as an adjective, describing Dave's boss. *Rest* (Choice *D*) is a noun, evidenced by the article, *the*, before it.

34. D: Summer is generic, so it doesn't require capitalization. Titles (*President*) are capitalized when they're specific and precede the person's name. It's similar to saying *Mr.* or *Mrs.*, followed by a person's name. Choice *A* is incorrect because *advanced history* should not be capitalized. It's already been established that *History 220* is the official name of the class, and *advanced* is indicating that the class is rigorous, especially in contrast to *entry-level*. Choice *B* is incorrect because *professor* should not be capitalized. It follows the name of the individual, and, therefore, does not qualify as a title. Choice *C* is incorrect because *army* and *navy* are specific to the British Empire, and, therefore, function as proper nouns.

35. D: This passage displays clarity (the author states precisely what he or she intended), fluency (the sentences run smoothly together), and parallelism (words are used in a similar fashion to help provide rhythm). Choice *A* lacks parallelism. When the author states, "the hero acts without thinking, is living in the moment, and is repressing physical and emotional pain," the words *acts*, *is living* and *is repressing* are in different tenses, and, consequently, jarring to one's ears. Choice *B* runs on endlessly in the first half ("Ernest Hemingway is probably the most noteworthy of expatriate authors since his concise writing style is void of emotion and stream of consciousness and has had a lasting impact on Americans which has resonated to this very day, and Hemingway's novels are much like in American cinema.") It demands some type of pause and strains the readers' eyes. The second half of the passage is choppy: "The hero acts. He doesn't think. He lives in the moment. He represses physical and emotional pain." For Choice *C*, leaving out *expatriate* is, first, vague, and second, alters the meaning. The correct version claims that Hemingway was the most notable of the expatriate authors while the second version claims he's the most notable of any author *ever*, a very bold claim indeed. Also, leaving out *stream of* in "stream of consciousness" no longer references the non-sequential manner in which most people think. Instead, this version sounds like all the characters in the novel are in a coma!

36. A: Books are italicized, like *Frankenstein*, and smaller works are put in quotation marks. A direct quotation takes a single set of quotation marks (" ") and a quote within a quote take a single set (' '). Choice *B* is incorrect because *Frankenstein* should be italicized, not put in quotation marks. In Choice *C*, the double and single-set quotation marks should be reversed. In Choice *D*, the comma is missing before the first quotation mark, and the period for the quote within a quote is on the outside of the quotation mark, not the inside. Punctuation belongs inside the quotation marks, regardless of whether it a single or double set.

37. B: Indefinite pronouns such as *everyone* always take the singular. The key is to delete unnecessary language mentally ("who has ever owned a pet and hasn't had help"), which allows one to better test the conjugation between noun and verb. In this case, *everyone* and *knows* are joined. Choice *A* is incorrect because *each* (another indefinite pronoun) is singular while the verb *have* is plural. In Choice *C*, *neither* is indefinite, so *is* should be *has*, not *have*. In Choice *D*, *One*, which is indefinite, is the noun. The prepositional phrase "of the very applauded and commended lecturers" can be removed from the sentence. Therefore, the singular *is* is needed, not *are*.

38. D: *Distraught* is an adjective because it describes *what* Sara (the noun) looks like. In Choice *A*, *never* is an adverb that modifies *is*. In Choice *B*, *after* is a preposition because it occurs before a noun, *class*, and establishes a relationship with the rest of the sentence. *Mess* (Choice *D*) is a noun.

39. C: Both second and third person points of view are represented. The phrases *one should have* and *it is* are in the third person. Typical third-person subjects include *he, she, him, her, they, one, person, people*, and *someone*. Second person voice is indicated in the second half of the passage by the words *you* and *your*. Second person is simple to identify because it is the *you* voice, in which the reader is directly addressed.

40. B: The word *conscience* means a sense of right and wrong. *Conscious* (Choice *A*) refers to a state of being awake and alert. *Consensus* (Choice *C*) means an opinion shared by many, and a *census* (Choice *D*) is a count of an area's population.

41. B: A simple sentence must contain three things: the subject, the verb, and the completed idea or thought. Once the nonessential clause "who is not yet sixty" is removed, one is left with, "Ted still easily fishes and camps, too." The combination of the verbs *fishes* and *camps* are known as compound verbs, but because there are no independent or dependent clauses combined, it is still considered simple. For Choice *A*, there's an independent clause ("Ted loves to rock climb") and a dependent clause ("even though he tore his rotator cuff.") *Even though* functions as a subordinate conjunction. For Choice *C*, there's two independent clauses ("Ted loves the outdoors" and "his wife is a homebody") joined by the compound conjunction *but*. For Choice *D*, there's two independent clauses ("Ted will also be retired soon" and "he likes to stay busy") joined with the conjunctive adverb *nevertheless*.

42. D: Here, the rules of plural possessive are followed, placing the apostrophe outside the *s*. The outside apostrophe confirms that there are multiple *businesses*, not just one, entertaining many *clients*. In Choice *A*, the word *women* is plural, so the apostrophe belongs before the added *s*; the correct usage is *women's*. For Choice *B*, knowing how to use *it's* versus *its* is critical. *It's* is always a contraction while *its* always shows ownership. In Choice *C*, the possessive is not in use at all.

43. C: For the prefix *anti-* to work in both situations, it must have the same meaning, one that generalizes to any word in the English language. *Oppose* makes sense in both instances. Antibiotics *oppose* bacteria, and antisocials *oppose* society. Choice A is illogical. *Reducing* the number of bacteria is somewhat logical, but *reducing* society doesn't make sense when considering the definition of antisocial. Choice B is not the best match for bacteria. *Revolt*, a word normally reserved for human opposition, sounds odd when paired with bacteria. Choice D might work for antibiotic (without bacteria) but doesn't work for antisocial (without society).

44. D: Shape is the best answer. If *conform* means to adjust behavior, *shape* could replace *conform*, as in the behavior was *re-shaped* or modified. The same goes for *inform*. New information *re-shapes* how one thinks about the world. Also, the word *shape* gives rise to the abstract idea that both behavior and information are malleable, like modeling clay, and can be molded into new forms. Choice A (*match*) works for *conform* (matching to society), but it doesn't work for *inform* (one cannot *match* information to a person). Choice B (*relay*) doesn't work for *conform* (there's no way to pass on new behavior), but it does work for *inform*, as to pass on new information. Choice C (*negate*) works for neither *conform* (the behavior is not being completely cancelled out) nor *inform* (the information is not being rescinded).

45. B: To arrive at the best answer (*surly*), all the character traits for Cindy must be analyzed. She's described as *happy* ("always has a smile on her face"), *kind* ("volunteers at the local shelter"), and *patient* ("no one has ever seen her angry"). Since Cindy's husband is the *opposite* of her, these adjectives must be converted to antonyms. Someone who is *surly* is *unhappy, rude,* and *impatient.* Choice A (*stingy*) is too narrow of a word. Someone could be *happy* and *kind*, for instance, but still be *stingy*. For Choice C, *scared*, to be plausible, the rest of the passage would need instances of Cindy being *bold* or *courageous*. Though she's certainly *kind* and *helpful*, none of those traits are modeled. Choice D (*shy*) also doesn't match. Someone who is *shy* could still be *happy, kind,* and *patient*.

46: A: *Grasp* is the best answer. It's important both in the New World and in Africa to ambulate or *move* (the word is used more than once), but only in the New World must mammals deal with dense vegetation and foliage. Choice B (*punch*) is incorrect because punching is unrelated to dealing with dense vegetation. *Prehensile tails* are designed to *grasp*. It's established in *both* environments that *movement* is critical to survival. Choice C (*move*) applies, again, to both jungle and savannah environments. Choice D (*walk*) would be applicable to savannahs, not environments populated with dense vegetation.

47. A: First person is the point of view represented. First person is known as the "I" voice. There are no "I's" in this passage, but the words *we* and *our* indicate first person plural. *We*, rationally, includes *I* and *other people*. *Our*, plural possessive, includes *mine* and *other's*. There is no evidence of second person (*you* voice), or third person (he, she, they). The narrator here is the "I," which means they are writing in first person.

48. B: "Make sure to clock out after your shift is through," includes both an independent and dependent clause. "Make sure to clock out" is the independent clause while "after your shift is through" is the dependent clause. *After* is the subordinate conjunction in this instance. Choice A is incorrect because "To make your fruit last longer" is a prepositional phrase, not a clause. "Keep it out of the sunlight" is an independent clause as well as an imperative command. For Choice C, "making a good fire" is considered a gerund phrase and is followed by the compound verbs *using* and *stacking*. Since there are no compound or complex sentences joined, it's considered a simple sentence. "Whenever possible," is an adverbial clause, not a dependent clause, so it's not classified as a complex sentence when paired with an independent clause ("Make sure to yield to oncoming traffic"). It, too, is a simple sentence.

49. B: *Accent* refers to the regional manner or style in which one speaks. *Ascent* refers to the act of rising or climbing. *Assent* means consensus or agreement. The people of Scotland have unique *accents* or dialects, and they're used to lofty *ascents* or climbs.

50. A: It is necessary to put a comma between the date and the year and between the day of the week and the month. Choice *B* is incorrect because it is missing the comma between the day of the week and the month. Choice *C* is incorrect because it adds an unnecessary comma between the month and date. Choice *D* is missing the necessary comma between day of the week and month.

Subtest III: Composition and Rhetoric; Reading Literature and Informational Texts

Writing Processes

Personal Writing Process

Teachers should create opportunities for students to evaluate both their own work and the work of their classmates. Teachers should reinforce the skills necessary for peer review, such as critical reading, revision skills, and collaboration. It's necessary to define the role of the peer reviewer as a reader, not an evaluator, so that students understand the goal is to offer helpful suggestions rather than grade the work like a teacher would. Students should learn that peer review is an essential step in the writing process. Revision strategies should be taught and the steps of the writing process reinforced.

Recognizing Research-Based Strategies for Teaching the Writing Process
Current trends in education have recognized the need to cultivate writing skills that prepare students for higher education and professional careers. To this end, writing skills are being integrated into other subjects beyond the language arts classroom. The skills and strategies used in language arts class, then, should be adaptable for other learning tasks. In this way, students can achieve greater proficiency by incorporating writing strategies into every aspect of learning.

To teach writing, it is important that writers know the writing process. Students should be familiar with the five components of the writing process:

- *Pre-writing*: The drafting, planning, researching, and brainstorming of ideas
- *Writing*: The part of the project in which the actual, physical writing takes place
- *Revising*: Adding to, removing, rearranging, or re-writing sections of the piece
- *Editing*: Analyzing and correcting mistakes in grammar, spelling, punctuation, formatting, and word choice
- *Publishing*: Distributing the finished product to the teacher, employer, or other students

The *writing workshop* is possibly the most common approach to teaching writing. It is an organized approach in which the student is guided by the teacher and usually contains the following components:

- *Short lesson* (~10 min) in which the teacher focuses on a particular aspect of the writing process—e.g., strategies, organization, technique, processes, craft—and gives explicit instructions for the task at hand

- *Independent writing time* (~30 min) in which the student engages in the writing activity and works through the process while receiving help from the teacher, writing in his/her own style on either a chosen topic or one assigned, and engaging with other students

- *Sharing* (~10 min) in which the student shares a piece of his or her work, either in a small group or as a class, and gains insight by listening to the work of other students

Another common strategy is *teacher modeling*, in which the student views the teacher as a writer and is therefore more apt to believe the teacher's instruction on the subject. To be a good writing teacher, the teacher must be a good writer. Therefore, it is important that the teacher practice his or her own writing on a somewhat regular basis through blogging, journaling, or creative writing, in order to keep his or her skills sharp. The following are some strategies for teacher writing:

- *Sharing written work*: This strategy is a good audio and/or visual learning technique. The teacher should frequently share personal writing with students so that the student recognizes the instructor as having authority on the subject. Many teachers also encourage feedback from the students to stimulate critical thinking skills.

- *Writing in front of students*: This strategy is very effective as a visual learning technique as the students watch as the teacher works through the writing process. This could include asking the students to provide a question or topic on which to write and then writing on blackboard or projector.

- *Encouraging real-world writing*: This is a kinesthetic teaching strategy in which the teacher urges students to write as frequently as possible and to share their written work with other students or an authentic audience. Teachers may also find it beneficial to show students their own blogs and other online media to demonstrate exactly how it's done. Students may also choose to model their writing after a published author, imitating his or her style, sentence structure, and word choices to become comfortable with the writing process.

Finally, a good thing for a student to have is a *writer's notebook*, which contains all the student's written work over the course of the curriculum, including warm-up assignments, drafts, brainstorming templates, and completed works. This allows the student to review previous writing assignment, learn from their mistakes, and see concrete evidence for improvement. Depending on the age group, many of the assignments could be performed on a word processor to encourage computer literacy.

Strengthening Writing

Identifying Strategies for Teaching Writing Tasks
There are over thirty research-proven strategies for teaching all components of the writing process through a variety of different tasks, the most comprehensive of which will be covered in this section.

Evidence shows that the most effective strategy for teaching writing is to have the students use the process-writing approach, in which they practice planning, writing, reviewing, editing, and publishing their work. Students should be taught how to write for a specific audience, take personal responsibility for their own work, and participate in the writing process with other students, such as a discussion-like setting where they can brainstorm together. Additionally, specific goals should be assigned, either classroom wide or to fit individual needs, through activities that encourage attention to spelling, grammar, sentence combination, and writing for specific audiences.

For pre-writing, students should also be exposed to the process of generating and organizing ideas before they set pen to paper, such as being given a specific topic and considering many different aspects associated with that topic using a *brainstorming web* or *mindmap*, visually dividing a project into main topics and subtopics. Teachers can help students by encouraging them to explore what they already know about a subject, topic, or genre. They can then illustrate how to go about researching and gathering information or data by using teacher modeling to access a variety of resources. Another research-based strategy is to require students to analyze and summarize a model text through writing, which encourages them to condense a composition into its main ideas and, in doing so, allows them to understand how these ideas were expressed and organized.

To teach the actual act of writing, *freewriting* is an effective writing warm-up activity as it requires nothing more than for the student to continually write uninterrupted for an allotted amount of time. One of the most common problems many students encounter is being uncertain what to write or how to begin. Freewriting creates a space in which the student does not have to worry about either of those things—they simply need to write. For this particular strategy, a teacher should avoid assigning a particular topic, genre, or format, nor should the student be encouraged or required to share what they have written so that they may write freely and without fear of judgment. After the allotted time for freewriting is up, students can then read back over what they have written and select the most interesting sentences and ideas to expand upon in a more organized piece of writing.

POWER Strategy for Teaching the Writing Process
The POWER strategy helps all students to take ownership of the writing process by prompting them to consciously focus on what they are writing.

The POWER strategy is an acronym for the following:

- Prewriting or Planning
- Organizing
- Writing a first draft
- Evaluating the writing
- Revising and rewriting

Prewriting and Planning
During the Prewriting and Planning phase, students learn to consider their audience and purpose for the writing project. Then they compile information they wish to include in the piece of writing from their background knowledge and/or new sources.

Organizing
Next, students decide on the organizational structure of their writing project. There are many types of organizational structures, but the common ones are: story/narrative, informative, opinion, persuasive, compare and contrast, explanatory, and problem/solution formats. Often graphic organizers are an important part of helping students complete this step of the writing process.

Writing
In this step, students write a complete first draft of their project. Educators may begin by using modeled writing to teach this step in the process. It may be helpful for beginning writers to work in small groups or pairs. Verbalizing their thoughts before writing them is also a helpful technique.

Evaluating
In this stage, students reread their writing and note the segments that are particularly strong or need improvement. Then they participate in peer editing. They ask each other questions about the piece. The peers learn to provide feedback and constructive criticism to help the student improve. Scoring rubrics are a helpful tool in this phase to guide students as they edit each other's work.

Revising and Rewriting
Finally, the student incorporates any changes she or he wishes to make based on the evaluating process. Then students rewrite the piece into a final draft and publish it however it best fits the audience and purpose of the writing.

Strategies to Clarify Meaning

Once a text has been introduced, teachers can help students understand its meaning through various tools. Graphic organizers, such as a KWL chart, can enhance reading comprehension by asking students to list what they know about the subject (K), what they want to know (W), and they have learned (L). Teachers should be aware of strategies that build reading comprehension and show students how to use them in critical reading and writing processes. Outlines are another strategy to help students plan what they want to write about. Often students will begin writing with a blank page. This can be frustrating and create writer's block. It is best to start with an outline or blueprint of the assignment. Teachers can make outlining assignments as brief or as detailed as they like, depending on the writing situation. A brief scratch outline can be a great way to get ideas on the page. A more formal detailed outline is an excellent step later in the planning process, which requires students to make important decisions about the direction of their paper.

When readers take notes throughout texts or passages, they are jotting down important facts or points that the author makes. Note taking is a useful record of information that helps readers understand the text or passage and respond to it. When taking notes, readers should keep lines brief and filled with pertinent information so that they are not rereading a large amount of text, but rather just key points, elements, or words. After readers have completed a text or passage, they can refer to their notes to help them form a conclusion about the author's ideas in the text or passage.

Text Types and Purposes

Writing Applications

The following steps help to identify examples of common types within the modes of writing:

- Identifying the audience—to whom or for whom the author is writing
- Determining the author's purpose—why the author is writing the piece
- Analyzing the word choices and how they are used

To demonstrate, the following passage has been marked to illustrate *the addressee*, the author's purpose, and word choices:

To Whom It May Concern:

I am extraordinarily excited to be applying to the Master of Environmental Science program at Australian National University. I believe the richness in biological and cultural diversity, as well as Australia's close proximity to the Great Barrier Reef, would provide a deeply fulfilling educational experience. *I am writing to express why I believe I would be an excellent addition to the program.*

While in college, I participated in a three-month public health internship in Ecuador, where I spent time both learning about medicine in a third world country and also about the Ecuadorian environment, including the Amazon Jungle and the Galápagos Islands. My favorite experience through the internship, besides swimming with sea lions in San Cristóbal, was helping to neutralize parasitic potable water and collect samples for analysis in Puyo.

Though my undergraduate studies related primarily to the human body, I took several courses in natural science, including a year of chemistry, biology, and physics as well as a course in a calculus. <u>I am confident</u> that my fundamental knowledge in these fields will prepare me for the science courses integral to the Masters of Environmental Science.

Having identified the *addressee*, it is evident that this selection is a letter of some kind. Further inspection into the author's purpose, seen in *bold*, shows that the author is trying to explain why he or she should be accepted into the environmental science program, which automatically places it into the argumentative mode as the writer is trying to persuade the reader to agree and to incite the reader into action by encouraging the program to accept the writer as a candidate. In addition to revealing the purpose, the use of emotional language—extraordinarily, excellent, deeply fulfilling, favorite experience, confident—illustrates that this is a persuasive piece. It also provides evidence for why this person would be an excellent addition to the program—his/her experience in Ecuador and with scientific curriculum.

The following passage presents an opportunity to solidify this method of analysis and practice the steps above to determine the mode of writing:

> The biological effects of laughter have long been an interest of medicine and psychology. Laughing is often speculated to reduce blood pressure because it induces feelings of relaxation and elation. Participating students watched a series of videos that elicited laughter, and their blood pressure was taken before and after the viewings. An average decrease in blood pressure was observed, though resulting p-values attest that the results were not significant.

This selection contains factual and scientific information, is devoid of any adjectives or flowery descriptions, and is not trying to convince the reader of any particular stance. Though the audience is not directly addressed, the purpose of the passage is to present the results of an experiment to those who would be interested in the biological effects of laughter—most likely a scientific community. Thus, this passage is an example of informative writing.

Below is another passage to help identify examples of the common writing modes, taken from *The Endeavor Journal of Sir Joseph Banks*:

10th May 1769 – THE ENGLISH CREW GET TAHITIAN NAMES

> We have now got the Indian name of the Island, Otahite, so therefore for the future I shall call it. As for our own names the Indians find so much dificulty in pronouncing them that we are forcd to indulge them in calling us what they please, or rather what they say when they attempt to pronounce them. I give here the List: Captn Cooke *Toote*, Dr Solander *Torano*, Mr Hicks *Hete*, Mr Gore *Toárro*, Mr Molineux *Boba* from his Christian name Robert, Mr Monkhouse *Mato*, and myself *Tapáne*. In this manner they have names for almost every man in the ship.

This extract contains no elements of an informative or persuasive intent and does not seem to follow any particular line of narrative. The passage gives a list of the different names that the Indians have given the crew members, as well as the name of an island. Although there is no context for the selection, through the descriptions, it is clear that the author and his comrades are on an island trying to communicate with the native inhabitants. Hence, this passage is a journal that reflects the descriptive mode.

These are only a few of the many examples that can be found in the four primary modes of writing.

Audience, Purpose, and Context

An author's *writing style*—the way in which words, grammar, punctuation, and sentence fluidity are used—is the most influential element in a piece of writing, and it is dependent on the purpose and the audience for whom it is intended. Together, a writing style and mode of writing form the foundation of a written work, and a good writer will choose the most effective mode and style to convey a message to readers.

Writers should first determine what they are trying to say and then choose the most effective mode of writing to communicate that message. Different writing modes and *word choices* will affect the tone of a piece—that is, its underlying attitude, emotion, or character. The argumentative mode may utilize words that are earnest, angry, passionate, or excited whereas an informative piece may have a sterile, germane, or enthusiastic tone. The tones found in narratives vary greatly, depending on the purpose of the writing. *Tone* will also be affected by the audience—teaching science to children or those who may be uninterested would be most effective with enthusiastic language and exclamation points whereas teaching science to college students may take on a more serious and professional tone, with fewer charged words and punctuation choices that are inherent to academia.

Sentence fluidity—whether sentences are long and rhythmic or short and succinct—also affects a piece of writing as it determines the way in which a piece is read. Children or audiences unfamiliar with a subject do better with short, succinct sentence structures as these break difficult concepts up into shorter points. A period, question mark, or exclamation point is literally a signal for the reader to stop and takes more time to process. Thus, longer, more complex sentences are more appropriate for adults or educated audiences as they can fit more information in between processing time.

The amount of *supporting detail* provided is also tailored to the audience. A text that introduces a new subject to its readers will focus more on broad ideas without going into greater detail whereas a text that focuses on a more specific subject is likely to provide greater detail about the ideas discussed.

Writing styles, like modes, are most effective when tailored to their audiences. Having awareness of an audience's demographic is one of the most crucial aspects of properly communicating an argument, a story, or a set of information.

Text Structures

Writing can be classified under four passage types: narrative, expository, technical, and persuasive. Though these types are not mutually exclusive, one form tends to dominate the rest. By recognizing the *type* of passage you're reading, you gain insight into *how* you should read. If you're reading a narrative, you can assume the author intends to entertain, which means you may skim the text without losing meaning. A technical document might require a close read, because skimming the passage might cause the reader to miss salient details.

1. *Narrative* writing, at its core, is the art of storytelling. For a narrative to exist, certain elements must be present. It must have characters. While many characters are human, characters could be defined as anything that thinks, acts, and talks like a human. For example, many recent movies, such as *Lord of the Rings* and *The Chronicles of Narnia*, include animals, fantastical creatures, and even trees that behave like humans. It must have a plot or sequence of events. Typically, those events follow a standard plot diagram, but recent trends start *in medias res* or in the middle (near the climax). In this instance, foreshadowing and flashbacks often fill in plot details. Along with characters and a plot, there must also be conflict. Conflict is usually divided into two types: internal and external. Internal conflict indicates the

character is in turmoil. Internal conflicts are presented through the character's thoughts. External conflicts are visible. Types of external conflict include a person versus nature, another person, and society.

2. *Expository* writing is detached and to the point, while other types of writing—persuasive, narrative, and descriptive—are lively. Since expository writing is designed to instruct or inform, it usually involves directions and steps written in second person ("you" voice) and lacks any persuasive or narrative elements. Sequence words such as *first*, *second*, and *third*, or *in the first place*, *secondly*, and *lastly* are often given to add fluency and cohesion. Common examples of expository writing include instructor's lessons, cookbook recipes, and repair manuals.

3. Due to its empirical nature, *technical* writing is filled with steps, charts, graphs, data, and statistics. The goal of technical writing is to advance understanding in a field through the scientific method. Experts such as teachers, doctors, or mechanics use words unique to the profession in which they operate. These words, which often incorporate acronyms, are called *jargon*. Technical writing is a type of expository writing but is not meant to be understood by the general public. Instead, technical writers assume readers have received a formal education in a particular field of study and need no explanation as to what the jargon means. Imagine a doctor trying to understand a diagnostic reading for a car or a mechanic trying to interpret lab results. Only professionals with proper training will fully comprehend the text.

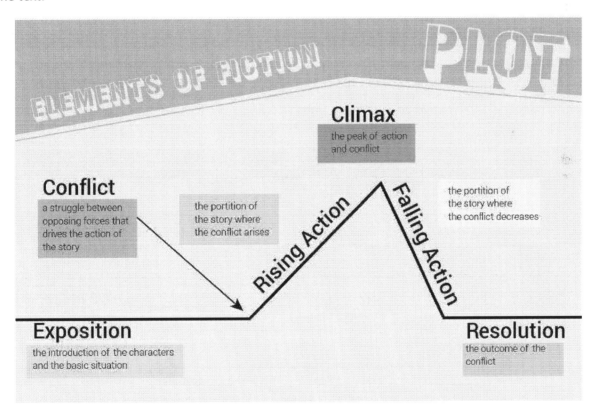

4. *Persuasive* writing is designed to change opinions and attitudes. The topic, stance, and arguments are found in the thesis, positioned near the end of the introduction. Later supporting paragraphs offer relevant quotations, paraphrases, and summaries from primary or secondary sources, which are then interpreted, analyzed, and evaluated. The goal of persuasive writers is not to stack quotes, but to develop original ideas by using sources as a starting point. Good persuasive writing makes powerful

arguments with valid sources and thoughtful analysis. Poor persuasive writing is riddled with bias and logical fallacies. Sometimes, logical and illogical arguments are sandwiched together in the same piece. Therefore, readers should display skepticism when reading persuasive arguments.

Organization of a Text
There are five basic elements inherent in effective writing, and each will be discussed throughout the various subheadings of this section.

- *Main idea*: The driving message of the writing, clearly stated or implied

- *Clear organization*: The effective and purposeful arrangement of the content to support the main idea

- *Supporting details/evidence*: Content that gives appropriate depth and weight to the main idea of the story, argument, or information

- *Diction/tone*: The type of language, vocabulary, and word choice used to express the main idea, purposefully aligned to the audience and purpose

- *Adherence to conventions of English*: Correct spelling, grammar, punctuation, and sentence structure, allowing for clear communication of ideas

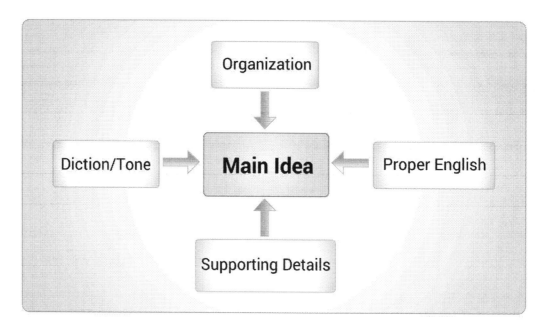

Developing Ideas in an Essay

To distinguish between the common modes of writing, it is important to identify the primary purpose of the work. This can be determined by considering what the author is trying to say to the reader. Although there are countless different styles of writing, all written works tend to fall under four primary categories: argumentative/persuasive, informative expository, descriptive, and narrative.

The table below highlights the purpose, distinct characteristics, and examples of each rhetorical mode.

Writing Mode	Purpose	Distinct Characteristics	Examples
Argumentative	To persuade	Opinions, loaded or subjective language, evidence, suggestions of what the reader should do, calls to action	Critical reviews Political journals Letters of recommendation Cover letters Advertising
Informative	To teach or inform	Objective language, definitions, instructions, factual information	Business and scientific reports Textbooks Instruction manuals News articles Personal letters Wills Informative essays Travel guides Study guides
Descriptive	To deliver sensory details to the reader	Heavy use of adjectives and imagery, language that appeals to any of the five senses	Poetry Journal entries Often used in narrative mode
Narrative	To tell a story, share an experience, entertain	Series of events, plot, characters, dialogue, conflict	Novels Short stories Novellas Anecdotes Biographies Epic poems Autobiographies

Introducing, Developing, and Concluding a Text Effectively

Almost all coherent written works contain three primary parts: a beginning, middle, and end. The organizational arrangements differ widely across distinct writing modes. Persuasive and expository texts utilize an introduction, body, and conclusion whereas narrative works use an orientation, series of events/conflict, and a resolution.

Every element within a written piece relates back to the main idea, and the beginning of a persuasive or expository text generally conveys the main idea or the purpose. For a narrative piece, the beginning is the section that acquaints the reader with the characters and setting, directing them to the purpose of the writing. The main idea in narrative may be implied or addressed at the end of the piece.

Depending on the primary purpose, the arrangement of the middle will adhere to one of the basic organizational structures described in the information texts and rhetoric section. They are cause and effect, problem and solution, compare and contrast, description/spatial, sequence, and order of importance.

The ending of a text is the metaphorical wrap-up of the writing. A solid ending is crucial for effective writing as it ties together loose ends, resolves the action, highlights the main points, or repeats the central idea. A conclusion ensures that readers come away from a text understanding the author's main idea. The table below highlights the important characteristics of each part of a piece of writing.

Structure	Argumentative/Informative	Narrative
Beginning	Introduction *Purpose, main idea*	Orientation *Introduces characters, setting, necessary background*
Middle	Body *Supporting details, reasons and evidence*	Events/Conflict *Story's events that revolve around a central conflict*
End	Conclusion *Highlights main points, summarizes and paraphrases ideas, reiterates the main idea*	Resolution *The solving of the central conflict*

Evaluating Arguments

A reader must be able to evaluate the argument or point the author is trying to make and determine if it is adequately supported. The first step is to determine the main idea. The main idea is what the author wants to say about a specific topic. The next step is to locate the supporting details. An author uses supporting details to illustrate the main idea. These are the details that provide evidence or examples to help make a point. Supporting details often appear in the form of quotations, paraphrasing, or analysis. Test takers should then examine the text to make sure the author connects details and analysis to the main point. These steps are crucial to understanding the text and evaluating how well the author presents his or her argument and evidence. The following graphic demonstrates the connection between the main idea and the supporting details.

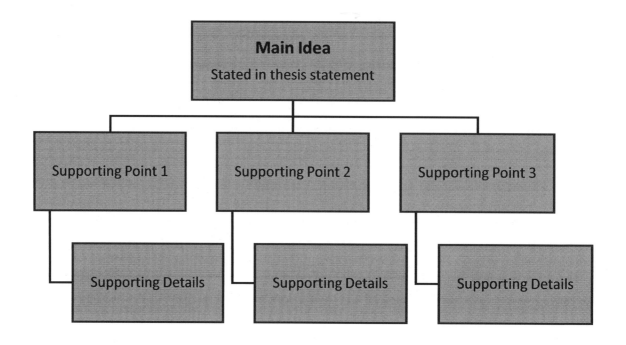

Evaluating Evidence

It is important to evaluate the author's supporting details to be sure that they are credible, provide evidence of the author's point, and directly support the main idea. Critical readers examine the facts used to support an author's argument and check those facts against other sources to be sure the facts are correct. They also check the validity of the sources used to be sure those sources are credible, academic, and/or peer- reviewed. A strong argument uses valid, measurable facts to support ideas.

Identifying False Statements

A reader must also be able to identify any *logical fallacies*—logically-flawed statements—that an author may make as those fallacies impact the validity and veracity of the author's claims.

Some of the more common fallacies are shown in the following chart.

Fallacy	Definition
Slippery Slope	A fallacy that is built on the idea that a particular action will lead to a series of events with negative results
Red Herring	The use of an observation or distraction to remove attention from the actual issue
Straw Man	An exaggeration or misrepresentation of an argument so that it is easier to refute
Post Hoc Ergo Propter Hoc	A fallacy that assumes an event to be the consequence of an earlier event merely because it came after it
Bandwagon	A fallacy that assumes because the majority of people feel or believe a certain way then it must be the right way
Ad Hominem	The use of a personal attack on the person or persons associated with a certain argument rather than focusing on the actual argument itself

Readers who are aware of the types of fallacious reasoning are able to weigh the credibility of the author's statements in terms of effective argument. Rhetorical text that contains a myriad of fallacious statements should be considered ineffectual and suspect.

Rhetorical Techniques

In an argument or persuasive text, an author will strive to sway readers to an opinion or conclusion. To be effective, an author must consider his or her intended audience. Although an author may write text for a general audience, he or she will use methods of appeal or persuasion to convince that audience. Aristotle asserted that there were three methods or modes by which a person could be persuaded. These are referred to as *rhetorical appeals*.

The three main types of rhetorical appeals are shown in the following graphic.

Ethos, also referred to as an *ethical appeal*, is an appeal to the audience's perception of the writer as credible (or not), based on their examination of their ethics and who the writer is, his/her experience or incorporation of relevant information, or his/her argument. For example, authors may present testimonials to bolster their arguments. The reader who critically examines the veracity of the testimonials and the credibility of those giving the testimony will be able to determine if the author's use of testimony is valid to his or her argument. In turn, this will help the reader determine if the author's thesis is valid. An author's careful and appropriate use of technical language can create an overall knowledgeable effect and, in turn, act as a convincing vehicle when it comes to credibility. Overuse of technical language, however, may create confusion in readers and obscure an author's overall intent.

Pathos, also referred to as a *pathetic* or *emotional appeal*, is an appeal to the audience's sense of identity, self-interest, or emotions. A critical reader will notice when the author is appealing to pathos through anecdotes and descriptions that elicit an emotion such as anger or pity. Readers should also beware of factual information that uses generalization to appeal to the emotions. While it's tempting to believe an author is the source of truth in his or her text, an author who presents factual information as universally true, consistent throughout time, and common to all groups is using *generalization*. Authors who exclusively use generalizations without specific facts and credible sourcing are attempting to sway readers solely through emotion.

Logos, also referred to as a *logical appeal*, is an appeal to the audience's ability to see and understand the logic in a claim offered by the writer. A critical reader has to be able to evaluate an author's arguments for validity of reasoning and for sufficiency when it comes to argument.

Informative/Explanatory Texts

Informative writing tries to teach or inform. Workplace manuals, instructor lessons, statistical reports and cookbooks are examples of informative texts. Informative writing is usually based on facts and is often void of emotion and persuasion. Informative texts generally contain statistics, charts, and graphs. Though most informative texts lack a persuasive agenda, readers must examine the text carefully to determine whether one exists within a given passage.

The key to developing a strong informative or explanatory written text is organization. It's not enough to simply state ideas and pile on reasoning. Readers will become confused and the focus of the writing will become lost in the jumbled content. This won't enhance argument or fully elucidate the ideas that are attempting to be explained. Therefore, creating an organized structure within the text will enable the information to flow clearly.

While style will add uniqueness to any text, the most efficient way to structure written work is around the use of reasoning. The writer's goal should be to present an idea or thesis, and then justify it by using selected examples that illustrate the reason for one's views. If one puts forth ideas and reasoning without demonstrating validity, the idea remains an opinion, not an argument.

A writer should be selective with the examples or proof they use. If the evidence doesn't strengthen the text, it should be taken out. Remember, it's not enough to simply list examples—it's crucial to use analysis to show the reader why the evidence supports the stance of the essay. Explaining what the evidence shows, why it's important, and how it substantiates the argument will allow the reader to understand the line of reasoning and recognize the validity of the claim.

The text should have an introduction, a body, and a conclusion. The conclusion, of course, will summarize and reaffirm the thesis or main idea. Therefore, from the beginning, the writing must be organized in a way that it leads to the conclusion. After the introduction, present evidence and analysis, then transition into the next piece of evidence that is even stronger than the last. This way, the text will have a clear writing pattern to follow and the argument will become stronger as the writing continues towards the conclusion.

Evidence in Literary Text

Text evidence is the information readers find in a text or passage that supports the main idea or point(s) in a story. In turn, text evidence can help readers draw conclusions about the text or passage. The information should be taken directly from the text or passage and placed in quotation marks. Text evidence provides readers with information to support ideas about the text so that they do not rely simply on their own thoughts.

Literary texts employ rhetorical devices. Figurative language like simile and metaphor is a type of rhetorical device commonly found in literature. In addition to rhetorical devices that play on the *meanings* of words, there are also rhetorical devices that use the *sounds* of words. These devices are most often found in poetry but may also be found in other types of literature and in non-fiction writing like speech texts.

Alliteration and *assonance* are both varieties of sound repetition. Other types of sound repetition include: anaphora, repetition that occurs at the beginning of the sentences; epiphora, repetition occurring at the end of phrases; antimetabole, repetition of words in reverse order; and antiphrasis, a form of denial of an assertion in a text.

Alliteration refers to the repetition of the first sound of each word. Recall Robert Burns' opening line:

> My love is like a red, red rose

This line includes two instances of alliteration: "love" and "like" (repeated *L* sound), as well as "red" and "rose" (repeated *R* sound). Next, assonance refers to the repetition of vowel sounds, and can occur anywhere within a word (not just the opening sound). Here is the opening of a poem by John Keats:

> When I have fears that I may cease to be

> Before my pen has glean'd my teeming brain

Assonance can be found in the words "fears," "cease," "be," "glean'd," and "teeming," all of which stress the long *E* sound. Both alliteration and assonance create a harmony that unifies the writer's language.

Another sound device is *onomatopoeia*, or words whose spelling mimics the sound they describe. Words like "crash," "bang," and "sizzle" are all examples of onomatopoeia. Use of onomatopoetic language adds auditory imagery to the text.

Readers are probably most familiar with the technique of *pun*. A pun is a play on words, taking advantage of two words that have the same or similar pronunciation. Puns can be found throughout Shakespeare's plays, for instance:

> Now is the winter of our discontent

> Made glorious summer by this son of York

These lines from *Richard III* contain a play on words. Richard III refers to his brother, the newly crowned King Edward IV, as the "son of York," referencing their family heritage from the house of York. However, while drawing a comparison between the political climate and the weather (times of political trouble were the "winter," but now the new king brings "glorious summer"), Richard's use of the word "son" also implies another word with the same pronunciation, "sun"—so Edward IV is also like the sun, bringing light, warmth, and hope to England. Puns are a clever way for writers to suggest two meanings at once.

Production and Distribution of Writing

Vocabulary

A writer's style is the way that he or she presents information through sentence structure, word choice, and even punctuation. Style is influenced by the writing situation and the intended audience. A writer's voice is an element of style that shows the writer's personality. It is what makes the writing unique to the writer. Voice and style can be developed through listening to examples of styles in other's writing. Developing an ear for different writing styles can help students to develop their own style.

Precision

People often think of precision in terms of math, but precise word choice is another key to successful writing. Since language itself is imprecise, it's important for the writer to find the exact word or words to convey the full, intended meaning of a given situation. For example:

> The number of deaths has gone down since seat belt laws started.

There are several problems with this sentence. First, the word *deaths* is too general. From the context, it's assumed that the writer is referring only to deaths caused by car accidents. However, without clarification, the sentence lacks impact and is probably untrue. The phrase "gone down" might be accurate, but a more precise word could provide more information and greater accuracy. Did the numbers show a slow and steady decrease of highway fatalities or a sudden drop? If the latter is true, the writer is missing a chance to make their point more dramatically. Instead of "gone down" they could substitute *plummeted, fallen drastically,* or *rapidly diminished* to bring the information to life. Also, the phrase "seat belt laws" is unclear. Does it refer to laws requiring cars to include seat belts or to laws requiring drivers and passengers to use them? Finally, *started* is not a strong verb. Words like *enacted* or *adopted* are more direct and make the content more real. When put together, these changes create a far more powerful sentence:

> The number of highway fatalities has plummeted since laws requiring seat belt usage were enacted.

However, it's important to note that precise word choice can sometimes be taken too far. If the writer of the sentence above takes precision to an extreme, it might result in the following:

> The incidence of high-speed, automobile accident related fatalities has decreased 75% and continued to remain at historical lows since the initial set of federal legislations requiring seat belt use were enacted in 1992.

This sentence is extremely precise, but it takes so long to achieve that precision that it suffers from a lack of clarity. Precise writing is about finding the right balance between information and flow. This is also an issue of conciseness (discussed in the next section).

The last thing to consider with precision is a word choice that's not only unclear or uninteresting, but also confusing or misleading. For example:

> The number of highway fatalities has become hugely lower since laws requiring seat belt use were enacted.

In this case, the reader might be confused by the word *hugely*. Huge means large, but here the writer uses *hugely* to describe something small. Though most readers can decipher this, doing so disconnects them from the flow of the writing and makes the writer's point less effective.

Conciseness

"Less is more" is a good rule to follow when writing a sentence. Unfortunately, writers often include extra words and phrases that seem necessary at the time but add nothing to the main idea. This confuses the reader and creates unnecessary repetition. Writing that lacks conciseness is usually guilty of excessive wordiness and redundant phrases. Here's an example containing both of these issues:

> When legislators decided to begin creating legislation making it mandatory for automobile drivers and passengers to make use of seat belts while in cars, a large number of them made those laws for reasons that were political reasons.

There are several empty or "fluff" words here that take up too much space. These can be eliminated while still maintaining the writer's meaning. For example:

- "Decided to begin" could be shortened to "began"
- "Making it mandatory for" could be shortened to "requiring"
- "Make use of" could be shortened to "use"
- "A large number" could be shortened to "many"

In addition, there are several examples of redundancy that can be eliminated:

- "Legislators decided to begin creating legislation" and "made those laws"
- "Automobile drivers and passengers" and "while in cars"
- "Reasons that were political reasons"

These changes are incorporated as follows:

> When legislators began requiring drivers and passengers to use seat belts, many of them did so for political reasons.

There are many general examples of redundant phrases, such as "add an additional," "complete and total," "time schedule," and "transportation vehicle." If asked to identify a redundant phrase on the test, look for words that are close together with the same (or similar) meanings.

Produce coherent writing by using clause-joining techniques (coordinators, subordinators, punctuation) to express logical connections between ideas

Coherent writing involves the use of clause-joining devices, such as the use of coordinators and punctuation such as semicolons and commas. Ideas should flow logically and fluidly and these skills should develop through writing instruction as well as by reading quality work. Writing skills are influenced by a number of factors. A student's personal experience, for example, can influence his or her voice writing. Socio-economic factors can also influence a student's writing skills and success. Early reading experiences can also be a factor in how writers develop their skills. Students who are regularly read to from a young age tend to have more developed vocabularies and better writing skills, while those that did not receive early literacy experiences are often not be as successful in their writing. These factors must be addressed and considered in the development of writing instruction in order to meet the needs of all students.

Coordinators and Subordinators
Using coordinators, or coordinating conjunctions, allows a writer to join two or more independent clauses that are of equal syntactic importance. This is done through the use of *but, and, for, or, nor, yet*, and *so*. Sometimes a comma is also necessary to correctly link two sentences correctly. For example:

> Tom was out late last night*, so* he took out the trash.

Note how both the coordinating conjunctions and comma are needed because these are two independent clauses: *Tom was late last night* and *he took out the trash*. The use of the coordinator and comma enable the author to combine two sentences in a way that makes grammatical sense.

Subordinate conjunctions function for two main reasons. The first is to transition between the ideas in a sentence, and the second is to reduce the significance of one clause over another so that the reader will identify the more important clause in a sentence. Subordinate conjunctions include *where, once, even though, before*, and several other words.

Subordinate conjunctions are essential in building complex sentences which contain an independent clause, which stands alone, and a subordinate clause, which cannot stand independently. Here's an example:

> We looked throughout the yard *where* Dill thought he left the ball

Note how the independent clause, *We looked throughout the yard,* is effectively connected with dependent clause *where Dill thought he left the ball.* The use of *where* not only indicates a thought transition but also indicates that the main focus of the sentence is looking throughout the yard.

End Punctuation

Periods (.) are used to end a sentence that is a statement (*declarative*) or a command (*imperative*). They should not be used in a sentence that asks a question or is an exclamation. Periods are also used in abbreviations, which are shortened versions of words.

- Declarative: The boys refused to go to sleep.
- Imperative: Walk down to the bus stop.
- Abbreviations: Joan Roberts, M.D., Apple Inc., Mrs. Adamson
- If a sentence ends with an abbreviation, it is inappropriate to use two periods. It should end with a single period after the abbreviation.

> The chef gathered the ingredients for the pie, which included apples, flour, sugar, etc.

Question marks (?) are used with direct questions (*interrogative*). An *indirect question* can use a period:

> Interrogative: When does the next bus arrive?

> Indirect Question: I wonder when the next bus arrives.

An *exclamation point (!)* is used to show strong emotion or can be used as an *interjection*. This punctuation should be used sparingly in formal writing situations.

> What an amazing shot!

> Whoa!

Commas

A *comma* (,) is the punctuation mark that signifies a pause—breath—between parts of a sentence. It denotes a break of flow. Proper comma usage helps readers understand the writer's intended emphasis of ideas.

In a complex sentence—one that contains a subordinate (dependent) clause or clauses—the use of a comma is dictated by where the subordinate clause is located. If the subordinate clause is located before the main clause, a comma is needed between the two clauses.

I will not pay for the steak, *because I don't have that much money.*

Generally, if the subordinate clause is placed after the main clause, no punctuation is needed. I did well on my exam because I studied two hours the night before. Notice how the last clause is dependent because it requires the earlier independent clauses to make sense.

Use a comma on both sides of an interrupting phrase.

I will pay for the ice cream, *chocolate and vanilla,* and I will eat it all myself.

The words forming the phrase in italics are nonessential (extra) information. To determine if a phrase is nonessential, try reading the sentence without the phrase and see if it's still coherent.

A comma is not necessary in this next sentence because no interruption—nonessential or extra information—has occurred. Read sentences aloud when uncertain.

I will pay for his chocolate and vanilla ice cream and I will eat it all myself.

If the nonessential phrase comes at the beginning of a sentence, a comma should only go at the end of the phrase. If the phrase comes at the end of a sentence, a comma should only go at the beginning of the phrase.

Other types of interruptions include the following:

- interjections: Oh no, I am not going.
- abbreviations: Barry Potter, M.D., specializes in heart disorders.
- direct addresses: Yes, Claudia, I am tired and going to bed.
- parenthetical phrases: His wife, lovely as she was, was not helpful.
- transitional phrases: Also, it is not possible.

The second comma in the following sentence is called an Oxford comma.

I will pay for ice cream, syrup, and pop.

It is a comma used after the second-to-last item in a series of three or more items. It comes before the word *or* or *and*. Not everyone uses the Oxford comma; it is optional, but many believe it is needed. The comma functions as a tool to reduce confusion in writing. So, if omitting the Oxford comma would cause confusion, then it's best to include it.

Commas are used in math to mark the place of thousands in numerals, breaking them up so they are easier to read. Other uses for commas are in dates (*March 19, 2016*), letter greetings (*Dear Sally,*), and in between cities and states (*Louisville, KY*).

Semicolons

A *semicolon (;)* is used to connect ideas in a sentence in some way. There are three main ways to use semicolons.

Link two independent clauses without the use of a coordinating conjunction:

> I was late for work again; I'm definitely going to get fired.

Link two independent clauses with a transitional word:

> The songs were all easy to play; therefore, he didn't need to spend too much time practicing.

Between items in a series that are already separated by commas or if necessary to separate lengthy items in a list:

> Starbucks has locations in Media, PA; Swarthmore, PA; and Morton, PA.

> Several classroom management issues presented in the study: the advent of a poor teacher persona in the context of voice, dress, and style; teacher follow-through from the beginning of the school year to the end; and the depth of administrative support, including ISS and OSS protocol.

Colons

A *colon* is used after an independent clause to present an explanation or draw attention to what comes next in the sentence. There are several uses.

Explanations of ideas:

> They soon learned the hardest part about having a new baby: sleep deprivation.

Lists of items:

> Shari picked up all the supplies she would need for the party: cups, plates, napkins, balloons, streamers, and party favors.

Time, subtitles, general salutations:

> The time is 7:15.

> I read a book entitled *Pluto: A Planet No More*.

> To whom it may concern:

Parentheses and Dashes

Parentheses are half-round brackets that look like this: ( ). They set off a word, phrase, or sentence that is an afterthought, explanation, or side note relevant to the surrounding text but not essential. A pair of commas is often used to set off this sort of information, but parentheses are generally used for information that would not fit well within a sentence or that the writer deems not important enough to be structurally part of the sentence.

> The picture of the heart (see above) shows the major parts you should memorize.
> Mount Everest is one of three mountains in the world that are over 28,000 feet high (K2 and Kanchenjunga are the other two).

See how the sentences above are complete without the parenthetical statements? In the first example, *see above* would not have fit well within the flow of the sentence. The second parenthetical statement could have been a separate sentence, but the writer deemed the information not pertinent to the topic.

The dash (—) is a mark longer than a hyphen used as a punctuation mark in sentences and to set apart a relevant thought. Even after plucking out the line separated by the dash marks, the sentence will be intact and make sense.

> Looking out the airplane window at the landmarks—Lake Clarke, Thompson Community College, and the bridge—she couldn't help but feel excited to be home.

The dashes use is similar to that of parentheses or a pair of commas. So, what's the difference? Many believe that using dashes makes the clause within them stand out while using parentheses is subtler. It's advised to not use dashes when commas could be used instead.

Ellipses
An *ellipsis* (...) consists of three handy little dots that can speak volumes on behalf of irrelevant material. Writers use them in place of words, lines, phrases, list content, or paragraphs that might just as easily have been omitted from a passage of writing. This can be done to save space or to focus only on the specifically relevant material.

> Exercise is good for some unexpected reasons. Watkins writes, "Exercise has many benefits such as...reducing cancer risk."

In the example above, the ellipsis takes the place of the other benefits of exercise that are more expected.

The ellipsis may also be used to show a pause in sentence flow.

> "I'm wondering...how this could happen," Dylan said in a soft voice.

Clausal and Phrasal Modifiers

Clauses
Clauses contain a subject and a verb. An *independent clause* can function as a complete sentence on its own, but it might also be one component of a longer sentence. *Dependent clauses* cannot stand alone as complete sentences. They rely on independent clauses to complete their meaning. Dependent clauses usually begin with a subordinating conjunction. Independent and dependent clauses are sometimes also referred to as *main clauses* and *subordinate clauses*, respectively. The following structure highlights the differences:

> Apiculturists raise honeybees because they love insects.

Apiculturists raise honeybees is an independent or main clause. The subject is *apiculturists*, and the verb is *raise*. It expresses a complete thought and could be a standalone sentence.

Because they love insects is a dependent or subordinate clause. If it were not attached to the independent clause, it would be a sentence fragment. While it contains a subject and verb—*they love*—this clause is dependent because it begins with the subordinate conjunction *because*. Thus, it does not express a complete thought on its own.

Another type of clause is a *relative clause*, and it is sometimes referred to as an *adjective clause* because it gives further description about the noun. A relative clause begins with a *relative pronoun*: *that, which, who, whom, whichever, whomever,* or *whoever.* It may also begin with a *relative adverb*: *where, why,* or *when.* Here's an example of a relative clause, functioning as an adjective:

The strawberries that I bought yesterday are already beginning to spoil.

Here, the relative clause is *that I bought yesterday*; the relative pronoun is *that*. The subject is *I*, and the verb is *bought*. The clause modifies the subject *strawberries* by answering the question, "Which strawberries?" Here's an example of a relative clause with an adverb:

The tutoring center is a place where students can get help with homework.

The relative clause is *where students can get help with homework*, and it gives more information about a place by describing what kind of place it is. It begins with the relative adverb *where* and contains the noun *students* along with its verb phrase *can get*.

Relative clauses may be further divided into two types: essential or nonessential. *Essential clauses* contain identifying information without which the sentence would lose significant meaning or not make sense. These are also sometimes referred to as *restrictive clauses*. The sentence above contains an example of an essential relative clause. Here is what happens when the clause is removed:

The tutoring center is a place where students can get help with homework.

The tutoring center is a place.

Without the relative clause, the sentence loses the majority of its meaning; thus, the clause is essential or restrictive.

Nonessential clauses—also referred to as *non-restrictive clauses*—offer additional information about a noun in the sentence, but they do not significantly control the overall meaning of the sentence. The following example indicates a nonessential clause:

New York City, which is located in the northeastern part of the country, is the most populated city in America.

New York City is the most populated city in America.

Even without the relative clause, the sentence is still understandable and continues to communicate its central message about New York City. Thus, it is a nonessential clause.

Punctuation differs between essential and nonessential relative clauses, too. Nonessential clauses are set apart from the sentence using commas whereas essential clauses are not separated with commas. Also, the relative pronoun *that* is generally used for essential clauses, while *which* is used for nonessential clauses. The following examples clarify this distinction:

Romeo and Juliet is my favorite play *that Shakespeare wrote.*

The relative clause *that Shakespeare wrote* contains essential, controlling information about the noun *play*, limiting it to those plays by Shakespeare. Without it, it would seem that *Romeo and Juliet* is the speaker's favorite play out of every play ever written, not simply from Shakespeare's repertoire.

> *Romeo and Juliet, which Shakespeare wrote*, is my favorite play.

Here, the nonessential relative clause—"which Shakespeare wrote"—modifies *Romeo and Juliet*. It doesn't provide controlling information about the play, but simply offers further background details. Thus, commas are needed.

Phrases

Phrases are groups of words that do not contain the subject-verb combination required for clauses. Phrases are classified by the part of speech that begins or controls the phrase.

A *noun phrase* consists of a noun and all its modifiers—adjectives, adverbs, and determiners. Noun phrases can serve many functions in a sentence, acting as subjects, objects, and object complements:

> *The shallow yellow bowl* sits on the top shelf.

> Nina just bought *some incredibly fresh organic produce*.

Prepositional phrases are made up of a preposition and its object. The object of a preposition might be a noun, noun phrase, pronoun, or gerund. Prepositional phrases may function as either an adjective or an adverb:

> Jack picked up the book *in front of him*.

The prepositional phrase *in front of him* acts as an adjective indicating which book Jack picked up.

> The dog ran into the back yard.

The phrase *into the backyard* describes where the dog ran, so it acts as an adverb.

Devices to Control Focus

Active and Passive Voice

Active voice is a sentence structure in which the subject performs the action of the sentence. The verbs of these sentences are called *active verbs*.

> The deer jumped over the fence.

In the example above, the deer is the one jumping. *Passive voice* is a sentence structure in which the object performs the action of the sentence. The verbs of these sentences are called *passive verbs*.

> The fence was jumped by the deer.

In this example, the fence is the subject, but it is not jumping over anything. The deer is still the one performing the action, but it is now the object of the sentence.

Passive voice is helpful when it's unclear who performed an action.

> The chair was moved.

While passive voice can add variety to writing, active voice is the generally preferred sentence structure.

Expletives and Concrete Subjects

Controlling the sentence is the art of keeping content direct and targeted. This can be aided by drawing the reader's focus to specific details in the text by avoiding expletives. Expletives are words that unnecessarily take up space and complicate the overall sentence. Here's an example:

> Alligators are likely to be inactive in winter.

Cutting out the unnecessary words will make the sentence more direct and increase the flow of the overall paragraph:

> Alligators are mostly inactive in winter.

Taking away *are* and *likely to be* streamlines the sentence and makes the main point of the sentence clearer.

Using concrete subjects will also enable the reader to pinpoint what's being talked about. This also personalizes and clarifies the subject matter. Here's an example:

> We went to the house.

This is very vague, it can be anyone's house, or it can be anywhere. Therefore, the sentence lacks clarity and control. This is easily remedied with a concrete subject such as:

> We went to Brian's house.

Now the sentence is more direct and the reader is aware of what's going on.

Using Varied and Effective Transitions

Transitions are the glue that holds the writing together. They function to purposefully incorporate new topics and supporting details in a smooth and coherent way. Usually, transitions are found at the beginnings of sentences, but they can also be located in the middle as a way to link clauses together. There are two types of clauses: independent and dependent as discussed in the language use and vocabulary section.

Transition words connect clauses within and between sentences for smoother writing. "I dislike apples. They taste like garbage." is choppier than "I dislike apples because they taste like garbage." Transitions demonstrate the relationship between ideas, allow for more complex sentence structures, and can alert the reader to which type of organizational format the author is using.

Transition words can be categorized based on the relationships they create between ideas:

- General order: signaling elaboration of an idea to emphasize a point—e.g., for example, for instance, to demonstrate, including, such as, in other words, that is, in fact, also, furthermore, likewise, and, truly, so, surely, certainly, obviously, doubtless

- Chronological order: referencing the time frame in which main event or idea occurs—e.g., before, after, first, while, soon, shortly thereafter, meanwhile

- Numerical order/order of importance: indicating that related ideas, supporting details, or events will be described in a sequence, possibly in order of importance—e.g., first, second, also, finally, another, in addition, equally important, less importantly, most significantly, the main reason, last but not least

- Spatial order: referring to the space and location of something or where things are located in relation to each other—e.g., inside, outside, above, below, within, close, under, over, far, next to, adjacent to

- Cause and effect order: signaling a causal relationship between events or ideas—e.g., thus, therefore, since, resulted in, for this reason, as a result, consequently, hence, for, so

- Compare and contrast order: identifying the similarities and differences between two or more objects, ideas, or lines of thought—e.g., like, as, similarly, equally, just as, unlike, however, but, although, conversely, on the other hand, on the contrary

- Summary order: indicating that a particular idea is coming to a close—e.g., in conclusion, to sum up, in other words, ultimately, above all

Sophisticated writing also aims to avoid overuse of transitions and ensure that those used are meaningful. Using a variety of transitions makes the writing appear more lively and informed and helps readers follow the progression of ideas.

Technology

Teachers are learning to adapt their writing instruction to integrate today's technology standards and to enhance engagement in the writing process. The key is to still build a strong foundation of the fundamentals of writing while using current technology. Gone are the days when writing relied solely on handwritten pieces and when the tools of the trade were pencils, paper, hardback dictionaries, and encyclopedias. Online resources are now the backbone of the writing experience. It is now possible to integrate photo, video, and other interactive components into a completed project to provide a well-rounded engagement with media. In order to have an education conducive to college and career readiness and success, students need online research and digital media writing skills.

There are many compelling reasons to teach students to be digitally aware and prudent users of technology when it comes to their writing. With current digital technology, the writing process has become a much more collaborative experience. In higher education and in career settings, collaborative skills are essential. Publishing and presenting are now simplified such that completed work is often read by a wide variety of audiences. Writing can be instantly shared with parents, peers, educators, and the general public, including experts in the field. Students are more apt to take an interest in the writing process when they know that others are reading their writing. Feedback is also simplified because so many platforms allow comments from readers. Teachers can be interactive with the students throughout the process, allowing formative assessment and integration of personalized instruction. Technology is simply a new vehicle for human connection and interactivity.

A student may be exposed to a plethora of technology, but this does not mean that she or he necessarily knows how to use it for learning. The teacher is still responsible for guiding, monitoring, and scaffolding the students toward learning objectives. It is critical that educators teach students how to locate credible information and to reliably cite their sources using bibliographies. Platforms and apps for online learning are varied and plentiful. Here are some ideas for how to use technology for writing instruction in the classroom:

- Use a projector with a tablet to display notes and classwork for the group to see. This increases instructional time because notes are already available rather than having to be written in real-time. This also provides the ability to save, email, and post classwork and notes for students and parents to access on their own time. A student can work at his or her own pace and still keep up with instruction. Student screens can be displayed for peer-led teaching and sharing of class work.

- More technology in class means less paperwork. Digital drop-boxes can be used for students to turn in assignments. Teachers can save paper, keep track of student revisions of work, and give feedback electronically.

- Digital media can be used to differentiate instruction for multiple learning styles and multiple skill levels. Instead of using standardized textbook learning for everyone, teachers can create and collect resources for individualizing course content.

- Inquiry- and problem-based learning is easier with increased collaborative capabilities provided by digital tools.

- Digital textbooks and e-readers can replace hardback versions of text that are prone to damage and loss. Students can instantly access definitions for new words, as well as annotate and highlight useful information without ruining a hardbound book.

- Library databases can be used to locate reliable research information and resources. There are digital tools for tracking citation information, allowing annotations for internet content, and for storing internet content.

- Mobile devices may be used in the classroom to encourage reading and writing when students use them to text, post, blog, and tweet.

- PowerPoint and other presentation software can be used to model writing for students and to provide a platform for presenting their work.

- Students can create a classroom blog, review various blog sites, and use blogs as they would diaries or journals. They can even write from the perspective of the character in a book or a famous historical person.

- Web quests can be used to help guide students on research projects. They can get relevant information on specific topics and decide what pieces to include in their writing.

- Students can write about technology as a topic. They can "teach" someone how to use various forms of technology, specific learning platforms, or apps.

- Students can create webpages, make a class webpage, and then use it to help with home-school communication.

- Online feedback and grading systems can be used. There are many to choose from. This may allow students to see the grading rubric and ask questions or receive suggestions from the teacher.

- Students and teachers can use email to exchange ideas with other schools or experts on certain topics that are being studied in the classroom.

- Game show-style reviews can be created for units of study to use on computers or on an overhead projector.

- A wiki website can be created that allows students to collaborate, expand on each other's work, and do peer editing and revision.

- Publishing tools can be used to publish student work on the web or in class newspapers or social media sites.

Conventions of Oral and Written Language

Linguistic Structure

Parts of Speech

The English language has eight parts of speech, each serving a different grammatical function.

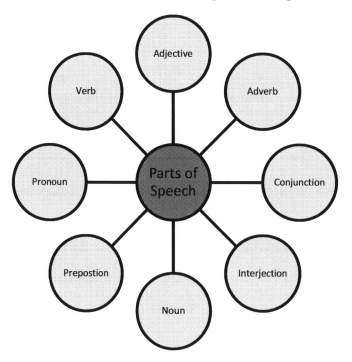

Verb

Verbs describe an action—e.g., *run, play, eat*—or a state of being—e.g., *is, are, was*. It is impossible to make a grammatically-complete sentence without a verb.

He *runs* to the store.

She *is* eight years old.

Noun

Nouns can be a person, place, or thing. They can refer to concrete objects—e.g., chair, apple, house—or abstract things—love, knowledge, friendliness.

> Look at the *dog*!

> Where are my *keys*?

Some nouns are *countable*, meaning they can be counted as separate entities—one chair, two chairs, three chairs. They can be either singular or plural. Other nouns, usually substances or concepts, are *uncountable*—e.g., air, information, wealth—and some nouns can be both countable and uncountable depending on how they are used.

> I bought three *dresses*.

> *Respect* is important to me.

> I ate way too much *food* last night.

> At the international festival, you can sample *foods* from around the world.

Proper nouns are the specific names of people, places, or things and are almost always capitalized.

> *Marie Curie* studied at the *Flying University* in *Warsaw, Poland*.

Object pronouns can function as the object of a sentence—me, us, him, her, them.

> Give the documents to *her*.

> Did you call *him* back yet?

Some pronouns can function as either the subject or the object—e.g., you, it. The subject of a sentence is the noun of the sentence that is doing or being something.

> *You* should try it.

> *It* tastes great.

Possessive pronouns indicate ownership. They can be used alone—mine, yours, his, hers, theirs, ours—or with a noun—my, your, his, her, their, ours. In the latter case, they function as a determiner, which is described in detail in the below section on adjectives.

> This table is *ours*.

> I can't find *my* phone!

Reflexive pronouns refer back to the person being spoken or written about. These pronouns end in -*self/-selves*.

> I've heard that New York City is gorgeous in the autumn, but I've never seen it for *myself*.

> After moving away from home, young people have to take care of *themselves*.

Indefinite pronouns are used for things that are unknown or unspecified. Some examples are *anybody, something,* and *everything.*

> I'm looking for *someone* who knows how to fix computers.

> I wanted to buy some shoes today, but I couldn't find *any* that I liked.

Conjunction

Conjunctions join words, phrases, clauses, or sentences together, indicating the type of connection between these elements.

> I like pizza, *and* I enjoy spaghetti.

> I like to play baseball, *but* I'm allergic to mitts.

Some conjunctions are *coordinating*, meaning they give equal emphasis to two main clauses. Coordinating conjunctions are short, simple words that can be remembered using the mnemonic FANBOYS: for, and, nor, but, or, yet, so. Other conjunctions are *subordinating*. Subordinating conjunctions introduce dependent clauses and include words such as *because, since, before, after, if,* and *while.*

Interjection

An *interjection* is a short word that shows greeting or emotion. Examples of interjections include *wow, ouch, hey, oops, alas,* and *hey.*

> *Wow*! Look at that sunset!

> Was it your birthday yesterday? *Oops*! I forgot.

Standard Conventions

Sentence Structure
Antecedents (Pronoun Reference)

An *antecedent* is the noun to which a pronoun refers; it needs to be written or spoken before the pronoun is used. For many pronouns, antecedents are imperative for clarity. In particular, many of the personal, possessive, and demonstrative pronouns need antecedents. Otherwise, it would be unclear who or what someone is referring to when they use a pronoun like *he* or *this.*

Pronoun reference means that the pronoun should refer clearly to one, clear, unmistakable noun (the antecedent).

Pronoun-antecedent agreement refers to the need for the antecedent and the corresponding pronoun to agree in gender, person, and number. Here are some examples:

> The *kidneys* (plural antecedent) are part of the urinary system. *They* (plural pronoun) serve several roles."

> The kidneys are part of the *urinary system* (singular antecedent). *It* (singular pronoun) is also known as the renal system.

Parallelism

Parallel structure occurs when phrases or clauses within a sentence contain the same structure. Parallelism increases readability and comprehensibility because it is easy to tell which sentence elements are paired with each other in meaning.

> Jennifer enjoys cooking, knitting, and to spend time with her cat.

This sentence is not parallel because the items in the list appear in two different forms. Some are *gerunds*, which is the verb + ing: *cooking, knitting*. The other item uses the *infinitive* form, which is to + verb: *to spend*. To create parallelism, all items in the list may reflect the same form:

> Jennifer enjoys cooking, knitting, and spending time with her cat.

All of the items in the list are now in gerund forms, so this sentence exhibits parallel structure. Here's another example:

> The company is looking for employees who are responsible and with a lot of experience.

Again, the items that are listed in this sentence are not parallel. "Responsible" is an adjective, yet "with a lot of experience" is a prepositional phrase. The sentence elements do not utilize parallel parts of speech.

> The company is looking for employees who are responsible and experienced.

"Responsible" and "experienced" are both adjectives, so this sentence now has parallel structure.

Verb Tense

Shifting verb forms entails conjugation, which is used to indicate tense, voice, or mood.

Verb tense is used to show when the action in the sentence took place. There are several different verb tenses, and it is important to know how and when to use them. Some verb tenses can be achieved by changing the form of the verb, while others require the use of helping verbs (e.g., *is, was,* or *has*).

Present tense shows the action is happening currently or is ongoing:

> I walk to work every morning.

> She is stressed about the deadline.

Past tense shows that the action happened in the past or that the state of being is in the past:

> I walked to work yesterday morning.

> She was stressed about the deadline.

Future tense shows that the action will happen in the future or is a future state of being:

> I will walk to work tomorrow morning.

> She will be stressed about the deadline.

Present perfect tense shows action that began in the past, but continues into the present:

> I have walked to work all week.

> She has been stressed about the deadline.

Past perfect tense shows an action was finished before another took place:

> I had walked all week until I sprained my ankle.

> She had been stressed about the deadline until we talked about it.

Future perfect tense shows an action that will be completed at some point in the future:
> By the time the bus arrives, I will have walked to work already.

Preferred Usage
Subject-Verb Agreement
In English, verbs must agree with the subject. The form of a verb may change depending on whether the subject is singular or plural, or whether it is first, second, or third person. For example, the verb *to be* has various forms:

> I am a student.

> You are a student.

> She is a student.

> We are students.

> They are students.

Errors occur when a verb does not agree with its subject. Sometimes, the error is readily apparent:

> We is hungry.

Is is not the appropriate form of *to be* when used with the third person plural *we*.

> We are hungry.

This sentence now has correct subject-verb agreement.

However, some cases are trickier, particularly when the subject consists of a lengthy noun phrase with many modifiers:

> Students who are hoping to accompany the anthropology department on its annual summer trip to Ecuador needs to sign up by March 31st.

The verb in this sentence is *needs*. However, its subject is not the noun adjacent to it—Ecuador. The subject is the noun at the beginning of the sentence—students. Because *students* is plural, *needs* is the incorrect verb form.

> *Students* who are hoping to accompany the anthropology department on its annual summer trip to Ecuador *need* to sign up by March 31st.

This sentence now uses correct agreement between *students* and *need*.

Another case to be aware of is a *collective noun*. A collective noun refers to a group of many things or people but can be singular in itself—e.g., family, committee, army, pair team, council, jury. Whether or not a collective noun uses a singular or plural verb depends on how the noun is being used. If the noun refers to the group performing a collective action as one unit, it should use a singular verb conjugation:

> The family is moving to a new neighborhood.

The whole family is moving together in unison, so the singular verb form *is* is appropriate here.

> The committee has made its decision.

The verb *has* and the possessive pronoun *its* both reflect the word *committee* as a singular noun in the sentence above; however, when a collective noun refers to the group as individuals, it can take a plural verb:

> The newlywed pair spend every moment together.

This sentence emphasizes the love between two people in a pair, so it can use the plural verb *spend*.

> The council are all newly elected members.

The sentence refers to the council in terms of its individual members and uses the plural verb *are*.

Overall though, American English is more likely to pair a collective noun with a singular verb, while British English is more likely to pair a collective noun with a plural verb.

Shift in Noun-Pronoun Agreement
Pronouns are used to replace nouns so sentences don't have a lot of unnecessary repetition. This repetition can make a sentence seem awkward as in the following example:

> Seat belts are important because seat belts save lives, but seat belts can't do so unless seat belts are used.

Replacing some of the nouns (*seat belts*) with a pronoun (*they*) improves the flow of the sentence:

> Seat belts are important because they save lives, but they can't do so unless they are used.

A pronoun should agree in number (singular or plural) with the noun that precedes it. Another common writing error is the shift in *noun-pronoun agreement*. Here's an example:

> When people are getting in a car, he should always remember to buckle his seatbelt.

The first half of the sentence talks about a plural (*people*), while the second half refers to a singular person (*he* and *his*). These don't agree, so the sentence should be rewritten as:

> When people are getting in a car, they should always remember to buckle their seatbelt.

Idiom
A figure of speech (sometimes called an idiom) is a rhetorical device. It's a phrase that is not intended to be taken literally.

When the writer uses a figure of speech, their intention must be clear if it's to be used effectively. Some phrases can be interpreted in a number of ways, causing confusion for the reader. Look for clues to the writer's true intention to determine the best replacement. Likewise, some figures of speech may seem out of place in a more formal piece of writing. To show this, here is an example:

Seat belts save more lives than any other automobile safety feature. Many studies show that airbags save lives as well, however not all cars have airbags. For instance, some older cars don't. In addition, air bags aren't entirely reliable. For example, studies show that in 15% of accidents, airbags don't deploy as designed, but on the other hand seat belt malfunctions happen once in a blue moon.

Most people know that "once in a blue moon" refers to something that rarely happens. However, because the rest of the paragraph is straightforward and direct, using this figurative phrase distracts the reader. In this example, the earlier version is much more effective.

Now it's important to take a moment and review the meaning of the word *literally*. This is because it's one of the most misunderstood and misused words in the English language. *Literally* means that something is exactly what it says it is, and there can be no interpretation or exaggeration. Unfortunately, *literally* is often used for emphasis as in the following example:

This morning, I literally couldn't get out of bed.

This sentence meant to say that the person was extremely tired and wasn't able to get up. However, the sentence can't *literally* be true unless that person was tied down to the bed, paralyzed, or affected by a strange situation that the writer (most likely) didn't intend. Here's another example:

I literally died laughing.

The writer tried to say that something was very funny. However, unless they're writing this from beyond the grave, it can't *literally* be true.

Note that this doesn't mean that writers can't use figures of speech. The colorful use of language and idioms make writing more interesting and draw in the reader. However, for these kinds of expressions to be used correctly, they cannot include the word *literally*.

Capitalization
Here's a non-exhaustive list of things that should be capitalized.

- The first word of every sentence
- The first word of every line of poetry
- The first letter of proper nouns (World War II)
- Holidays (Valentine's Day)
- The days of the week and months of the year (Tuesday, March)
- The first word, last word, and all major words in the titles of books, movies, songs, and other creative works (In the novel, *To Kill a Mockingbird*, note that *a* is lowercase since it's not a major word, but *to* is capitalized since it's the first word of the title.)
- Titles when preceding a proper noun (President Roberto Gonzales, Aunt Judy)

When simply using a word such as president or secretary, though, the word is not capitalized.

Officers of the new business must include a *president* and *treasurer*.

Seasons—spring, fall, etc.—are not capitalized.

North, *south*, *east*, and *west* are capitalized when referring to regions but are not when being used for directions. In general, if it's preceded by *the* it should be capitalized.

> I'm from the South.

> I drove south.

Understanding Dialect and its Appropriateness

While students should come away from class feeling supported in their linguistic diversity, the reality is that certain forms of language are viewed differently depending on the context. Lessons learned in the classroom have a real-life application to a student's future, so he or she should know where, when, and how to utilize different forms of language.

For students preparing for college, knowledge of the conventions of Standard English is essential. The same is true for students who plan to enter professional job fields. Without necessarily having a word for it, many students are already familiar with the concept of *code-switching*—altering speech patterns depending upon context. For example, a person might use a different accent or slang with neighborhood friends than with coworkers or pick up new vocabulary and speech patterns after moving to a new region, either unconsciously or consciously. In this way, speakers have an innate understanding of how their language use helps them fit into any given situation.

Instructors can design activities that help students pay attention to their language use in a given context. When discussing a novel in class, students might be encouraged to spend a few minutes freewriting in a journal to generate ideas and express their unedited thoughts. Later, though, students will then be asked to present those thoughts in a formal writing assignment that requires adherence to Standard English grammar, employing academic vocabulary and expressions appropriate to literary discussions. Alternatively, students might design an advertisement that appeals to teenagers and another one that appeals to adults, utilizing different language in each. In this way, students can learn how to reformulate their thoughts using the language appropriate to the task at hand.

Awareness of dialect can also help students as readers, too. Many writers of literary fiction and nonfiction utilize dialect and colloquialisms to add verisimilitude to their writing. This is especially true for authors who focus on a particular region or cultural group in their works, also known as *regionalism* or *local color literature*. Examples include Zora Neale Hurston's *Their Eyes Were Watching God* and the short stories of Kate Chopin. Students can be asked to consider how the speech patterns in a text affect a reader's understanding of the characters—how the pattern reflects a character's background and place in society. They might consider a reader's impression of the region—how similar or different it is from the reader's region or what can be inferred about the region based on how people speak. In some cases, unfamiliar dialect may be very difficult for readers to understand on the page but becomes much more intelligible when read aloud—as in the reading of Shakespeare.

Reading passages together in class and then finding recordings or videos of the dialect presented in the text can help familiarize students with different speech patterns. And of course, students should also consider how use of dialect affects the audience or if it is directed to a specific audience. Who was the intended audience for *Their Eyes Were Watching God*, a novel that recreates the speech patterns of African Americans in early 1900s Florida? How might the novel be understood differently by readers who recognize that dialect than by readers who are encountering it for the first time? What would be lost if the characters didn't converse in their local dialect? Being alert to these questions creates students who are attuned to the nuances of language use in everyday life.

Research to Build and Present Knowledge

Research Questions

The purpose of all research is to provide an answer to an unknown question. Therefore, all good research papers pose the topic in the form of a question, which they will then seek to answer with clear ideas, arguments, and supporting evidence.

A *research question* is the primary focus of the research piece, and it should be formulated on a unique topic. To formulate a research question, writers begin by choosing a general topic of interest and then research the literature to determine what sort of research has already been done—the *literature review*. This helps them narrow the topic into something original and determine what still needs to be asked and researched about the topic. A solid question is very specific and avoids generalizations. The following question is offered for evaluation:

> What is most people's favorite kind of animal?

This research question is extremely broad without giving the paper any particular focus—it could go any direction and is not an exceptionally unique focus. To narrow it down, the question could consider a specific population:

> What is the favorite animal of people in Ecuador?

While this question is better, it does not address exactly why this research is being conducted or why anyone would care about the answer. Here's another possibility:

> What does the animal considered as the most favorite of people in different regions throughout Ecuador reveal about their socioeconomic status?

This question is extremely specific and gives a very clear direction of where the paper or project is going to go. However, sometimes the question can be too limited, where very little research has been conducted to create a solid paper, and the researcher most likely does not have the means to travel to Ecuador and travel door-to-door conducting a census on people's favorite animals. In this case, the research question would need to be broadened. Broadening a topic can mean introducing a wider range of criteria. Instead of people in Ecuador, the topic could be opened to include the population of South America or expanded to include more issues or considerations.

Methods of Inquiry and Investigation

With a wealth of information at your fingertips in this digital age, it's important to know not only the type of information you're looking for, but also in what medium you're most likely to find it. Information needs to be specific and reliable. For example, if you're repairing a car, an encyclopedia would be mostly useless. While an encyclopedia might include information about cars, an owner's manual will contain the specific information needed for repairs. Information must also be reliable or credible so that it can be trusted. A well-known newspaper may have reliable information, but a peer-reviewed journal article will have likely gone through a more rigorous check for validity. Determining bias can be helpful in determining credibility. If the information source (person, organization, or company) has something to gain from the reader forming a certain view on a topic, it's likely the information is skewed. For example, if you are trying to find the unemployment rate, the Bureau of Labor Statistics is a more credible source than a politician's speech.

Print and Digital Sources

Identifying Relevant Information During Research
Relevant information is that which is pertinent to the topic at hand. Particularly when doing research online, it is easy for students to get overwhelmed with the wealth of information available to them. Before conducting research, then, students need to begin with a clear idea of the question they want to answer.

For example, a student may be interested in learning more about marriage practices in Jane Austen's England. If that student types "marriage" into a search engine, he or she will have to sift through thousands of unrelated sites before finding anything related to that topic. Narrowing down search parameters, then, can aid in locating relevant information.

When using a book, students can consult the table of contents, glossary, or index to discover whether the book contains relevant information before using it as a resource. If the student finds a hefty volume on Jane Austen, he or she can flip to the index in the back, look for the word *marriage* and find out how many page references are listed in the book. If there are few or no references to the subject, it is probably not a relevant or useful source.

In evaluating research articles, students may also consult the title, abstract, and keywords before reading the article in its entirety. Referring to the date of publication will also determine whether the research contains up-to-date discoveries, theories, and ideas about the subject or is outdated.

Evaluating the Credibility of a Print or Digital Source
There are several additional criteria that need to be examined before using a source for a research topic.

The following questions will help determine whether a source is credible:

Author
- o Who is he or she?
- o Does he or she have the appropriate credentials—e.g., M.D, PhD?
- o Is this person authorized to write on the matter through his/her job or personal experiences?
- o Is he or she affiliated with any known credible individuals or organizations?
- o Has he or she written anything else?

Publisher
- o Who published/produced the work? Is it a well-known journal, like National Geographic, or a tabloid, like The National Enquirer?
- o Is the publisher from a scholarly, commercial, or government association?
- o Do they publish works related to specific fields?
- o Have they published other works?
- o If a digital source, what kind of website hosts the text? Does it end in .edu, .org, or .com?

Bias
- o Is the writing objective? Does it contain any loaded or emotional language?
- o Does the publisher/producer have a known bias, such as Fox News or CNN?

- o Does the work include diverse opinions or perspectives?
- o Does the author have any known bias—e.g., Michael Moore, Bill O'Reilly, or the Pope? Is he or she affiliated with any organizations or individuals that may have a known bias—e.g., Citizens United or the National Rifle Association?
- o Does the magazine, book, journal, or website contain any advertising?

References
- o Are there any references?
- o Are the references credible? Do they follow the same criteria as stated above?
- o Are the references from a related field?

Accuracy/reliability
- o Has the article, book, or digital source been peer reviewed?
- o Are all of the conclusions, supporting details, or ideas backed with published evidence?
- o If a digital source, is it free of grammatical errors, poor spelling, and improper English?
- o Do other published individuals have similar findings?

Coverage
- o Are the topic and related material both successfully addressed?
- o Does the work add new information or theories to those of their sources?
- o Is the target audience appropriate for the intended purpose?

Interpreting and Applying Findings

It can be daunting to integrate so many sources into a research paper while still maintaining fluency and coherency. Most source material is incorporated in the form of quotations or paraphrases, while citing the source at the end of their respective references. There are several guidelines to consider when integrating a source into writing:

- The piece should be written in the author's voice. Quotations, especially long ones, should be limited and spaced evenly throughout the paper.

- All paragraphs should begin with the author's own words and end with his or her own words; quotations should never start or end a paragraph.

- Quotations and paraphrases should be used to emphasize a point, give weight to an idea, and validate a claim.

- Supporting evidence should be introduced in a sentence or paragraph, and then explained afterwards: *According to Waters (1979)* [signal phrase], *"All in all, we're just another brick in the wall" (p.24). The wall suggests that people are becoming more alienated, and the bricks symbolize a paradoxical connection to that alienation* [Explanation].

- When introducing a source for the first time, the author's name and a smooth transition should be included: *In Pink Floyd's groundbreaking album The Wall, Roger Waters argues that society is causing people to become more alienated.*

- There should be an even balance between quotations and paraphrases.

- Quotations or paraphrases should never be taken out of context in a way that alters the original author's intent.

- Quotations should be syntactically and grammatically integrated.

- Quotations should not simply be copied and pasted in the paper. Rather, they should be introduced into a paper with natural transitions.

  - As argued in Johnson's article...
  - Evidence of this point can be found in Johnson's article, where she asserts that...
  - The central argument of John's article is...

Integrating Information

Identifying the Components of a Citation

Citation styles vary according to which style guide is consulted. Examples of commonly-used styles include MLA, APA, and Chicago/Turabian. Each citation style includes similar components, although the order and formatting of these components varies.

MLA Style

For an MLA style citation, components must be included or excluded depending on the source, so writers should determine which components are applicable to the source being cited. Here are the basic components:

- Author—last name, first name
- Title of source
- Title of container—e.g., a journal title or website
- Other contributors—e.g., editor or translator
- Version
- Number
- Publisher
- Publication date
- Location—e.g., the URL or DOI
- Date of Access—optional

APA Style

The following components can be found in APA style citations. Components must be included or excluded depending on the source, so writers should determine which components are applicable to the source being cited.

The basic components are as follows:

- Author—last name, first initial, middle initial
- Publication date
- Title of chapter, article, or text
- Editor— last name, first initial, middle initial
- Version/volume
- Number/issue
- Page numbers
- DOI or URL
- Database—if article is difficult to locate
- City of publication

- State of publication, abbreviated
- Publisher

Chicago/Turabian Style

Chicago/Turabian style citations are also referred to as note systems and are used most frequently in the humanities and the arts. Components must be included or excluded depending on the source, so writers should determine which components are applicable to the source being cited. They contain the following elements:

- Author—last name, first name, middle initial
- Title of chapter or article—in quotation marks
- Title of source
- Editor—first name, last name
- Page numbers
- Version/volume
- Number/issue
- Page numbers
- Date of access
- DOI
- Publication location—city and state abbreviation/country
- Publisher
- Publication Date

<u>Citing Source Material Appropriately</u>

The following information contains examples of the common types of sources used in research as well as the formats for each citation style. First lines of citation entries are presented flush to the left margin, and second/subsequent details are presented with a hanging indent. Some examples of bibliography entries are presented below:

Book

- MLA

  Format: Last name, First name, Middle initial. *Title of Source*. Publisher, Publication Date.

  Example: Sampson, Maximus R. *Diaries from an Alien Invasion*. Campbell Press, 1989.

- APA

  Format: Last name, First initial, Middle initial. (Year Published) *Book Title*. City, State: Publisher.

  Example: Sampson, M. R. (1989). *Diaries from an alien invasion*. Springfield, IL: Campbell Press.

  Chicago/Turabian

  Format: Last name, First name, Middle initial. *Book Title*. City, State: Publisher, Year of publication.

  Example: Sampson, Maximus R. *Diaries from an Alien Invasion*. Springfield, IL: Campbell Press, 1989.

A Chapter in an Edited Book

- MLA

  Format: Last name, First name, Middle initial. "Title of Source." *Title of Container*, Other Contributors, Publisher, Publication Date, Location.

  Example: Sampson, Maximus R. "The Spaceship." *Diaries from an Alien Invasion*, edited by Allegra M. Brewer, Campbell Press, 1989, pp. 45-62.

- APA

  Format: Last name, First Initial, Middle initial. (Year Published) Chapter title. In First initial, Middle initial, Last Name (Ed.), *Book title* (pp. page numbers). City, State: Publisher.

  Example: Sampson, M. R. (1989). The Spaceship. In A. M. Brewer (Ed.), *Diaries from an Alien Invasion* (pp. 45-62). Springfield, IL: Campbell Press.

- Chicago/Turabian

  Format: Last name, First name, Middle initial. "Chapter Title." In Book Title, edited by Editor's Name (First, Middle In. Last), Page(s). City: Publisher, Year Published.

  Example: Sampson, Maximus R. "The Spaceship," in *Diaries from an Alien Invasion*, edited by Allegra M. Brewer, 45-62. Springfield: Campbell Press, 1989.

Article in a Journal

- MLA

  Format: Last name, First name, Middle initial. "Title of Source." *Title of Container*, Number, Publication Date, Location.

  Example: Rowe, Jason R. "The Grief Monster." *Strong Living*, vol. 9, no. 9, 2016, pp 25-31.

- APA

  Format: Last name, First initial, Middle initial. (Year Published). Title of article. *Name of Journal, volume*(issue), page(s).

  Example: Rowe, J. R. (2016). The grief monster. *Strong Living, 9*(9), 25-31.

- Chicago/Turabian:

  Format: Last name, First name, Middle initial. "Title of Article." *Name of Journal* volume, issue (Year Published): Page(s).

  Example: Rowe, Jason, R. "The Grief Monster." *Strong Living* 9, no. 9 (2016): 25-31.

Page on a Website

- MLA

  Format: Last name, First name, Middle initial. "Title of Article." *Name of Website*, date published (Day Month Year), URL. Date accessed (Day Month Year).

  Example: Rowe, Jason. "The Grief Monster." *Strong Living Online*, 9 Sept. 2016. http://www.somanylosses.com/the-grief-monster/html. Accessed 13 Sept. 2016.

- APA

  Format: Last name, First initial. Middle initial. (Date Published—Year, Month Day). Page or article title. Retrieved from URL

  Example: Rowe, J. W. (2016, Sept. 9). The grief monster. Retrieved from http://www.somanylosses.com/ the-grief-monster/html

- Chicago/Turabian

  Format: Last Name, First Name, Middle initial. "Page Title." *Website Title*. Last modified Month day, year. Accessed month, day, year. URL.

  Example: Rowe, Jason. "The Grief Monster." *Strong Living Online*. Last modified September 9, 2016. Accessed September 13, 2016. http://www.somany losses.com/ the-grief-monster/html.

In-Text Citations

Most of the content found in a research paper will be supporting evidence that must be cited in-text, i.e., directly after the sentence that makes the statement. In-text citations contain details that correspond to the first detail in the bibliography entry—usually the author.

- MLA style - In-text citations will contain the author and the page number (if the source has page numbers) for direct quotations. Paraphrased source material may have just the author.
  - According to Johnson, liver cancer treatment is "just beyond our reach" (976).
  - The treatment of liver cancer is not within our reach, currently (Johnson).

- o The narrator opens the story with a paradoxical description: "It was the best of times, it was the worst of times" (Dickens 1).
- APA Style - In text citations will contain the author, the year of publication, and a page marker—if the source is paginated—for direct quotations. Paraphrased source material will include the author and year of publication.
  - o According to Johnson (1986), liver cancer treatment is "just beyond our reach" (p. 976).
  - o The treatment of liver cancer is not within our reach, currently (Johnson, 1986).
- Chicago Style - Chicago style has two approaches to in-text citation: notes and bibliography or author-date.
  - o Notes – There are two options for notes: endnotes—provided in a sequential list at the end of the paper and separate from bibliography—or footnotes provided at the bottom of a page. In either case, the use of superscript indicates the citation number.
    - ▪ Johnson states that treatment of liver cancer is "just beyond our reach." [1]
    - ▪ 1. Robert W. Johnson, Oncology in the Twenty-first Century (Kentville, Nova Scotia: Kentville Publishing, 1986), 159.
  - o Author-Date – The author-date system includes the author's name, publication year, and page number.
    - ▪ Johnson states that treatment of liver cancer is "just beyond our reach" (1986, 159).
    - ▪ Research shows that liver cancer treatment is not within our reach, currently (Johnson 1986, 159).

Constructed-Response Questions

Below, each question will have two reading selections. Read the selections below, then write a constructed-response answer of 800 to 1000 words for each question.

Question 1

Passage A
Excerpt from *Preface to Lyrical Ballads* by William Wordsworth (1800)

> From such verses the Poems in these volumes will be found distinguished at least by one mark of difference, that each of them has a worthy *purpose.* Not that I always began to write with a distinct purpose formerly conceived; but habits of meditation have, I trust, so prompted and regulated my feelings, that my descriptions of such objects as strongly excite those feelings, will be found to carry along with them a *purpose.* If this opinion be erroneous, I can have little right to the name of a Poet. For all good poetry is the spontaneous overflow of powerful feelings: and though this be true, Poems to which any value can be attached were never produced on any variety of subjects but by a man who, being possessed of more than usual organic sensibility, had also thought long and deeply. For our continued influxes of feeling are modified and directed by our thoughts, which are indeed the representatives of all our past feelings; and, as by contemplating the relation of these general representatives to each other, we discover what is really important to men, so, by the repetition and continuance of this act, our feelings will be connected with important subjects, till at length, if we be originally possessed of much sensibility, such habits of mind will be produced, that, by obeying blindly and mechanically the impulses of those habits, we shall describe objects, and utter sentiments, of such a nature, and in such connexion with each other, that the understanding of the Reader must necessarily be in some degree enlightened, and his affections strengthened and purified.

Passage B
Excerpt from Tradition and the Individual Talent by T.S. Eliot (1921)

> If you compare several representative passages of the greatest poetry you see how great is the variety of types of combination, and also how completely any semi-ethical criterion of "sublimity" misses the mark. For it is not the "greatness," the intensity, of the emotions, the components, but the intensity of the artistic process, the pressure, so to speak, under which the fusion takes place, that counts. The episode of Paolo and Francesca employs a definite emotion, but the intensity of the poetry is something quite different from whatever intensity in the supposed experience it may give the impression of. It is no more intense, furthermore, than Canto XXVI, the voyage of Ulysses, which has not the direct dependence upon an emotion. Great variety is possible in the process of transmution of emotion: the murder of Agamemnon, or the agony of Othello, gives an artistic effect apparently closer to a possible original than the scenes from Dante. In the *Agamemnon,* the artistic emotion approximates to the emotion of an actual spectator; in *Othello* to the emotion of the protagonist himself. But the difference between art and the event is always absolute; the combination which is the murder of Agamemnon is probably as complex as that which is the voyage of Ulysses. In either case there has been a fusion of elements. The ode of Keats contains a number of feelings which have nothing particular to do with the nightingale, but which the nightingale, partly, perhaps, because of its attractive name, and partly because of its reputation, served to bring together.

Write a critical essay where you analyze the two passages above, using specific evidence from the text. Assume that your audience knows about literary criticism. In your essay:

- Identify a valid theme that the two passages share

- Compare and contrast the perspectives of each author

- Examine the literary techniques used by the authors, including genre, figurative elements, and rhetorical devices, to express their perspectives on the theme

- Draw a conclusion that dictates how the literary techniques affect the ideas portrayed in the text.

Question 2

This excerpt is adaptation from Our Vanishing Wildlife, *by William T. Hornaday*

Three years ago, I think there were not many bird-lovers in the United States, who believed it possible to prevent the total extinction of both egrets from our fauna. All the known rookeries accessible to plume-hunters had been totally destroyed. Two years ago, the secret discovery of several small, hidden colonies prompted William Dutcher, President of the National Association of Audubon Societies, and Mr. T. Gilbert Pearson, Secretary, to attempt the protection of those colonies. With a fund contributed for the purpose, wardens were hired and duly commissioned. As previously stated, one of those wardens was shot dead in cold blood by a plume hunter. The task of guarding swamp rookeries from the attacks of money-hungry desperadoes to whom the accursed plumes were worth their weight in gold, is a very chancy proceeding. There is now one warden in Florida who says that "before they get my rookery they will first have to get me."

Thus far the protective work of the Audubon Association has been successful. Now there are twenty colonies, which contain all told, about 5,000 egrets and about 120,000 herons and ibises which are guarded by the Audubon wardens. One of the most important is on Bird Island, a mile out in Orange Lake, central Florida, and it is ably defended by Oscar E. Baynard. To-day, the plume hunters who do not dare to raid the guarded rookeries are trying to study out the lines of flight of the birds, to and from their feeding-grounds, and shoot them in transit. Their motto is—"Anything to beat the law, and get the plumes." It is there that the state of Florida should take part in the war.

The success of this campaign is attested by the fact that last year a number of egrets were seen in eastern Massachusetts—for the first time in many years. And so to-day the question is, can the wardens continue to hold the plume-hunters at bay?

Write a critical essay in which you analyze this passage. Assume that your audience is educated, and use evidence from the text. In your essay:

- Summarize the main point of the argument
- Evaluate the author's reasoning
- Describe the methods of persuasion and rhetorical devices
- Identify the audience; who is the author writing to?
- Answer whether or not the passage is effective in persuading the audience.

Subtest IV: Communications: Speech, Media, and Creative Performance

Non-Written Communication

Oral Performance

Oral performance is an important part of any curriculum, as it presents an opportunity for students to become comfortable speaking in front of a group. As early as Kindergarten, students should be introduced to the skills of speaking and listening in a variety of contexts. Teachers can model and reinforce the necessary skills of oral communication such as speaking audibly, providing details, and answering questions. Students should have practice in a variety of age-appropriate situations from an impromptu sharing activity to a formal, prepared debate with a classmate. Oral presentation can enhance literacy through read aloud activities, and be an extension of the writing process when students present information they have compiled or written themselves. Oral presentations can be individual or collaborative, and include multimedia components. Students should also be able to identify the components of oral presentations, recognizing aspects such as a speaker's purpose, intended audience, and tone. Types of oral performance are as follows:

Type	Features	Examples
Impromptu	Spur of the moment, no preparation	An interview, a sharing activity
Extemporaneous	Acknowledge the audience with few words, minimal prep time	Changing direction in a presentation to interest readers, responding to a question or interruption of the speech
Persuasive	Influence the audience's opinion, argue a point, provide evidence, preparation required	Prepared speech on a pre-determined subject
Expository	Inform and explain a topic, focuses on presentation of facts, requires prep time, includes organizational patterns like cause/effect, comparison	Prepared speech on a pre-determined subject
Interpretive	Interpret the deeper meaning of a piece of literature, prep time required to read and analyze source	Oral performance may or may not be prepared in advance of reading a piece of literature
Debate	Includes proposition and opposition format, often timed, prep time typically required on subject	Moderated debate between two individuals or two teams on a pre-determined subject

Performance Skills

Teaching students to present and speak to an audience involves teaching them how to structure a presentation so that it is appropriate for the task, purpose, and audience. *Task* is what the students are required to do with their presentation. *Purpose* is the reason for the presentation and how it will achieve the outcome of the task. *Audience* is whom the presentation is for, the population it is trying to reach, and why it is specifically for that group. Some presentation tips that teachers should impart to students are as follows:

- During student preparation, students should ask themselves: "Why am I giving this presentation?" "What do I want people to take away from the presentation?" and "How much does my audience already know about the topic?"

- Presentations should be structured with an effective introduction, covering each item on their agenda succinctly, and wrapping up with a memorable conclusion.

- Presentations should be given with clarity and impact. The audience won't remember everything a student presents, so he or she needs to highlight the key points clearly and concisely and then expand and illustrate as needed.

- Visual aids should be used to enhance the presentation without causing distractions – such as useless images and animated transitions between slides – from the information.

- Presentations should be given without memorization. Students should be charged with becoming more familiar with their content and to "test drive" the presentation beforehand.

- Appropriate pauses should be used during presentations to help the audience better absorb the information.

- Various techniques can be employed if there is a "stumbling point" or a piece of information is forgotten during the presentation.

Speaker/Audience Interrelationship

<u>Understanding Effective Delivery of a Speech or Presentation</u>
Good public speakers all have several characteristics in common. It is not enough to simply write a speech, but it must also be delivered in a manner that is both engaging and succinct. The following qualities are inherent to good public speaking.

Confidence is possibly the most important attribute a speaker can have. It instills trust in the listener that the person knows what he or she is talking about and that he or she is credible and competent. Confidence is displayed by making brief eye contact—about 2-3 seconds—with different members of the audience to demonstrate that the speaker is engaged. It is also displayed in his or her tone of voice—strong, light-hearted, and natural. A nervous speaker can easily be identified by a small, quivering voice. Confidence is also conveyed by the speaker facing the audience; turning one's back may demonstrate insecurity.

Authenticity is another quality of an effective speaker, as it makes a person more relatable and believable to the audience. Speeches that are memorized word-for-word can give the impression of being inauthentic as the monologue does not flow quite naturally, especially if the speaker accidentally fumbles or forgets. Memorizing speeches can also lead to a monotonous tone, which is sure to put the audience to sleep, or worse, a misinterpreted tone, which can cause the audience to stop listening entirely or even become offended. Therefore, speeches should be practiced with a natural intonation and not be memorized mechanically.

Connection with the audience is another important aspect of public speaking. Speakers should engage with their listeners by the use of storytelling and visual or auditory aids, as well as asking questions that the audience can participate in. Visual and auditory aids could range from an interesting PowerPoint presentation to a short video clip to physical objects the audience can pass around to a soundtrack. The use of appropriate humor also allows the audience to connect with the speaker on a more personal level and will make the speech sound more like a conversation than a one-sided lecture. Speakers who are passionate about their subject inspire their listeners to care about what they're saying; they transfer their energy into the audience. This level of connection will encourage their listeners to want to be there.

Succinctness and *purposeful repetition* ensures that the audience's attention remains focused on the message at hand. Repeating the overall point of the speech in different ways helps listeners remember what the speaker is trying to tell them, even when the speech is over. A speech that is longer than necessary will cause listeners to become bored and stop absorbing information. Keeping the speech short and sweet and leaving more time for questions at the end will ensure that the audience stays engaged.

There are many different styles a speaker can utilize, but the most important thing speakers should keep in mind is maintaining a connection with the audience. This will help ensure that the audience will remain open and focused enough to hear and absorb the message.

Evaluating a Speaker

It is necessary for students to be able to effectively evaluate many components of a speech in order to comprehend its overall message. Point of view refers to the perspective from which a speech is presented. The reader should consider the author's stance on a subject, or his or her position. They should also consider the use of rhetoric or argument in order to deliver the message. A speaker may use causal analysis (the exploration of causes and effects), or analogical reasoning (making a comparison with familiar scenarios to explain new one) to present an argument. A speaker may also use evidence to support his or her point. The use of reasoning and rhetoric should be examined for their effectiveness in proving a point. Premises refer to the proposition on which an argument is based or for which a conclusion may be drawn. These are the facts of the argument that the speaker believes. These must be evaluated for truthfulness before a conclusion is drawn about the argument. Another important factor in the evaluation of a speech is word choice. This can help listeners understand the intended audience based on the language used. Tone and tone of voice can also influence the speaker's message. Students should be able to recognize different tones such as irony, sarcasm, or humor and what effects the tone has on the speaker's overall argument.

Communication Skills

Speaking, listening, reading, and writing are all intimately connected as essential elements of literacy development. As social beings, students begin to recognize that with effective literacy skills, their social, emotional, and physical needs can be met, and their curiosity can be satisfied. They also begin to learn that they can develop communication skills to answer questions that others pose. This can be an exciting and self-affirming realization for young students. In order to encourage literacy development, educators should ensure that all activities in the classroom involve meaningful language and literacy experiences. Each child learns at a unique pace and in a unique way. With this sensitivity in place, classroom activities should be as differentiated as possible.

Developing Listening Skills

Actively teaching good listening skills is essential in the classroom. Behaviors should not be expected that have not been taught. Students need to learn the difference between what an excellent listener does and what poor listening behaviors are. Good listening skills that should be taught include:

- Focusing on the speaker, looking them in the eye, and choosing not to interrupt.

- Looking at the speaker to indicate that the student is ready to hear what the speaker has to say and to pick up body language cues and facial expressions.

- Giving nonverbal signals that the student is listening (e.g., nods, smiles).

- Giving verbal signals that indicate interest in the speaker (e.g., repeating back what is heard to indicate understanding).

- Subtly matching the energy and emotional level of the speaker to indicate understanding.

- Choosing not to make side comments or to focus on other things occurring in the room.

Some strategies for teaching these skills in the classroom include, but are not limited to:

- Providing pre-listening activities, such as teaching new vocabulary words, outlining what students will be hearing, distributing study guides or pre-listening questions, and teaching students the objectives of the listening activity beforehand.

- Avoiding repeating directions multiple times. Teachers are often inclined to repeat steps and directions several times before allowing students to begin working. This is counterproductive because it teaches students that they do not have to listen the first time. Students should be taught that the teacher will say things only once and they are expected to listen, but they may ask for clarification. Students should also be taught to seek other sources of finding the instructions.

- Modeling good listening and speaking skills in the classroom because students learn by watching and emulating others. Teachers need to consistently model choosing not to interrupt and focusing their full attention on the speaker. They also need to model speaking clearly with proper grammar and foster an environment in the classroom of good peer modeling as well.

- Teaching students to take notes, write down questions, and report on or paraphrase what they have heard the speaker say. Students should be given active listening activities to complete during and after the listening task.

- Giving students multiple methods to contribute to conversations. Some students are not inclined to speak in front of others. In such cases, it may be helpful to allow them to give other signals of understanding such as "thumbs up," "thumbs sideways," "thumbs down," or sign language for "yes" and "no" answers.

- Encouraging the use of technology in the classroom to allow students to blog, tweet, or use quiz show-style games to indicate understanding of what they heard.

Developing Speaking Skills

Similar to listening skills, students also need to be taught speaking and presenting skills. Students need to learn such skills as:

- How to introduce themselves effectively
- How to make appropriate eye contact with listeners
- How to begin a conversation and keep it going
- How to interact with various types of audiences
- How to answer questions in an interview
- How to stand and deliver a speech with confidence
- How to ask for and answer questions during a presentation

The following strategies can help teach conversational and speaking skills:

- Students can be taught to use "conversation enhancers" when working with others. Some examples are: "Really?" "Wow!" "That's interesting" "Tell me more about …" "Can you say that in another way?" "Tell me what you are thinking …" and "Can you add to my idea?"

- Good conversational skills can be modeled as frequently as possible in one- to two-minute one-on-one dialogues with students. This is especially important for the introverted and shy students.

- A safe speaking environment can be fostered by teaching good manners to listeners, and by challenging students who are disrespectful listeners to act in a different way.

- Students should be asked open-ended questions that have no right or wrong answer and that invite lengthy answers instead of just "yes" or "no" responses.

- "I don't know" should not be accepted for an answer. Students should be taught that their thinking is valued rather than whether they *know* something.

- Students should be taught how to take turns in the classroom fairly and to not interrupt one another.

- Students should be instructed not to read their presentations word for word, and to speak toward the audience instead of toward the project or PowerPoint slide.

- Videos of good and poor presentations can be shown as models for students to critique.

- Students should be taught to build in humor and good non-verbal communication into their presentations.

- Students should be shown how to curb involuntary habits such as repeating themselves or saying "um" or "like" too much.

Presenting Information, Findings, and Supporting Evidence

Giving a speech requires knowing the components that make it effective for listeners. Depending on the subject matter and grade level, students must be able to present their own perspective on a subject using oral presentation techniques. It's important for students to use logical organization so the speech is easy to follow. Students should also be able to present facts and research in a way that shows their own perspective on the subject matter. The speaker should present any opposing viewpoints as a way of strengthening their own argument. This can be done through refuting these perspectives or pointing out their weaknesses. Students should know their audience and purpose before planning a speech, and consider them as they develop their viewpoint. It is necessary to consider what the audience knows and needs to know when developing an argument, and to consider how they may receive the message of the speech. Style should also be considered when giving a speech to be sure it is appropriate to the task. For example, a formal speech presenting a report on scientific findings would require a more formal style than an impromptu sharing activity in front of the group.

<u>Appropriate Organization to Purpose and Audience</u>
All information should be presented with a clear beginning, middle, and end. Distinct organization always makes any work more clear, concise, and logical. For a presentation, this should involve choosing a primary topic and then discussing it in the following format:

- Introducing the speaker and the main topic
- Providing evidence, supporting details, further explanation of the topic in the main body
- Concluding it with a firm resolution and repetition of the main point

The beginning, middle, and end should also be linked with effective transitions that make the presentation flow well. For example, a presentation should always begin with an introduction by the speaker, including what he/she does and what he/she is there to present. Good transitional introductions may begin with statements such as *For those who do not know me, my name is...*, *As many of you know, I am...* or *Good morning everyone, my name is ___, and I am the new project manager*. A good introduction grabs the attention and interest of the audience.

After an introduction has been made, the speaker will then want to state the purpose of the presentation with a natural transition, such as *I am here to discuss the latest editions to our standard of procedure...* or *This afternoon, I would like to present the results of our latest findings*. Once the purpose has been identified, the speaker will want to adhere to the main idea announced. The presenter should be certain to keep the main idea to one sentence as too much information can confuse an audience; an introduction should be succinct and to the point.

Supporting information should always be presented in concise, easy-to-read formats such as bullet points or lists—if visual aids are presented during the presentation. Good transitions such as *Let's begin with...* or *Now to look at...* make the presentation flow smoothly and logically, helping listeners to keep ideas organized as they are presented. Keeping the material concise is extremely important in a presentation, and visual aids should be used only to emphasize points or explain ideas. All the supporting information should relate back to the main idea, avoiding unnecessary tangents.

Finally, a firm conclusion involves repeating the main point of the presentation by either inspiring listeners to act or by reiterating the most important points made in the speech. It should also include an expression of gratitude to the audience as well as transition to opening the floor for questions.

Reflective Narrative

A reflective narrative is a memoir of a personal experience. A reflective narrative should identify a specific event or experience that had an impact on the writer. Potentially a lesson was learned or the writer was changed in some way from this event, and students should be able to convey the broader theme in the narrative. Typically, students can make connections to the incident and its meaning in the conclusion of the narrative. In order to make a reflective narrative interesting and meaningful to the reader, writers should include certain elements such as sensory language. Sensory language invokes all of the senses in order to paint a picture in the reader's mind. Students should also learn the skill of observation to reinforce descriptive elements of narrative writing. Other narrative techniques such as pacing and the use of dialogue should also be reinforced by teachers. For example, dialogue should be used sparingly, and only when the words spoken are very important. It can be used to show the relationship between characters as well.

Planning and Presenting an Argument

Before beginning any writing, it is imperative that a writer have a firm grasp on the message he or she wishes to convey and how he or she wants readers to be affected by the writing. For example, does the author want readers to be more informed about the subject? Does the writer want readers to agree with his or her opinion? Does the writer want readers to get caught up in an exciting narrative? The following steps are a guide to determining the appropriate type of writing for a task, purpose, and audience:

- Identifying the purpose for writing the piece
- Determining the audience
- Adapting the writing mode, word choices, tone, and style to fit the audience and the purpose

It is important to distinguish between a work's purpose and its main idea. The essential difference between the two is that the *main idea* is what the author wants to communicate about the topic at hand whereas the *primary purpose* is why the author is writing in the first place. The primary purpose is what will determine the type of writing an author will choose to utilize, not the main idea, though the two are related. For example, if an author writes an article on the mistreatment of animals in factory farms and, at the end, suggests that people should convert to vegetarianism, the main idea is that vegetarianism would reduce the poor treatment of animals. The primary purpose is to convince the reader to stop eating animals. Since the primary purpose is to galvanize an audience into action, the author would choose the argumentative writing mode.

The next step is to consider to whom the author is appealing as this will determine the type of details to be included, the diction to be used, the tone to be employed, and the sentence structure to be used. An audience can be identified by considering the following questions:

- What is the purpose for writing the piece?
- To whom is it being written?
- What is their age range?
- Are they familiar with the material being presented, or are they just being newly introduced to it?
- Where are they from?
- Is the task at hand in a professional or casual setting?
- Is the task at hand for monetary gain?

These are just a few of the numerous considerations to keep in mind, but the main idea is to become as familiar with the audience as possible. Once the audience has been understood, the author can then adapt the writing style to align with the readers' education and interests. The audience is what determines the *rhetorical appeal* the author will use—ethos, pathos, or logos. *Ethos* is a rhetorical appeal to an audience's ethics and/or morals. Ethos is most often used in argumentative and informative writing modes. *Pathos* is an appeal to the audience's emotions and sympathies, and it is found in argumentative, descriptive, and narrative writing modes. *Logos* is an appeal to the audience's logic and reason and is used primarily in informative texts as well as in supporting details for argumentative pieces. Rhetorical appeals are discussed in depth in the informational texts and rhetoric section of the test.

If the author is trying to encourage global conversion to vegetarianism, he or she may choose to use all three rhetorical appeals to reach varying personality types. Those who are less interested in the welfare of animals but are interested in facts and science would relate more to logos. Animal lovers would relate better to an emotional appeal. In general, the most effective works utilize all three appeals.

Finally, after determining the writing mode and rhetorical appeal, the author will consider word choice, sentence structure, and tone, depending on the purpose and audience. The author may choose words that convey sadness or anger when speaking about animal welfare if writing to persuade, or he or she will stick to dispassionate and matter-of-fact tones, if informing the public on the treatment of animals in factory farms. If the author is writing to a younger or less-educated audience, he or she may choose to shorten and simplify sentence structures and word choice. If appealing to an audience with more expert knowledge on a particular subject, writers will more likely employ a style of longer sentences and more complex vocabulary.

Depending on the task, the author may choose to use a first person, second person, or third person point of view. First person and second person perspectives are inherently more casual in tone, including the author and the reader in the rhetoric, while third person perspectives are often seen in more professional settings.

Media Analysis and Applications

Media Forms

Media sources can influence the way students experiences the world, and thus, their voice in their writing and communication. Visual images seen on television, the Internet, and in magazines, can have a powerful impact on the way children view themselves and the world. Teachers should consider the magnitude of media's impact on students, and assess whether they are being overexposed to negative images such as violence, sexuality, and alcohol or drug use. Steps should be taken to help students understand the role of the media and visual imagery in their self-concept, and to help promote a healthy self-image apart from these sources. Beyond the classroom, media impacts society at large. Teachers should encourage discussions about the influence of various media forms and messages on the culture and attitudes of the society in which they are displayed. It can be interesting and helpful to compare media from different countries, such as evaluating the similarities and differences in magazine ads from various countries. The marketing strategies and appeals can differ, reflecting different ideals and priorities.

Evaluating Strategies of Media

Mass media refers to the various methods by which the majority of the general public receives news and information. Mass media includes television, newspapers, radio, magazines, online news outlets, and social media networks. The general public relies on mass media for political knowledge and cultural socialization, as well as the majority of their knowledge of current events, social issues, and political news.

Evolution of Mass Media
- Until the end of the nineteenth century, print media such as newspapers and magazines was the only form of mass communication.

- In the 1890s, after the invention of the radio, broadcast media become a popular form of communication, particularly among illiterate people.

- In the 1940s, television superseded both print and broadcast media as the most popular form of mass media.

- In 1947, President Harry Truman gave the first political speech on television.

- In 1952, Dwight Eisenhower was the first political candidate to air campaign ads on television.

- Today, the Internet is the most widespread mass media technology, and citizens have instant access to news and information, as well as interactive platforms on which they can communicate directly with political leaders or share their views through social media, blogs, and independent news sites.

Influence of Mass Media on Politics

Mass media has a powerful effect on public opinion and politics. Mass media:

- Shapes public interests
- Enables candidates to reach voters wherever they are
- Determines what is and is not considered important in society based on how it prioritizes events and issues
- Provides the context in which to report events
- Is paid for by advertisers who may pressure news outlets to suppress or report information in their own interests

Persuasive Speech in Media

Media communications have enabled us to become more informed about current events and trends. News reports are constantly streaming, and web articles are breaking virtually every minute. It's important to think analytically in order to understand fact over opinion. Identifying when persuasive language is being used and applying reason to isolate the facts from such language is key.

A lot of reporting today is heavily laden with persuasive language that angles towards an individual's perspective or contains facts along with an opinion. The writer or broadcaster's tone, diction, and even grammatical choices can indicate whether they're trying to influence people. It's crucial to identify when facts and proof are presented. This is usually the simplest, most basic reporting:

Bank officials confirm that over $12K was stolen from the Wells Fargo last night.

This is a simple statement of what happened. We know it happened because the bank workers confirmed it. The information is delivered in an organized way, with information being presented alongside corroborating evidence. This is not persuasive—this is fact. The tone of the writer is also neutral and logical, presenting information without any kind of bias.

Persuasive writing can be identified by shifts in tone and diction. The writer or reporter may seem more sympathetic, accusatory, or critical, and their word choices may evoke emotion rather than a logical conclusion. Exaggerations or dramatic word use also indicate persuasive tactics. Adjectives, adverbs, and alliteration can also be used in persuasive language. Let's look at the following example:

> The suspect, probably a disgruntled worker or customer, greedily jeopardized the bank's well-being. This adds further proof why body scans must be stationed at bank entrances.

Note the colorful descriptions of *disgruntled* and *greedily*. While these are conceivably true descriptions of the criminal, these evoke emotion in readers. The truth is that the suspect is uncertain, and the writer is guessing. This also doesn't note the exact motivation for the thief, but rather speculates. The second sentence is mostly persuasive, and one can see that the writer has written a statement calling for action. While this incident could be used to justify the new security measure, the media story clearly shifted from describing an incident to using the incident to persuade people to support body scans.

Aesthetic Effects of Media Presentation

Media aesthetics include light, color, 2- and 3-dimensional space, time, motion, and sound. Knowing these elements of media can help students to create their own more effective presentations. Students should understand the role each of these elements in the effectiveness of media presentations. For example, playing music during a presentation can create a mood for the viewer, and elicit a desired emotion. It's also important for students to know how to manipulate aesthetics for desired effect in their own media presentations.

<u>Advantages and Disadvantages of Different Media</u>
Each visual aid has its advantages and disadvantages and should be used sparingly to avoid distracting the audience. Visual aids should be used to emphasize a presentation's message, not overwhelm it.

Microsoft PowerPoint is currently the most commonly used visual aid. It allows for pictures, words, videos, and music to be presented on the same screen and is essentially just a projection of a computer screen, allowing easy and quick access to all forms of media as well as the Internet. However, a PowerPoint presentation should not be overwhelmed with information, such as text-heavy slides, as audience members will spend more time reading the slides than listening to the speaker. Conversely, they may avoid reading it entirely, and the presentation will serve no purpose. A PowerPoint presentation that uses too many animations and visual elements may also detract from the presence of the speaker.

Handouts are a great way for the audience to feel more involved in a presentation. They can present lots of information that may be too much for a PowerPoint, and they can also be taken home and reviewed later. The primary disadvantage of handouts is that the audience may choose to read rather than to listen, thus missing the main points the speaker is trying to make, or they may decide not to read it at all. The best handouts are those that do not contain all the information of a presentation, but allow for the audience to take notes and complete the handout by listening or asking questions.

Whiteboards and *blackboards* are excellent for explaining difficult concepts by allowing the audience to follow along with a process and copy down their own version of what is being written on the board. This visual aid is best used to explain concepts in mathematics and science. The main problem with the board, however, is that there can be limited space, and if the presenter runs out of room, he or she will have to erase the content written on the board and will be unable to refer back to it later. He or she may also have to wait for the entire audience to write the information down, which slows down the presentation.

Overhead projectors are wonderful in that a speaker can use a prepared transparency and draw images or add words to emphasize or explain concepts. They can also erase these additions but still keep the original content if they wish to alter their method to fit the audience or provide further explanations. Similar to PowerPoint presentations, overhead projections should limit the amount of text to keep the audience focused on listening.

Physical objects are a useful way to connect with the audience and allow them to feel more involved. Because people interact with the physical world, physical objects can help solidify understanding of difficult concepts. However, they can be distracting if not properly introduced. If they are presented too early or are visible during the presentation, the audience will focus on the objects, wondering what purpose they may serve instead of listening to the speaker. Objects should instead be hidden until it is time to show them and then collected when they are no longer useful.

Videos are a great way to enliven a presentation by giving it sound, music, flow, and images. They are excellent for emphasizing points, providing evidence for ideas, giving context, or setting tone. The major issue with videos is that the presenter is unable to speak at this point, so this form of media should be used sparingly and purposefully. Also, overly-long videos may lose the audience's attention.

Effective public speakers are aware of the advantages and disadvantages of all forms of media and often choose to utilize a combination of several different types to keep the presentations lively and the audience engaged.

Diverse Media

Students should be able to solve problems and make decisions through the use of multiple informational sources. It is important for students to be able to analyze sources for credibility and relevance, evaluate them for any bias or inaccuracies, and ultimately synthesize them to generate an answer or make a decision. The more diverse the sources, the more comprehensive the answer or decision will be. One area where this is especially important is in Internet research. Students must be able to discern between many sources and choose the most reliable information to integrate. One way for students to glean an answer from multiple sources is through cross-referencing. When a fact is repeated in many credible sources, especially a variety of different types of sources, it can generally be accepted as true. Students should also know the criteria for evaluating a source's credibility, such as author credentials, peer-reviewed status, and timeliness of the information. As other media become more prevalent, such as videos and social media posts, students must also be able to identify what makes these types of sources credible and how to integrate them with more traditional sources.

Using Technology Tools for Effective Communication
Different technological tools serve different functions. To function in the developing world, students need to learn and understand *digital literacy*—the knowledge, dexterity, and critical thinking skills involved in using technology to create, evaluate, and present information. The best techniques for instructing students on choosing and using technological tools involve educating them on the advantages and disadvantages of each, demonstrating how to use them, breaking down their different aspects, assigning students homework or projects in which they will utilize different technological resources, and instructing them on when it is appropriate to use each kind. The most common types of tools used for communication are as follows:

- Smartphones/apps
- Email

- Microsoft Office
- iMovie
- Skype
- Twitter
- Facebook
- Instagram
- Google Drive
- Various blogging websites
- Online bulletin boards
- Wikis

A good way to introduce students to varying technological tools is by using them in the classroom. It would be helpful to teach students how to use a PowerPoint presentation, for example, by giving a PowerPoint presentation. If a student asks a question to which the teacher does not know the answer, they can discover the answer together by using a reliable source on the Internet, projecting the process on the board, so that they can see exactly how it's done. Students can also receive homework and updates on school and classroom events through a personal blog or class bulletin board the teacher has designed so that they may become familiar with using online communication. Students can also be assigned to use personal blogs to practice and improve their writing skills.

The most effective method for learning new skills is a hands-on approach. Students can be educated on the pros and cons of each technological tool, but the best way for them to learn is to allow them to find out for themselves by assigning projects and asking them to give the reasoning behind choosing a specific tool. For example, they may be asked to do a project on some aspect of the Revolutionary War by choosing a media format. Ideas may include the following:

- Doing a presentation
- Filming and editing a video re-enactment of a great battle
- Writing a script in Microsoft Word or in a Google doc and having classmates act it out
- Creating Facebook statuses from the viewpoints of the forefathers in modern colloquial language
- Having a "Twitter war" between the British and the Colonials
- Asking various people to participate in a collaborative Wiki or Google Doc in which many people give their versions of aspects of the Revolutionary War
- Writing a blog narrating life as a soldier
- Posting photos of the signing of the Declaration of Independence

Students can then give their presentations to the classroom so that students can learn about the topic through different presentation styles.

Another way to engage students in using technology is to have them communicate with each other through the various methods of communication—e.g., starting a class Google Doc, creating a classroom Facebook group, or using a discussion board. This is also an excellent opportunity to encourage students to use Standard English through all methods of communication to enhance their writing skills and instill a sense of professionalism, which they will need throughout their lives.

For example, requiring that all students use complete sentences, proper spelling, and grammar through Facebook, Twitter, or blogs associated with homework or projects will encourage them to do so in their daily lives as well. Another example is requiring that students select tweets from their favorite celebrities or politicians, analyze their meaning and purpose, correct their grammar and spelling, and re-tweet them in the correct way. There are countless ways in which technology can be used in the classroom to enhance students' understanding of digital communication; all it requires is a little creativity.

Strategic Use of Digital Media

Students can use digital media to make their presentations more effective. They should know how to integrate media that is appropriate to the intended audience, enhances purpose, and uses appropriate style and tone for the task. Digital media should be integrated strategically to be effective. Teachers can model this through their own presentations, and help students to recognize how digital media can spark an audience's interest, and highlight key facts. A well-placed video or photograph, for example, can illustrate a presenter's message and have a deeper impact on the audience than a simple lecture would. Students should understand the impact of visual, auditory, and interactive features in a presentation in order to deliver their message and keep the audience interested in the subject matter.

Evaluating Technology-Based Strategies
It is hard to find a technological tool that will not be useful for students to explore. The more a student engages with the numerous different types of technology, the more digitally literate that student will become. Each type is effective and brings value to the table in its own way. When evaluating the effectiveness of a specific technology-based strategy, it's important to consider how this method is enhancing the student's digital literacy, as well as their critical thinking and communication skills. It is also necessary to evaluate the technology itself by asking relevant questions:

- Is it appropriate for the average age of the students in the classroom?
- Is it user friendly?
- Does it work consistently?
- Are there multiple ways to get help on learning how to use it?
- Are there trouble-shooting options?
- Does it have good reviews?
- Is it relevant to the content of the curriculum?
- Does it support and align to the learning objective?
- Is it more distracting than it is useful?
- Is it a tool that is/will be used often in the real world?
- Can it be used for more than one project or assignment?

One very effective teaching strategy is *collaborative learning*, in which two or more students work together to develop a project, work through an idea, or solve a problem. This method allows for students to play off each other's strengths and different experiences and learn how to communicate with their classmates to achieve goals. Technology can be used for collaborative learning in Google Drive, Skype, Google Hangouts, Neapod, Padlet, and Periscope, in creating PowerPoint presentations together, or by conducting surveys with websites like Survey Monkey.

Another effective teaching method is *discussion*, in which students are given a topic or create a topic themselves and then use technology to engage in discourse. This can be done via discussion boards, such as ProBoards or Boardhost, or done live through programs such as Skype or Hangouts. Discussion strategies are extremely effective for enhancing communication skills and digital literacy.

A third method is *active learning*, in which the student engages in activities such as reading, writing, or teaching the subject to another student. Blogging is a great way to encourage active learning as it provides a medium through which students can reflect on what they've learned and respond to comments posted by the teacher or other students. Most of the suggestions made in the previous section—making presentations, creating video re-enactments, writing scripts, having mock Twitter or Facebook comment wars—are all forms of active learning. These types of activities solidify events, ideas, and skills in a student's mind in a way that memorization or flashcards do not as they utilize many different types of thinking and interaction.

One method that a teacher may employ depending on the class and circumstances is *distance learning*. Distance learning is any type of teaching method in which the student and teacher are not in the same place simultaneously. Many professors utilize distance learning through different kinds of technologies, including a live virtual lecture, computer simulations, interactive discussions, and virtual/audio learning environments. These strategies have their advantages in that one teacher can teach a large number of students and multiple locations, and students can communicate with fellow classmates across the globe.

Auditory learning is a strategy in which a student learns through listening. This typically happens via recorded lectures that can be downloaded as podcasts onto a classroom website, discussion board, or some other audio-simulated learning environment. *Visual learning* is learning through watching, in which ideas and concepts are illustrated through images, videos, or by observing a teacher complete a task, explain a concept, or solve a problem. This can be achieved through recorded videos, cartoons, virtual lectures, or by sitting in the classroom. Additionally, *kinesthetic learning* is active learning through physical interaction with an object or actively solving a problem, as opposed to passively listening or watching.

Every student has a different learning style which is unique to them—some learn better through listening while others learn better through doing. The best teaching methods employ all different learning strategies so that all the senses are engaged and every student has a chance at learning material based on their individual learning needs. Technology offers educators the tools do that.

Dramatic Performance

Rehearsal Strategies

Students should be able to identify and employ the components of a dramatic performance production. Putting on a play provides a unique opportunity to practice teamwork skills and use knowledge of staging techniques to produce a fully-rounded performance.

Students can be involved in all aspects of the planning and staging of a production including scheduling, set design, casting, acting, and stage directions. Teachers should offer students the opportunity to participate in a variety of roles in order for them to learn all aspects of the production and creative process. Plays are not only meant to be read, but performed, and the experience of producing, staging, and acting in a play is an invaluable experience that goes beyond simply reading a textbook. It can offer students a far more impactful, lasting experience of the work.

Character Analysis

Character analysis refers to studying the description of a character to determine a deeper meaning behind his or her motivation. It involves finding out who the character is and why he or she behaves in a certain manner. Students should pay attention to the description of a character, such as his or mannerisms, the words he or she uses, and how the character interacts with other characters. They should also consider what challenges the character faces and how he or she overcomes them. It's also important to consider the choices a character makes, and how the character ultimately resolves the issues he or she faces in a dramatic work. Studying these details can help an actor know how to play the role of this character, not just on the surface, but with a deeper understanding of who the character really is. This in itself is a very creative process, because while the character might be written with key features and motivations, the actor must actually take on these aspects to bring the character to life.

Performing the character entails body language and voice in order to flesh the character out. This also means that there are several ways to interpret how to physically embody character attributes. Students should take the core traits of the character and explore how they might behave under the similar circumstances. For example, Macbeth is a character that is seemingly torn in his desire for the Scottish crown and whether or not to murder Duncan. This hesitation can be highlighted in moments of physical unease, or even how he delivers lines. An actor might choose to pause more in Macbeth's soliloquy or earlier lines, or perhaps to deliver the lines in a reflective manner to show Macbeth's inner dialogues.

Characters like Macbeth also change dramatically as the play goes on. This is an excellent opportunity to demonstrate change through a shift in performance. An actor can move more confidently to reflect a character's new purpose or even deliver a softened tone to show how a character is being pacified. The key is to not deliver a monotone performance, but rather to reflect the shifting dynamics of how a real individual would react to the situations presented in the play.

Preparing for the role is key but this will be for naught if the audience has trouble discerning the performance. The audience must clearly hear and see the performance. Some vocal techniques include using good posture and breathing to project one's voice. It is also important to focus on articulation and audibility for the audience's understanding of a vocal performance.

Informing Play Production Choices

Dramatic works include both dialogue and stage directions that are meant to inform the production of the play. Dialogue tells what an actor says, while stage directions show how the character should behave. It is this behavior that informs the reader or audience of how a character feels. In addition to showing character behavior, stage directions include information on intended lighting, costumes, scenery, and sound/music. This information must all be considered in the production of the play to produce what the playwright intended. Teachers can help students decipher the intended meaning behind the text of the play, such as the central theme or motivations of a character to inform acting choices, scenery and set design, and the overall tone and mood of the production.

It's also important to recognize the conventions of the play category—a tragedy is fundamentally different than a comedy. Both types will influence the tone of the play, the characters, lighting, and ultimately the direction of the entire work. In tragic plays, humor is used to lighten the mood after particularly dark scenes.

Stage Directing

Stage directions refer to the parts of a dramatic play script that tell what the actors should do, as opposed to dialogue, which tells what actors should say. Stage directions are an important part of the production of a play, as they inform the audience of how characters feel. Students should be aware of the fundamentals of stage directions, such as the parts of the stage and blocking (where characters stand on the stage). They should also consider the tempo of a play, which is the pace at which the story unfolds. A stage director should also be keenly aware of the dramatic arc and how it is portrayed on the stage. Rising and falling action can be enhanced by the actions and placement of the characters, which a stage director is ultimately responsible for in the production.

Oral Performance Traditions

Oral performance traditions are an integral part of the language arts curriculum, and students should become comfortable with the fundamentals of these traditions. Students begin learning these traditions from an early age through nursery rhymes, poems, and songs. Teachers can model and reinforce oral performance skills such as tone, inflection, emotion, and volume control with students through storytelling and recitation of poems. They should also provide ample opportunities for students to practice these skills in small and large group settings.

Special focus should be on how the various forms of oral tradition differ and the history behind their use. This will also inform students of why the format, dialogue, symbolism, and diction varies in different forms of oral performance. For example, an epic poem was originally performed or sung to a broad audience. It wasn't until much later that these poems were written down because they were part of oral traditions, being passed on purely through memory and word-of-mouth.

Poetry relies on specific devices in addition to rhyme such as alliteration, repetition, and meter. Meter is unique to poetry, song, and some plays because of its use to create a linguistic pattern. This is what enables people to pass on the first stories, including epic poems, through oral tradition. The use of rhyme and meter are not seen in regular stories. Instead, fiction stories use prose but still utilize artistic devices such as similes and metaphors to add meaning to the work.

Constructed-Response Questions

Read the questions below then write a response of 75 to 125 words.

Question 1

During a class, one student gives an oral performance wherein they attempt to persuade the audience to agree with them on a subject. Write a response in which you:

- Identify an example of a rhetorical device that a student might give in a persuasive speech; and
- Identify one way in which the speaker can draw the audience in rather than the audience just listening.

Question 2

A student admits that she doesn't know how to effectively organize her speech. Write a response in which you:

- Show her the appropriate organization to purpose and audience; and
- Give a brief example of what this would look like.

Question 3

Your students are having trouble understanding the role technology plays for academic purposes. You have given multiple lectures on the different mediums of technology, but you figure the students should have some hands-on experience. To address this, the teacher considers the following three pieces of technology:

- Google docs
- Facebook group
- Blogging

Select one of these depicted above and write a response in which you:

- Describe how this technology is able to be both entertaining and educational; and
- Explain why this strategy is likely to help students understand the role of technology in academia.

Question 4

A high school student has been asked to write an essay over a common myth and ways to debunk that myth that won't alienate the audience. The student's draft appears below:

The Myth of Head Heat Loss

It has recently been brought to my attention that most people believe that 75% of your body heat is lost through your head. I had certainly heard this before, and am not going to attempt to say I didn't believe it when I first heard it. It is natural to be gullible to anything said with enough authority. But the "fact" that the majority of your body heat is lost through your head is a lie.

Let me explain. Heat loss is proportional to surface area exposed. An elephant loses a great deal more heat than an anteater, because it has a much greater surface area than an anteater. Each cell has mitochondria that produce energy in the form of heat, and it takes a lot more energy to run an elephant than an anteater.

So, each part of your body loses its proportional amount of heat in accordance with its surface area. The human torso probably loses the most heat, though the legs lose a significant amount as well. Some people have asked, "Why does it feel so much warmer when you cover your head than when you don't?" Well, that's because your head, because it is not clothed, is losing a lot of heat while the clothing on the rest of your body provides insulation. If you went outside with a hat and pants but no shirt, not only would you look silly, but your heat loss would be significantly greater because so much more of you would be exposed. So, if given the choice to cover your chest or your head in the cold, choose the chest. It could save your life.

Write a response in which you:

- Describe one type of revision the student could make to improve the draft; and
- Explain why this type of revision would enhance the effectiveness of the essay.

Dear CSET English Test Taker,

We would like to start by thanking you for purchasing this study guide for your CSET English exam. We hope that we exceeded your expectations.

Our goal in creating this study guide was to cover all of the topics that you will see on the test. We also strove to make our practice questions as similar as possible to what you will encounter on test day. With that being said, if you found something that you feel was not up to your standards, please send us an email and let us know.

We would also like to let you know about other books in our catalog that may interest you.

CSET Mathematics

This can be found on Amazon: amazon.com/dp/1628454571

CSET Multiple Subject

amazon.com/dp/1628454504

CBEST

amazon.com/dp/1628454121

NES Elementary Education

amazon.com/dp/1628454334

We have study guides in a wide variety of fields. If the one you are looking for isn't listed above, then try searching for it on Amazon or send us an email.

Thanks Again and Happy Testing!
Product Development Team
info@studyguideteam.com

Interested in buying more than 10 copies of our product? Contact us about bulk discounts:

bulkorders@studyguideteam.com

FREE Test Taking Tips DVD Offer

To help us better serve you, we have developed a Test Taking Tips DVD that we would like to give you for FREE. **This DVD covers world-class test taking tips that you can use to be even more successful when you are taking your test.**

All that we ask is that you email us your feedback about your study guide. Please let us know what you thought about it – whether that is good, bad or indifferent.

To get your **FREE Test Taking Tips DVD**, email freedvd@studyguideteam.com with "FREE DVD" in the subject line and the following information in the body of the email:

  a. The title of your study guide.

  b. Your product rating on a scale of 1-5, with 5 being the highest rating.

  c. Your feedback about the study guide. What did you think of it?

  d. Your full name and shipping address to send your free DVD.

If you have any questions or concerns, please don't hesitate to contact us at freedvd@studyguideteam.com.

Thanks again!

Made in the USA
San Bernardino, CA
27 February 2019